The Way of

the Storyteller

THE WAY

OF

THE STORYTELLER

BY

RUTH SAWYER

THE VIKING PRESS

NEW YORK

372.64
S271

COPYRIGHT 1942, 1962 BY RUTH SAWYER
ALL RIGHTS RESERVED
FIRST PUBLISHED BY THE VIKING PRESS, INC. IN MARCH 1942
PUBLISHED SIMULTANEOUSLY IN CANADA BY
THE MACMILLAN COMPANY OF CANADA LIMITED
FOURTEENTH PRINTING DECEMBER 1969
LIBRARY OF CONGRESS CATALOGUE NUMBER: 62-15697
SBN 670-75244-4

Acknowledgments for the use of copyrighted material will be found at
page vi, which is made a part of this copyright page.

Printed in U.S.A. by The Colonial Press Inc.

TO THE MEMORY OF TWO GREAT STORYTELLERS,

Marie Shedlock

OF BOULOGNE AND TUNBRIDGE WELLS

AND

Johanna

OF COUNTY DONEGAL,

THIS BOOK IS DEDICATED IN DEEP HUMILITY

ACKNOWLEDGMENTS

The author wishes to thank Charles Scribner's Sons for permission to quote passages from *Success in Music and How to Achieve It* by Henry Finck and from William Butler Yeats's introduction to *Gods and Fighting Men* by Isabella Augusta Gregory (Lady Gregory); The Macmillan Company for a verse from Vachel Lindsay's "Eden in Winter" in *Collected Poems*; Farrar and Rinehart for a passage from Bertil Malmberg's *Ake and His World*; Houghton Mifflin Company for a passage from Josephine Preston Peabody's *The Piper*; Simon and Schuster for a passage from John Cowper Powys's *The Enjoyment of Literature*; and Miss Dorothy Thompson and *Life* magazine for a passage from her speech and article "There Was a Man."

Acknowledgment is made as follows for material incorporated in two new chapters, added in 1962:

"Daniel Boone," from *A Book of Americans* by Rosemary and Stephen Vincent Benét (Holt, Rinehart and Winston, Inc.), Copyright 1933 by Rosemary and Stephen Vincent Benét, Reprinted by permission of Brandt & Brandt; "An Old Woman of the Roads," from *Poems* by Padraic Colum, Copyright 1916 by Padraic Colum, Reprinted by permission of the author; "Poetry" from *Poems for Children* by Eleanor Farjeon, Copyright 1938 by Eleanor Farjeon, Reprinted by permission of J. B. Lippincott Company and Harold Ober Associates; "General Store," from *Taxis and Toadstools* by Rachel Field, Copyright 1926 by Rachel Field, Reprinted by permission of Doubleday & Company, Inc.; "Dirge for a Righteous Kitten," from *The Collected Poems of Vachel Lindsay*, Copyright 1914 by The Macmillan Company, Renewed 1942 by Elizabeth C. Lindsay, and "Abraham Lincoln Walks at Midnight," from *The Congo and Other Poems* by Vachel Lindsay, Copyright 1914 by The Macmillan Company, Renewed 1942 by Elizabeth C. Lindsay, Reprinted by permission of The Macmillan Company; "Five Chants" and "Conversation," from *Far and Few* by David McCord, Copyright 1941, 1952 by David McCord, Reprinted by permission of Little, Brown & Co.; "Sea Fever," from *Salt-Water Poems and Ballads* by John Masefield, Copyright 1912 by The Macmillan Company, Renewed 1940 by John Masefield, Reprinted by permission of The Macmillan Company, New York, and The Society of Authors, London; "The Piper," from *Transition and Transcription* by Seumas O'Sullivan, Reprinted by permission of H. R. Carter Publications, Ltd., Belfast; "The Ox and the Donkey's Carol" and "Christmas Carol for the Dog," from *Frost for St. Brigid* by Sister Maris Stella, C.S.J., Copyright 1949, Sheed & Ward, Inc., New York, and reprinted by their permission; "Song of the Fairy Child," in *Land of the Heart's Desire* from *The Collected Plays of William Butler Yeats*, Copyright 1934, 1952 by The Macmillan Company, Reprinted by permission of The Macmillan Company, New York, and A. P. Watt & Sons, London.

Contents

Chapters

Stories

CONTENTS

An Introduction

I think fit to tell thee these following truths, That I did neither undertake nor write nor publish . . . this Discourse to please myself. . . . And I wish the Reader also to take notice that in writing of it I have made myself a recreation of a recreation; and that it might prove so to him and not to read dull and tediously, I have in several places mixt some . . . innocent, harmless mirth. . . . And I am the willinger to justify the pleasant part of it because . . . the whole Discourse is . . . a picture of my owne disposition.

—IZAAK WALTON

An Introduction

I CAN find no abler or more understanding person to speak my introduction for me than Izaak Walton, he of *The Compleat Angler*. Within the very narrow space of his book he has done a rare thing—he has established a perfect balance between master and apprentice, the one who has something to teach and the one who has much to learn. I believe all teachers, all masters, all adventurers in art would give much to do this as well. In substance he has said:

Come out from under your four walls and roof. Declare a holiday. Take the road with me to Thatch House—that admirable hostelry where good companions gather, where at the end of the day you will find a good telling of tales, a good singing of ballads, linen sheets that look white and smell of lavender, and you can listen to the refrain of Coridon's song: "Then care away and wend along with me." Stand with me at mid-day, in the open, where the sun casts no shadow, and let us together consider all things concerning our art—that which lies back of us—the antiquity of it, that which lies ahead of us—the great promise of it, and that which lies close about us and claims our immediate attention. I would have you know that tingling mood which comes to all who share the best that they have found. I would have you honor this art, and those who have gone before—who have set it in high places. Let your eye be single in all that it looks upon. And let us both share that humility which is at once the boon and the true grace of all who learn together.

Memory is a pleasant and profitable performance of the mind; so is intellectual appreciation. These as compared to the imagination, however, are but pale and sterile accomplishments; I mean for the artist, and for those who prefer to enjoy art rather than to analyze it. So it is your imagination I would conjure, and your emotions. This is no intellectual accomplishment, this book. I have no wish to prove anything, nor could I if I wished. If there be a place for this book on storytelling, it must be of adventure along the way of one storyteller. It must be built upon the feelings which have outlived memory. It must tell a story.

Wisely says the philosopher in James Stephens's *The Crock of Gold:* "I have learned . . . that the head does not hear anything until the heart has listened, and what the heart knows today the head will understand tomorrow."

And there is that delicious thing that James Stephens says on his own account: "A community of Leprecauns without a crock of gold is a blighted and merriless community. . . . A Leprecaun is of more value to the Earth than is a Prime Minister."

Thrice blessed is that child who comes early under the spell of the traditional storyteller, one who holds unconsciously to the ancient and moving power of her art. I was such a child. No fairy godmother could have hung over my cradle with richer gifts than Johanna, my Irish nurse. She had the art by nature and inheritance. The blood of the old seanachies ran in her veins; and there are no peoples with a richer folk-inheritance than the Gaels. I can hear Johanna saying: "Tales or tunes, ye'll find none better anywhere than what we have in Ireland." And she might have added: "And nowhere will you find them better told or sung."

Stories were year-round with Johanna; yet she had the strong instinct for "telling-time"; either the time was ripe for a story or it was not. She was as true in this as nature herself, who can tell without failing snow-drop-time, robin-time, ripe-strawberry-time. She honored her art too greatly to offer a story as a premium for good behavior, nor did she fling it as a sop to a child in tantrums. She saw to it that the telling never sank into the commonplace. I think Johanna wore her pride in the story and the telling of it with the same grace and gesture as did any ancient poet entering the dun of the five kings of Ireland. I can hear her giving the traditional ending: "Take it, and may the next one who tells it better it."

I never bring Johanna back into the present, that story-telling does not become the living art she made it. Hers was the gift of establishing a spiritual balance at the end of a day. I can feel the comfortable refuge of her lap. It hollowed deeper than any lap I had ever sat in. I can see her face, fairy-ridden. I can hear the soft Irish burr on her tongue which made the words join hands and dance, making a fairy ring that completely encircled me. I can hear her begin the tale of "Wee Meg Barnileg," knowing it already well myself, and feeling the stinging mortification of Meg's own behavior, which might well have been mine. But Johanna pointed no moral and drew no application. There was the tale—I could take it or leave it; and always I took it.

Truly thrice blessed is the child who has experienced such art through the listening-years. For these are the years a child can be so easily played on, when to be filled to the brimming means that the years ahead will never run dry. Now I believe it is the easiest thing in the world to tell a story—and the hardest to be a fine storyteller.

The best I have had of the unconscious art of the storyteller I have had from Johanna; and the best of the conscious art I have had from Marie Shedlock. How often down the years I have pictured what a festival there might have been had Marie Shedlock of Boulogne and Tunbridge Wells, and Johanna of County Donegal ever come together for an evening of storytelling.

I have been writing this book for a long time. Year after year I have watched it slough its shell like a shedder lobster, and start a new one. When I first began it our children were very young. It was a tradition with us every spring—March to April—to bring out Kenneth Grahame's *The Wind in the Willows* and begin again: "The Mole had been working very hard all the morning, spring-cleaning his little home."

Often there were other children sitting with us beside the fire; and that was good. Often another grandmother came to join ours; and that was very good. But best of all was when some tired neighbor dropped in on an errand and stayed; one who, like Mole, had never before deserted spring

cleaning for spring itself. Then it was that a homely, everyday miracle took place. The children undertook between
them to tell what had gone before in the book; and this
joyous, eager effort at storytelling drew us together into
that same kind of spiritual fellowship that was Mole's and
Rat's and Badger's.

Much of the book was beyond the intellectual understanding of our youngest. But nothing that could gain the
heart was lost: the humankindliness of Rat, the absurdities
of Toad, all the snug intimacies of life along the River
Bank. There was one part of the book that we approached
with reservation, almost with fear. Each spring when we
came to "The Piper at the Gates of Dawn" we wondered,
to ourselves of course, if for this one more time it would
bring the same lift of the spirit, the same sense of benedic-
tion, the same tremendous and overpowering awe at finding ourselves again in the presence of the Friend and Helper.

Our youngest once said: "I can divide our town up in
two—those who know Mole and Rat and Badger, and those
who don't." Those who have broken fairy-bread with Kenneth Graname have this feeling. Among all who have to do
with children, with their books and storytelling, it is those
who have missed *The Wind in the Willows* and the Piper
that I would draw into calling distance of the Willow Wren.
I would have them all embark with Rat and Mole on their
search for little Portly. For I take it to be a great and moving experience, one which none can afford to miss, to watch
with those of the River Bank while the moon lifts itself from
the earth and swings clear of its moorings, to explore every

patch of reeds, every runnel, in that silent, silvery kingdom. And at last, at dawn, to hear with Rat the first notes of that far-away piping; to feel the spirit leap to it; to know the full heritage of wonder; to listen, to understand for the space of the piping, even to forget afterward what one has heard and seen.

That I believe is part of every sacrament. It is enough to stand for the short breathing-space of the vision and look upon what is divine and imperishable and to know that it is true; to be able to say with Rat: "Afraid! Of *Him?* O, never, never! And yet—O, Mole, I am afraid!"

This is no book on how to tell stories and what to tell. It is a call to go questing, an urge to follow the way of the storyteller as pilgrims followed the way of Saint James in the Middle Ages, not for riches or knowledge or power, but that each might find "something for which his soul had cried out." I believe it to be something that transcends method, technique—the hows and the whys. It is, in the main, spiritual experience which makes storytellers. So strongly do I believe this that it seems to me when such experience is lacking all efforts toward expression, through the medium of any art, become but "sounding brass or tinkling cymbal."

Storytelling—A Folk-Art

Oh, sir, doubt not but that Angling is an Art, and an Art worth your learning: the Question is rather whether you be capable of learning. . . . For he that hopes to be a good Angler must not only bring an inquiring, searching, observing wit, but he must bring also a large measure of hope and patience and a love and propensity to the Art itself . . . but having once got and practised it, then doubt not but that Angling will prove to be so pleasant that it will prove like Vertue, a reward to itself.

—IZAAK WALTON

Storytelling—A Folk-Art

IN THE days of the guilds each man who had become master of his craft had two major concerns: to uphold the standard of workmanship within his guild, and to act as teacher, director, and inspirer of the apprentices.

I wish there might be a guild for storytellers today where master and apprentices might work together for the upholding of their art. Painters of the sixteenth and seventeenth centuries worked so, as did the silversmiths, the coachmakers. Only under such intimate and daily contact does it seem to me there can be pressed out that constant exchange of ideas that is so essential to any form of interpretation.

I am feeling this lack very strongly at the moment. I may have my own ideas, and express them. But I shall at best be able to reach little beyond the covers of this book for those ideas and feelings that are affecting others interested in storytelling. What comes back to me will come at random, and this is a great pity; for to play with an idea, to pass it from this one to that, to draw from it what is substantial and good and to discard the rest, here is what makes for that clarity of understanding upon which and by which one's art is built.

Twenty years ago good fortune brought the master of a guild to our door. He was from Bavaria, little, very old, and his face shrunken and colored like a pickled peach. He had come to measure our davenport for re-covering. With painstaking care he got out of his coat and into his apron of blue-and-white-striped ticking, adjusted his pincushion, his shears, hung his tape measure about his neck. He got only as far as measuring the front; and there he sat, on his heels, his tape measure dangling from one hand, while he told me about guilds—his guild. "I could cry when I think how it was in the old country. Money! We did not know what money was. We were sheltered; we were fed; we were taught. We lived only for our work—the rightness and beauty of it. We honored the guild, the master, and our patron saint. We knew if we were good, industrious boys we would be masters some day. Then it would be our turn to pass on to the apprentices the best of what we had learned, what we had invented for ourselves. That was the way it was. But what have I to pass on to the boys of this country who work for me? Money! That is all they want. No pride, no honor. Money—to earn and to spend."

Time went by on slippered feet. He told of the little town by the Danube where he had been born, of the long journey when he was twelve to Würzburg, where he began his apprenticeship under "a hard but a good master." And finally when, as an under-master, he went to the palace of King Ludwig. What a king! Mad? Never. They called him mad to make it easier to get his throne from him—those Germans! How he hated Bismarck! How he worshiped Ludwig! Did I know that every year the king had all who worked for him take part in an opera? Those who could sing were in the chorus. Those who played instruments made up the orchestra. A conductor from Dresden was brought to direct. The soloists came from the big cities. The great Wagner came; they were friends, those two— Ludwig and Wagner. For a week fete was held; then everybody went back to his work.

What the Bavarian upholsterer said at the last I have always remembered: "All the goodness, the lift of the heart that we got out of playing in those operas, we would put back into our work—in the draperies and tapestries we hung, in the cabinets we made. Nothing was lost. That is how it should be when you have experienced something great and beautiful. *Gnädige Frau,* something of those operas will go into your sofa."

The upholsterer was right—nothing is lost. I feel this strongly. My experience with storytelling has been rich, varied, and of long duration; and what I have to contribute must come out of this, rather than from any abstract ideas I may have gathered along the way. I feel vitally the presence of those mythical apprentices in an equally mythical guild who need direction and inspiration, an invitation to clear and sound thinking, if they are to accomplish anything with a traditional art in the present-day world.

In the main I have found students divided into two groups—those who want to learn largely by experimentation and their own efforts, who are willing to try and try again, even if they fail, or knowing they will fail; and those others who want specific direction, who would have a definite rule-of-thumb to go by. For the latter, if they remain rule-of-thumb persons, I have little to give. I think they will be able to tell stories but I doubt if they will be true storytellers.

Once somebody gave me a cook-book. It was compiled from what the editor called "basic recipes." Now, I consider cooking an art; it calls for imagination, ingenuity, natural aptitude. To ask an artist to work on basic recipes alone seems to me to belittle the greatest quality he has—his creative power. I want none of them. I can feel no anticipation for honey-bread, for crêpes Suzette, made on a basic recipe; I have none to give for storytelling.

The art of storytelling lies within the storyteller, to be searched for, drawn out, made to grow. It is compounded of certain invariables and these can be stated. Experience—that faring forth to try one's mettle. I have already spoken of this, with more to come later. The building of background—that conscious reaching out and participation in all things that may contribute to and illuminate one's art. Creative imagination; the power to evoke emotion; a sense of spiritual conviction. Finally a gift for selection. This last comes partly out of experience, the innumerable times of trying out a story and summing up the consequences. But the secret of the gift lies in the sixth sense of the true storyteller. Here is an indefinable something that acts as does the nose for the winetaster, as fingertips for the textile expert, as absolute pitch for the musician. I think one may be born with this; but it is far more likely to become ingrained after years of experience. Blessed be he who acquires it; for to judge stories for telling on the basis of critical discrimination alone leads to a barren performance.

While these are essentials, there is one fact about storytelling that must, like time, be taken by the forelock if there is to be intelligent as well as emotional satisfaction in becoming a storyteller. First must come a clear understanding of what storytelling is and what it is not. I know of so many who go stumbling along with little or no conception of what it is all about. They may be extremely successful at telling some stories, and extremely dreary at telling others. They have never made themselves think. They have liked to tell stories; and no one has kept them from it. This seems to have been all that mattered. It is far easier to dabble than to make oneself think through to some purpose, to comprehend the nature and demands laid upon one when one undertakes an art. What does storytelling require?

Most important is the right approach. Storytelling is a folk-art. To approach it with the feelings and the ideas of an intellectual or a sophisticate is at once to drive it under the domination of mind and critical sense. All folk-arts have grown out of the primal urge to give tongue to what has been seen, heard, experienced. They have been motivated by simple, direct folk-emotions, by imágination; they have been shaped by folk-wisdom. To bring a sophisticated attitude to a folk-art is to jeopardize it. Or rather, it is to make it into something that it is not. To the unpracticed, unthinking public there is no difference between dramatic reading, recitation, and storytelling. But to one who knows, dramatic reading and recitation belong to a comparatively modern and sophisticated age, and storytelling to one of the oldest traditional arts, having its roots in the beginnings of articulate expression. I think it is a common experience among storytellers of long standing to have the millstones of dramatic reading and recitation hung about their necks. Sometimes worse. The wife of a university president once said to me: "I haven't any parlor tricks. I wish you'd stay a week and give me some lessons in storytelling."

Every traditional storyteller I have heard—and I have gone into many countries to find them—has shown above everything else that intense urge to share with others what has already moved him deeply. "I will tell you a story that has given me good laughter for years," said the Spanish peasant before he told "The Flea." "When I think I am losing faith in my fellow-men I tell myself again this legend," said the Breton priest who told the Christmas story of Bo'Bossu. "Look," said Johanna, "this is your birthday. I am giving you a pink bowl to eat your porridge from. But that's the small, little part of it. I'm giving you mostly a tale about a peddler. It has kept my heart warm in a country which is a long distance from an Irish turf fire."

Not a clever sharing of the mind alone, but rather a sharing of heart and spirit: I think storytelling must do this if it is to endure.

To be a good storyteller one must be gloriously alive. It

is not possible to kindle fresh fires from burned-out embers.
I have noticed that the best of the traditional storytellers
whom I have heard have been those who live close to the
heart of things—to the earth, the sea, wind and weather.
They have been those who knew solitude, silence. They
have been given unbroken time in which to feel deeply, to
reach constantly for understanding. They have come to
know the power of the spoken word. These storytellers have
been sailors and peasants, wanderers and fishermen. They
have said with old Ivan in the story of "The Deserted
Mine": "Earth—water—darkness—they are all in God's
hands."

It is good to remember that there lies in this folk-art
much to quicken the spirit, that through and by the practice of it have been kept alive those experiences and imag-
inings which have made possible the eternal re-births of the
human race in the midst of maraudings, conquerings, sub-
jugations of tribe by tribe, of nation by nation.

I believe storytelling to be not only a folk-art but a living
art; and by that I mean much. Music in all its forms is a
living art in that it becomes a reality only when it is played.
Dancing is a living art, for it lives only while you watch the
movement, grace, interpretation of the dancer. So is it with
storytelling: it lives only while the story is being told. True,
child or adult can sometimes go to a book and read the story
again for himself; a good and an abiding thing to do, but
not the same thing.

I once watched a drab and dirty tinker tell a story about
the fairies at a Donegal crossroads. He gathered a crowd in

no time. Words became living substance for all who listened. That tight-fisted man by the name of Teig was born before our eyes; so were the fairies. A multitude of wee red caps took visible form. We caught our own red caps and took the voyage with Teig. For the duration of the story nothing lived but the story, neither listeners nor storyteller. When it was over, we saw again that the tinker was drab and dirty, that he was a tinker, haggling for trade; and we became, each of us, the child, the priest, the schoolmaster, the Yankee we had been before.

There is something definite about this story of Teig, as with all that I have got from a traditional storyteller. I tell it always from my memory of the telling at the crossroads. Then it is an easy and creative bit of telling. But if I should have to go to the printed page for it I know I should find it an overwhelming effort to blow the breath of life back into Teig and the fairies. I think it is this kind of miracle every storyteller must perform when he takes the story from the printed page, if it is to be true art and satisfying. Everyone who reads performs this miracle for himself to a certain extent.

The gift for storytelling comes as part of our racial inheritance; but that may mean less than nothing. It is not the legacy that is important; it is the way we feel about it and the use we make of it. One may inherit books and have little of the art of reading. One may inherit land and have no love for it. The point is that anyone can tell stories. Every human being tells many stories throughout the day, tells of a book he has read, of a play he has seen, of a street incident; but this being able to tell stories is a very different affair from being a storyteller, as I have said before.

Lineva in her introduction to *Peasant Songs of Great Russia* wrote:

It is because the whole power of the peasant song lies in free improvisation that the practiced execution of a folk-song, even by the best artists, cannot compare with the best peasant performance. . . . I am convinced that until we live in our song as every true artist lives in his work our execution will seem weak and pale.

And while I am quoting, let me give you Henry Finck, in his *Success in Music:*

No matter what Paderewski plays, he usually seems to be improvising, to follow the inspiration of the moment, to create the music while he performs it. His playing is the negation of the mechanical in music. When ordinary pianists play a Liszt rhapsody there is nothing in their performance that a musical stenographer could not note down just as it is played. But what Paderewski plays could not be put down on paper. . . . It is precisely these unwritten and unwritable things that constitute the soul of music and the instinctive command of which distinguishes a genius from a mere player.

Everyone can recall certain impressions such as these. I have heard great artists sing Negro spirituals; but I never knew the compelling beauty, the creative force in them, until I heard a hundred Negro prisoners in the federal prison in West Virginia sing on the heights below the Allegheny Mountains at sunrise on Easter Morning "Were You There When They Crucified My Lord?" Everyone who listened lived through the Crucifixion, the laying in the tomb, the Resurrection.

That is living art. That is creative art. That is what I believe can be brought to the art of storytelling were there more to feel impelled to bring it. Sorry indeed are the performance and the performer when all that is given is what a public stenographer could note down on paper. Or let me put it in another way—when all that is given in the telling is no more than what may lie already on the printed page.

If storytelling be the art we have granted it to be, then should we not accept it on the same terms on which we accept all art, and free it at the outset from all moral and utilitarian purpose? In this there is no intention of not recognizing or not understanding the broad educational value of storytelling. What I am decrying is the telling of stories to impart information or to train in any specified direction. The sooner this unhampering be accomplished the more positive and direct will be the approach to our goal, which I take to be creative.

I honestly believe no true artist ever put into concrete form a great and living idea with the primary impulse of educating humanity, or building its character, one jot or one tittle. To link moral purpose to any art is both absurd and sterile. In the past it has been with a kind of horror that I watched eager and intelligent young minds being thumb-screwed under the belief that storytelling could not stand alone as an art, that its reason for existence depended on some extraneous motive. Like many another I have been stormed with protests about the use of fairy tales. Child psychologists have done their best to create havoc in the field of children's stories and literature; especially would they step in and dilute, remedy, or bar altogether that which has sprung, living, from the spiritual loins of the race or from the creative pen of those who knew the true nature of childhood far better than the psychologist. I have been told that the story of "The Three Bears" conditions a child to fear; that "Red Riding Hood" conditions against grandmothers; that "Jack and the Beanstalk" induces a fixation for stealing. And well do I remember the young mother who once came to me asking for a list of stories which would keep Jerry from running away.

No one questions the vivid effect a story well told can have on the imagination of a child. Without purpose or effort young minds will be led out, stimulated, winged by the sharing of stories aloud, and to a far greater degree than when read alone and to oneself. But I hold with Sir Walter Scott, who warned a hundred and fifty years ago against putting a child's mind into the stocks, making it rigid, inflexible, by submitting to it only prescribed material. The whole process of growing up is the process of reaching out avidly for the world, to gain experience, to learn, to evaluate.

I was once nearly assaulted by an indignant mother who told me she had been telling some of Parker Fillmore's stories to her little girl of eight, on my recommendation, and had thereby produced a state of hysteria. The particular tale that caused the hysteria was "The Shoemaker's Apron." Yet here is a theme which has provided substance for one of the most delightful books and most moving of recent plays, *On Borrowed Time*. Upon inquiry I discovered the child was a border case, nervously. Her parents had preyed upon her sensibilities with their own fears and efforts to guard her from every possible dissonance of life. At eight years of age she could not stand the strain of having the devil put up in the pear tree.

Now if a child, through the misfortune of maladjustment, or parental over-concern, or illness, becomes highly nervous, I would accept it as a pathological case and treat it accordingly. But there is no reason to bar from the vigorous and buoyant minds of normal children legitimate folk-experience and fancies. Not that I champion "Red Riding Hood" or "The Three Bears" as great stories. But I do champion the cause of leaving healthy minds free, ungyved and soaring. I do hold it to be foolish and dangerous for adults to distrust this freedom for children, while they themselves distrust the substance and value of folk-literature.

There is another attitude toward storytelling which has disturbed me. It is the well-meaning protest which goes up from many of the normal schools, library schools, kindergarten training classes, against making the preparation of the storyteller appear hard. There are too many teachers who, feeling that their students have to master the intricate studies of pedagogy and cataloguing and Froebel, would therefore simplify what they judge to be the byproducts of training. There is no time to give much thought or direction to storytelling; therefore it must be made to appear easy, pleasant, that parlor trick the wife of the university president took it to be.

I come from old New England stock, the work-hard, die-hard kind. Instinctively I resent this attitude. Why should anything that is worth doing and doing well be made to appear easy when it is not? Why try to fool young people? Why so belittle an art that may prove an asset and a reward unto itself to any teacher and children's librarian? How much better to set students right as to the nature of story-telling, build up an attitude of integrity and effort toward it. And then say: Here is something you can learn as you go along. Apply everything that comes your way to a better understanding and use of it. Be your own teacher and your own critic, develop that love and propensity for it that can bring such immeasurable returns. We can give you a starting-point; go on from here with a stout heart.

I trust youth. I trust it to the point of not being too easily fooled by the "make it pleasant and easy" approach. I trust it to choose, if choice be honestly presented, the hard way of the storyteller if it brings in the end that satisfaction and pride of sound accomplishment. "Springes to catch woodcocks." I have detested them as much as Shakespeare did, and as I believe youth does.

The pity of it is that this matter of learning slowly, con-tinuously, is not brought often enough and with sufficient force and conviction before the potential storytellers of today to win them at the start. It makes in the end for the slipshod storyteller, the lazy storyteller, the half-hearted storyteller. It provides a deadly and vicious cycle of picking a story out of some collection, learning it by rote, telling it, and going back to the collection again. It is a dreadful thing to think about—a kind of additional limbo to Dante's inferno. It means that the true significance of storytelling is lost, or never discovered. It means there is never a knowing of the untold joy of the artist in taking substance, giving it form and color, blowing the breath of life into it, and then watching it take on life for others.

Storytelling is not for remedial purpose or for training. It is not a mechanical process to be made easy and pleasant. It is not a means of presenting limited material to the minds of children. It is an art demanding the utmost of your capacity and mine for living and understanding; it is dependent upon our power of creation; it asks for integrity, trust, and vision.

As in all arts, there may be a wide variation in the style and execution of the artist. The Basque captain did not tell his story in any way like the Donegal tinker, the fisherman on the Brittany coast told of the Kerrigans very differently from the way Johanna told of Wee Meg Barnileg. There must inevitably be a highly individual approach to each story. Creative imagination reaches for new material in diversified ways. It grasps it, makes it over, each time differently. Herein lies the living quality of it, that it is never the same, never repetitive.

Under all good storytelling there lies the common denominator of racial inheritance. Whether we have it by

conscious acquisition or not, there it is. I think it important to look into this inheritance and see how far it concerns
us today.

Years ago a middle-aged boy in my club at Greenwich
talked with me quietly one night after the story hour, when
the others had gone on to shoot craps and loiter in the back
alleys. "I like to listen to stories," he said, "but I like to do
something better. I like to tell them. I read more than the
other boys. Sometimes I tell them stuff out of books I've
read. Sometimes I pretend the stories happened to me. I
say 'I' instead of 'he' or using the guy's name. It isn't lying.
It's making believe. I like to feel I've had some wonderful
adventures. Some day I'm going out to get me some real
adventures."

Last year in a women's federal prison, a woman said
almost the same thing to me. I had been talking about
some of the new books. "I like the way you tell about
them," she said. "I like to tell stories myself." She was one
of the slickest confidence women operating in this country.
It took Edgar Hoover three years to get her. She had interested me considerably and so I asked: "What kind of
stories do you like to tell?"

"Mostly about myself—always did." She laughed with
apology and much amusement. "When I was a kid I used
to make up all kinds of stories about the things I wanted
to do—told them to folks as if they'd been Gospel truth.
I'd tell 'em how I walked the wire in some circus, how I'd
traveled south with some medicine show, how I'd rode a

white horse in Buffalo Bill's Wild West. Sometimes folks believed me; sometimes they didn't. It didn't matter; I always got a big kick out of it." She stopped there; and I waited. Finally it came out: "You know, I've often wondered if the rest of my life wasn't a kind of answer to those stories. After telling about it so long I had to run away and get going. You know—do something."

I did know; and she had done plenty. The interesting thing to me was the fact that she, like the Greenwich boy, had laid the universal pattern for storytelling. Strong and universal as the urge has always been to listen to a story, the urge to tell it has been stronger. And back of these has been the primal urge to do something—to adventure. It was whip-lash to Stevenson. It sent Stefansson and Du Chaillu to the extremes of the earth. It sent Rockwell Kent a-voyaging. It is out of this play of action against consequence that storytelling has developed.

And so I hold it to be both wise and interesting to go back to the beginning of race expression and lay out something of the pattern of this development. I have been digging at these beginnings of storytelling for more years than I can count. I have learned very little. I am no anthropologist, and only a fair-to-middling researcher. But I have been enchanted by what I have found. It seems worth sharing this in the hope that it may be a stimulus to others, sending them farther afield, to know the thrill of fresh discovery, to gather for others, to give back something, be it ever so little, in return for that wealth contributed by the past.

I know of no other group of artists. be they painters,

architects, composers, who have not gone into their own pasts, keen to gather all that had a bearing on their art. But I have found too few storytellers in this country who have looked beyond the hand that compiled or wrote their favorite collection of stories for them.

The Antiquity of It

Whining like forest dogs,
Rustling like budding trees,
Bubbling like thawing springs,
Humming like little bees,
Crooning like Maytime tides,
Chattering parrot words,
Crying the panther's cry,
Chirping like mating birds,
Thus, thus, we learned to speak. . . .

—VACHEL LINDSAY, "Eden in Winter"

(Reprinted from *Collected Poems* by Vachel
Lindsay, by permission of The Macmillan
Company, publishers)

The Antiquity of It

I AM writing this at the beginning of a raw, colorless
January. From my hilltop I can look westward over slate
roofs and chimney pots to farmland checkered brown and
green, the brown of fields plowed, ready for spring planting,
and the green of winter wheat. Between my hilltop and the
westing farms lies Cayuga Lake, meaning in the Iroquois
tongue: "Where we draw up our boats." Two hundred
years ago the Cayugas with their neighboring tribe the
Onondagas fished, hunted, marauded, smoked their peace-
pipes, made their treaties, told their tribal stories on the
shores of the lake. These stories were as old then as the
beaten trails which now mark a state highway and the main
road to a great university.

It is not hard to sweep aside the slate roofs and these centuries and draw the Indians back into their own country.
I can see the saffrons and browns of their longhouse showing among the naked trunks of maple and poplar, with here
and there the blur of an evergreen, set in one of those many
creeks which feed the lake. I can see the spirals of smoke
curling from a council fire. As dry fagots are thrown on, I
can picture face after face springing out in sharp relief;

lithe, crouched bodies, half naked, wrapped in blankets or skins, circling the fire. I can smell the sweet, pungent odor of smoldering wild-apple or pine-knots that hang in the air and from across the lake I can hear the fluted call of a loon winter-locked.

There comes the soft slithering of a moccasin over loose shale: the medicine man or one of the ancient wise ones of the tribe comes to take his place. Around his neck hangs the string of bears' teeth, numbering the tales he knows. He may carry his own drum or an apprentice may carry it, one who is learning the tribal tales and the art of telling them. The drum sets the rhythm for the chanting; it marks the pauses; it beats gloriously for the ending.

All this is as reality to me, for I heard not long ago one of the few surviving chieftains of the Onondagas tell some of his legends. I watched him slowly emerge from the shell of his civilized self-consciousness and become the inspired, traditional storyteller of the past. In his eyes I watched this picture grow which I have given you.

If you have been born in some European country it should not be hard for you to bring back your own native storyteller in this wise, whether he be scald or minnesinger, troubadour, pinkerdd, or seanachie. Their stories are still being told in cabin and croft, by the old men and women. These storytellers, like the Indian, stand out clear-cut and familiar along the road to the past. It is far back of these I would have you go, to where the first crude gropings toward storytellings had their inception. We have no records of them; the storytellers themselves stand blurred like trees at the far end of a forest trail. Fortunately there are rather recent records gathered by careful researchers among isolated tribes whose present development has not gone much beyond the primitive stage of our own. Beginning with these, we have a series of records covering nearly every stage of savage groping toward articulate expression, and from these we can get a fairly satisfactory picture of the beginnings of storytelling.

Our knowledge is not definite as to the beginning of language, nor do I think it greatly matters. There may have been language of a sort while man lived isolated in cave or tree, hunted alone, fought for his mate and young, and feared every other living thing. Or it may not have come until later, when men banded together for their common welfare and tribal life began.

It is enough if we remember that long before there was adequate language to express actions, emotions, and ideas, there had been intelligent purpose. People had been doing certain things for certain reasons for thousands of years and there existed an accumulation of experience that took a higher form than mere instinct. Experience began to be remembered. After thousands of years of action there began to be reaction, involving emotions, ideas, and the faculty to reason. As I have already said, it is out of this play of action and reaction that storytelling began.

The first primitive efforts at conscious storytelling consisted of a simple chant, set to the rhythm of some daily tribal occupation such as grinding corn, paddling canoe or kayak, sharpening weapons for hunting or war, or ceremonial dancing. They were in the first person, impromptu, giving expression to pride or exultation over some act of bravery or accomplishment that set the individual for the moment apart from the tribe. From the mass of material at hand I give three illustrations. These show a natural progression toward prose narrative. They are from three widely different hunting tribes, all of them extemporaneous outbursts following some specific event.

In each case one can readily imagine the successful tribesman swept by his sense of importance, glorying in his strength and prowess. The first might have been shouted to the swing of the paddle so that watchers on land or ice might hear; the second chanted by the spokesman of the hunters, stepping out of the circle round the fire in the center of the kraal; the third spoken after a feast, a general vaunting or exploiting, to remind fellow-tribesmen whose was the hunting and the quarry.

> I, Keokok, have slain a bear.
> Ayi—ayi—ayi—
> A great bear, a fierce bear,
> Ayi—ayi—ayi—
> With might have I slain him.
> Ayi—ayi—ayi—
> Great are the muscles of my arm—
> Strong for spear throwing—
> Strong for bear slaying—
> Strong for kayak going—
> I, Keokok, have slain a bear.
> Ayi—ayi—ayi—
>
> (An Innuit chant from Greenland)

Hunting it was good,
Hunting it was good.

We have killed a beast,
We have killed a beast.

Now we have something to eat,
Now we have something to eat. . . .

etc.

(P. Ehrenreich, "The Botocudos, a Tapuya
Tribe of Southern Brazil," *Zeitschrift für
Ethnologie*, 1887.)

The third is from the Dinkas, a Negroid tribe in the Eastern
Sudan:

I have a red bull with twisted horns;
He is so big that men can sit and rest in his shadow.
He went into the land of the people and ate their beans.
The land trembled because of him.
My father is a proud man at my greatness:
Like a lion am I and my enemies are scattered before me.
"Where," said he, "is there another like my son?"

(S. L. Cummins, *Journal of Anthropology*, 1904.)

You may find it interesting to compare these with a
Hebrew chant from Ecclesiastes, and then with an example
of unconscious rhythmic prose chanted by a four-year-old
boy of today:

I made great works; I builded me houses; I planted me vineyards. . . .
I made me pools of water, to water therewith the wood that
bringeth forth trees:

I got me servants and maidens, and had servants born in my
house;

Also I had great possessions of great and small cattle above all
that were in Jerusalem before me. . . .

So I was great, and increased more than all that were before
me in Jerusalem. . . .

(Ecclesiastes ii:4, 6, 7, 9)

Winter is gone.
I am out with my red engine;
It is full of electric-city,
It makes the headlights shine.
Today I planted my prune-pits,
Tomorrow-day they will grow.
The world is full of sunshine,
It is on my engine,
It is on my planted prune-pits,
I can feel it shining on my stomach.
Mother and I will pick the prunes
And I will eat them for my supper.

It may seem a far cry from an African Negro of this gen-
eration to "one who spoke in an assembly" two thousand
years ago, and then back to an American boy of today; but
they come together on a common plane of development, as
far as outward expression shows. Each is intensely concerned with himself—what he does and what he thinks
about it and what others may think. It is the legitimate
stage of blowing one's own trumpet, reaching not for the
moon but for the limelight. Those who have had much to
do with young children know how, for a certain period, they
will express themselves continually in this sing-song fashion.

Often small bodies undulate to the rhythm, often words are set to the swing of their play. The chant about the red engine was timed to the regular pushing, forward and backward, of the train. Every mother, I believe, could give innumerable illustrations from her own children.

With savage as with child, this narrow focus of interest upon himself begins to widen. The circle grows until it includes first his tribe or his family, then those closely related to them. Here are the beginnings of social interest and intercourse. Here develops a willingness to listen as well as to tell; and gradually narrative comes to adopt the third person.

One of the indicative points in arrested development in childhood is the inability to pass beyond this first-person focus, to become social-minded. As adults we become greatly concerned when this period in a child lengthens beyond its normal limit. An amusing incident with a neighbor's child comes to mind. In spite of a younger sister, the little girl clung tenaciously to her egotistical domination of every situation.

One day the two children passed the house on their way home from an adventure with a snake in a near-by meadow. The older child told the story in crisp sentences, and briefly it ran thus: "I went to the lower meadow, you know where, by the brook. I was running by a big rock when I saw a long, black snake. I was terribly frightened but I caught up a big stick and I went for him. He didn't hurt me. I made him run away and when he was gone I came home."

After she had finished, the small one asked with a good

deal of puzzlement: "But, Susie, where was me and my stick?"

As our primitive ancestors grew less subjective in their interest and curiosity they began to reach out of themselves toward life in general. At the beginning they were no more concerned with the universe and its laws than our dog is today. The sun may rise or set, or have an eclipse; seasons may rotate; it may rain continuously, the flats lie under water, and the creeks overflow their beds; or drought may come and the land lie parched. All this disturbs our collie not a whit. And so it was when the race was very young and life meant little more than survival.

But in time man began to wonder and to fear; and in consequence there came to be a propitiatory worship of the elements and the unseen forces behind them. Each tribe created its own ceremonials with their contemporary chants and charms. Chants to these unseen powers for benefits and protection; charms to ward off famine, pestilence, ill-luck. Leadership developed quickly—strong fearless men dominated; and these were propitiated and lauded, only in lesser degrees than the deities or demons.

This period, therefore, that marks the transition from first to third person, marks as well the beginnings of hero tale and myth. I give you two illustrations. The first is a chant from the Commi, a Negroid tribe of West Africa. It is a description of White Man, whom they believed in the beginning to be part hero, part god, living under the water and worthy of special propitiation.

In the blue palace of the deep sea
Dwells a creature strange.
His skin is white as salt,
His hair long and tangled as seaweed.
He is greater than the princes of the earth;
He is clothed with the skin of fishes,
Fishes more lovely than birds.
His house is built of rods and brass;
His garden is a forest of tobacco;
On his soil are white beads scattered
Like sand grains on the seashore.

(W. W. Reade, *Savage Africa*)

The second is the simplest form of myth. It comes from the Besis, a tribe of the Malay Peninsula.

Sun is a woman. She is tied by a rope which her lord is always hauling. Moon is a woman. She is the wife of Moyang-Bertang. Moonman is the enemy of mankind. He is always knotting strings by which he can snare men. He fails. Why? Some friendly mice are always gnawing the strings. Stars are Moon's children. At one time Sun had as many. They feared man could not stand so much heat so they agreed to eat their children. Moon did not eat her Stars. She hid them from Sun. Sun ate hers. Moon then brought out her family. Sun was very angry. She chased Moon to kill her. She has chased Moon ever since.

(Skeat and Blagden, *Pagan Races of the Malay Peninsula*)

During these early racial beginnings of storytelling, story was not distinct from poetry. These arts had a common inception, and music and dancing were associated with them. The chants were often accompanied by an instrument of some sort, dry bones rubbed together or beaten against stretched rawhide, or dried sinews stretched over a bent or hollowed piece of wood and strummed with the fingers. If the narrative was not timed to some occupational rhythm it was generally set to the swaying of the body and slow-measured movements of the feet.

As the third-person narrative became the more popular form, stories began to be told for the sole purpose of entertainment. Storytelling took its place as a part of tribal entertainment. After the hunt or a successful war foray, during a feast or afterward, those who could tell stories best told them to those who liked best to listen. As tribal life grew beyond the state of simple hunting and hand-to-mouth living into pasturing, planting, utensil-making, weaving, and simple government, the tribesmen were no longer satisfied with a casual remembering and recounting of traditional stories and events. A feeling for what we call historical record came into existence, a sense of its importance to the tribe. After generations of every man's being his own storyteller it became apparent that one man would have to give all his time and resourcefulness to keeping the records of tribal wanderings, to perpetuating the names and the deeds of the great men of the tribe. After generations of haphazard storytelling it was inevitable that it should begin to develop as an art, with certain ones showing more talent than others, until the chief and the wise old ones of the tribe chose a certain man among them who should tell tales and do nothing else. The chosen one was relieved of all tribal duties; others took over his share of the hunting, shelter-providing, fighting, so that he might be free to make war chants, charms, and stories, free to develop that art of extemporizing the feats of their heroes, and finally to tell tales for the amusement of the tribe.

Here we find the beginnings of the medicine man, the shaman, and the chief priest. Simple methods for keeping the records of tribal events and hero tales were devised: strings of shells, bears' or tigers' teeth, notches in sticks, knots in sinews or fiber, and, in the North, pieces of seal or walrus tusk and fish bones tied with sinews.

Out of the recording of hero events grew the hero cycles or sagas. Out of growing imagination came the impulse to exaggerate and idealize. Where history failed, imagination stepped in; for with the increasing capacity to wonder had come the capacity to invent. As storytelling came to be more and more a source of entertainment, as tribe vied with tribe to outdo each other in their records of achievement, storytellers began to fabricate a richer, more colorful pattern than facts could produce. In this way came the transition from the purely historical tale to the traditional and finally to the purely imaginative tale, what we now call the folktale.

The mythical tale grew in the same way—out of the first primitive chants to propitiate and to praise and out of the efforts of primitive men to answer their own wonderings. The race was tremendously concerned in the origin of man and the creation of the earth. A few concerned themselves with the origin of deity, but for the most part they accepted deity as an awesome fact, not to be inquired into. Gradually they became concerned in the whys and wherefores of all natural laws.

Correlated with the development of the myth and hero tale was a third type, the beast or totem story. This grew out of an inborn sense of animism and the everlasting wondering as to whether animals were created before men or afterward, with spirits or without. It was inevitable to give animals and humans an interchange of attributes, to foist upon the creatures the weaknesses, foibles, and rascality of humankind. We find an early creeping in of crude satire in connection with these beast tales. What the storyteller dared not attempt at the expense of his fellow-tribesmen he could safely convey in animal terms for those whom the skin would fit. Out of these beast tales grew a permanent literary form which we find in the *Jataka* or *Rebirth Stories,* the *Panchatantra, The Golden Ass,* the *Epic of Reynard the Fox,* the American *Bre'r Rabbit,* the North American Indian tales of Manabozho, the Great White Rabbit, Eskimo tales, and innumerable others.

With storytelling as a definite form of tribal entertainment, with the storyteller chosen and self-trained for his office, we find the beginnings of a conscious literary form. A distinction began to be made between prose and metrical narrative. Storytellers gave attention to ways of saying things; they studied the effects of presentation upon their listeners. Certain types of stories gained by rhythmic presentation; certain other types fared better if given in terse, strong prose. And along with this growing appreciation of form and its effect came a new type of story—the ethical tale.

This was told largely for its effect upon the tribe. Originally there had been only chants to bravery, to tribal loyalty and honor. Now stories were told for a deeper purpose, to instill into the minds and natures of the youths the standards of tribal behavior—respect for the elders, protection of the women and children, sacrifice for the chief—and the practical benefits of religious worship, good conduct, and personal chastity. Like the beast tales these found a later permanent literary form in fables, allegories, parables, and legends.

Lest this brief presentation of the growth of the ethical tale, and its purpose, appears in contradiction to that statement made earlier in the book, deploring the telling of stories for moral or utilitarian purpose, let me make clear what I mean.

Among primitive peoples that groping toward what we call ethical consciousness had its definite place in tribal growth. Out of it grew a more or less conscious recognition that certain behavior was necessary for the welfare of all. This being so, certain standards for individual conduct were laid down by the elders or wise ones for the young to follow; and it was natural that these should take the form of stories, fables, parables, allegories. What they said in the main was: Act in this wise—and this will happen. Fail to do this and you will pay for it. Definite teaching provided a part of the schooling called for in the early days of human development. It was schooling then even as it is schooling now.

But such schooling has no kinship with that art of story-telling to which we are holding fast today.

I think there can be little doubt that the boys and girls of the wandering tribes of five and six thousand years ago were as bored by these "behavior tales," as our boys and girls of today would be if we attempted to offer them as substitutes for the stories that delight and enchant.

This covers the period of primitive storytelling, that which stands far back at the blurred end of the trail. There follow thousands of years of transition. We come to a time in ancient storytelling when stories were no longer per-petuated by word of mouth alone. Clay tablets began to be made; the use of picture and symbol became widespread, from the cave drawings of the Cro-Magnons in Western Europe to the famous stone prism recording the events in the reign of Sennacherib over Babylon.

There began to be commerce; and a great making over of conquered tribes into dominating nations. Wherever merchandise was carried, wherever armies marched to battle, storytellers went and with them a great weaving and distributing of story material.

Pattern for the Past

Children play at being great and wonderful people, at the ambitions they will put away for one reason or another before they grow into ordinary men and woman. Mankind as a whole had a like dream once; everybody and nobody built up the dream bit by bit, and the ancient storytellers are there to make us remember what mankind would have been like, had not fear and the failing will and the laws of nature tripped up its heels. . . . I have read in a fabulous book that Adam had but to imagine a bird and it was born into life, and that he created all things out of himself by nothing more important than an unflagging fancy; and heroes who can make a ship out of a shaving have but little less of the divine prerogatives.

—WILLIAM BUTLER YEATS, in his preface to Lady Gregory's *Gods and Fighting Men*

Pattern for the Past

I HAVE an old belief—true or not as it may be—and that is that the first definite challenge to the art of the story-teller came when stories began to be written down, when for the first time tales were no longer handed on as living substance, from mouth to mouth, no longer expelled on the breath of one storyteller to be drawn in on the breath of another. Among primitive peoples it is believed possible to sustain life this way; the spirit about to depart may be held by one who breathes life out of himself in through the lips of the dying one.

There is a kind of death to every story when it leaves the speaker and becomes impaled for all time on clay tablets or the written and printed page. To take it from the page, to create it again into living substance, this is the challenge—not only for the storytellers from 4000 B.C. through the Middle Ages, but for the storyteller of today. It is well to remember this, to keep oneself primed for this challenge, for the greater bulk of storytelling material comes to the modern storyteller off the printed page.

The first written record we have of storytelling in ancient times is that collection of Egyptian tales on papyri known

as the *Tales of the Magicians*. The majority of scholars date
it as far back as 4000 B.C. It tells of how the sons of Cheops,
the great builder of pyramids, entertained their father with
strange stories. When one son finished, a second took his
place that he might tell yet a stranger tale.

Here we find the original grouping of stories around a
central idea. Two or three thousand years afterward the
compiler or compilers of *The Thousand and One Nights*
borrowed the device for these Arabian tales. Somadeva borrowed it for his *Ocean of Story;* the compilers for the *Gesta
Romanorum;* Boccaccio for his *Decameron;* Chaucer for
his *Canterbury Tales;* and so on *ad infinitum.* For nearly
six thousand years it has proved a popular way of holding a
collection of stories together, and listeners have never tired
of it.

Beginning with the sons of King Cheops, the ancient
storytellers gather from every corner of the earth in bewildering numbers. To give them all the variety and color
and sweep of imagination that they deserve their story
would have to be told as the Finnish Romani story of the
nativity was told—by the stars. One can imagine Capella
calling across the sky to Aldebaran: "Look! Yonder I see a
desert encampment. For days the tribe has been wandering
to find fresh pasturage for their sheep. Now they reach the
oasis. They have slaked their thirst at the well, they have
gathered fresh dates, and creatures are grazing while the
herdboys watch and the men pitch their tents. Women prepare the evening meal. They know they have nearly reached
the end of their wanderings; across this corner of Arabia

lies a river and, beyond that, wide stretches of green pasturage. There is much rejoicing among the tribes. When
supper is over, they will make a thank offering to their god,
Jehovah."

And Aldebaran calling back: "Look! I can see young
shepherds making their fire of dried palm-fiber and roots
and huddling about it, their cloaks drawn close about them
against the cold of the desert night. I see a head herdsman
of the tribe joining them. He squats on his heels and begins
the telling of a story to lessen the tedium of these longest
hours between midnight and dawn. Come, hearken to the
tale."

So did the tribes of Israel tell of Terah, the father of
Abraham, and of those legends supposed to have been
gathered in the lost books of the Apocrypha; recorded by
the early Hebrews but never found by Hebrew scholars.
There was no doubt about the amazing gift of these early
wandering storytellers. It might be said of them that they
were as rich in imagination as in herds and flocks; that they
gathered their legends as later their kings gathered precious
metals and stones. A thousand years afterward their stories
were carried to the four corners of the earth to be raveled
out and woven again into the folk-tales of other peoples.

Another thousand years pass and one can hear Vega, in
the northern sky, calling across to Sirius, in the lower sky:
"Look! Can you see Rome reaching over the face of the
earth like outstretched fingers on a mighty hand? Can you
see her gathering more mercenaries and sending her legions
into Carthage, Gaul, and Britain? There are slaves to row

her galleys into the waters about Africa Media, Asia Minor, Arabia. They whisper among themselves stories of their gods. I see hairy barbarians, coming to the Roman camps at night. They tower like giants over the fires while they tell tales to the legionaries, in exchange for food. I see women slaves, the daughters of conquered kings, sitting in the atrium of conquerors' houses, telling to the Roman children tales from Greece, from Egypt, from Palestine, Gaul, and Britain. I can see conquered artisans telling their tales to each other over the forge, the loom, and in the quarry."

Of Roman storytellers there are scant records; and the Romans themselves created little early literature. But they were the greatest distributors. While they were hiring mercenaries, marching armies across Europe, subjecting tribes and nations, they were casting a tremendous melting-pot into which was going most of the lore of the Eastern Hemisphere.

Next to the Romans, as distributors, come the gypsies. We know little about their origin—probably Hindu. That they wandered from the east westward, that their language shows Sanskrit or Prakrit source, that they claim descent from the first Pharaoh—that is as near to the facts as we can come. It is of interest, however, that the early Egyptians called themselves "Romi," meaning men; and it is more than probable that the words Rom and Romani of the gypsies were from this source.

Legend is rife about them. They are spoken of in the Apocryphal Book of Adam; and there is one legend to the effect that they were the children of Ishmael, son of Hagar, the cast-out wife of Abraham. Like the Romans, they created very little. Their literature was thieved and made over, as were their cloaks; yet they have added much in color and intricacy to the pattern. Old chronicles, manuscripts, and tales of the Middle Ages speak often of them. They were prized for their music, their storytelling and prophecies; they were tolerated for their skill as coppersmiths, farriers, and horsebreakers. But they carried rascally tongues and they were too light-fingered to be allowed long encampment in any community. So they eternally wandered, as under a curse. Here today, gone tomorrow. If you wish to get any idea of how far they traveled, with what countries they identified themselves to the extent of learning the language and establishing permanent camps, read the *Journal of the Gypsy Lore Society*. They have left their imprint on almost every country: Turkey, Afghanistan, Algeria, Spain, Finland, the British Isles, the Americas. In olden times kings feasted them, monasteries opened their doors to them, overlords granted them living-space among their serfs. Vagabonds always, but vagabonds with silver tongues and imaginations. I heard two Irish tinkers tell stories once at a crossroads in County Fermanagh, and I shall never forget it.

There is a third source of distribution throughout the Eastern Hemisphere which should be remembered: the pilgrims and crusaders of the Middle Ages. Especially did they cover the old pilgrim way of Saint James, leading down through France, around the Cantabrian Coast to the city of Santiago de Compostela in Galicia, Spain. Kings and friars, palmers and knights, commoners and rogues traveled together. The distances between rest-houses were great; the way, long and tedious. Think of the sharing of tales there must have been as they traveled. Unfortunately there was no recorder along the way of Saint James such as Geoffrey Chaucer on the way to Canterbury. But even lacking a Chaucer, tales were brought from the four corners of Christendom, were exchanged along the road, and carried east or north again. There are some rare legends surviving of Saint James himself; and today he who goes searching through Galicia will find storytellers repeating old Celtic tales, Frankish tales, Danish tales. Alcuin, that monastic clerk to King Charlemagne, in his chronicle told of these pilgrims and the storytellers but nothing of the stories.

I like to remember that hundreds of years afterward George Borrow came along part of that same pilgrim way, selling his Bibles. He was shipwrecked off the Cantabrian Coast and very nearly did not get to Spain.

At two geographical extremes we find a common type of storyteller developing: the Aeolic minstrel of Greece and the scald of the North. These are heroic figures, chanters of war ballads, epics, and sagas. With both groups the prose narrative grew slowly; it was the metrical story that enthralled them, both as composers and as reciters. The Iceland poet was not unlike the later troubadour. He became vassal to some king or earl, sang for him, fought for him, recounted his deeds and, if he survived him after the battle, sang his death-song for him.

While Roman legions were still conquering, while gypsies

were wandering hither and yon, while viking ships were doing battle on the high seas and Homer's successors were making epics, reciting war ballads and festival hymns, there were coming into existence two schools of storytelling among kindred peoples. These were the Gaelic school of ollamhs in Ireland, and the Cymric school of bards in Wales. To Ireland more than to Wales came scholars from all over the world to be trained in the arts of composition and recitation.

The ollamhs had nine divisions, each bearing a different name and holding a distinct office. They were historians, keepers of genealogies, poets, writers of heroic stories or loidhes, judges of the people, teachers of wit, wisdom, and satire, and tellers of tales. Youths entered as apprentices and attached themselves to some one master, in much the same fashion that apprentices attached themselves to the master of some craft in the time of the guilds. Often they made the journey on foot, facing innumerable dangers and hardships. They remained for years while they passed from master to master. Sometimes they stayed permanently, like Saint Patrick, making Ireland their homeland and becoming known as native bards or seanachies. Patrick himself made poetry—good poetry.

To the seanachie was given the historical tale, and he had to know one hundred and seventy-eight. These included stories of famous cattle raids, voyages, the stealing of wives, the crowning of kings, the winning of championships and adventure with the sidhe or fairies. A record of these has been kept in one of the ancient books of Ireland. The seanachie it was who preserved by word of mouth all that went later into the making of the *Book of the Dun Cow.*

The loidhes or hero sagas were chanted in the Gaelic minor scale of five notes. Later I tell of hearing John Hegarty, then one of the oldest living seanachies, chant a loidhe of Oisin on the hills of Donegal. The night before we had heard a banshee call from the other side of the moor; and she had in her caoining the same notation. Was it the banshee who taught those men of pagan times their eerie way of blending words and music? Was it from her caoining that the Irish learned their minor scale? I have often wondered. William Butler Yeats has given the notation of a banshee's cry in his *Irish Fairy Tales.* But when I heard John Hegarty he sounded exactly like the banshee.

A master owned certain stories which no apprentice could tell without his permission. I remember Mary Austin once told me that the Navajos owned songs and song-poems in the same sense.

In ancient Ireland, once a year, a truce was declared between the warring clans. Along the five white roads to Tara, seat of the High King, came chieftains and champions, bards, storytellers, harpers and pipers, to compete for rank in their several arts. Each clan had its chief ollamh and seanachie, and woe to the latter if he did not have a fresh tale to tell when the king called for it. The penalty for this could be death if the king willed it. Here is a good tale within a tale, put in, as the Irish would say, for diversion.

Attached to Fionn MacCumhal and the Fianna was a certain famous seanachie. Tales he had thick on his tongue.

Now the season was Samhain, and the gathering was at Tara, and for three nights there had been feasting and harping and the long hours of tale-telling. And the day came when the High King commanded the telling to be that night by the chief seanachie of the Fianna. The man was at his wit's end, for he owned not one new tale; and to take one from another seanachie was against the law. A heavy horror crept into his heart that sank it like a stone: "Decent man, decent man," he said over and over to himself, "go out and find yourself a tale or you'll never be seeing tomorrow's sun."

Out he went toward the Hill of Tara, where the tall green forest does be growing. Along the edge of the woods he tramped, making one foot to go before the other, and finding nothing at all of importance in his mind out of which to make a tale. After him ran Bran, Fionn's hound, which everyone does be knowing was born of a woman, sired by a fairy. Suddenly out of a thicket sprang a snow-white doe; and on the instant Bran was baying it. Forgetting his own trouble the seanachie was after them both. Running, running fast was he now; and in time to see the doe change to a white wood-pigeon, and take the air; while Bran, the hound changed to a gray falcon, pursuing her.

Across the sky and back again went the chase, the seanachie watching it hard with the two eyes. Gaining the near-by stream he saw the pigeon change to a trout and take the current, swimming down with it, while the falcon changed to a great buck-salmon, going after the trout. So change after change went on, the pursuer never slacking speed after the pursued, until the seanachie found himself not far from the dun of the king and beside him stood Bran, Fionn's hound, again, and beside him the queen of the sidhe. And what she said was this: "Teller of tales, decent man that you are, go you to the feast with a contented mind. Have you not now a fresh tale to be telling?"

(For those who would have a fine feeling for the early storytelling in Ireland let them be reading "The Poet's Fee" by Ella Young, a story published in the *Horn Book* in 1939, May–June issue. Ireland has no more perfect example of the traditional storyteller's art today than that which is Ella Young's. Her pen and her voice keep pace in wonder and pure artistry.)

The leaders of the Welsh bards were the pinkerdd, and their apprentices were the mabinogs, from which name we get the *Mabinogion*. In the beginning mabinogion meant simply those tales that had to be known by every apprentice before he could become a master storyteller; we erroneously associate the name today with those stories which make up the Arthurian cycle.

It is interesting to go back over a thousand years and see what the ranking and the worth of a storyteller were. A pinkerdd was assigned the tenth chair from the king; he was equal in rank to the court smith. His value was sixscore and six kine. The price of his ransom or indemnity was sixscore and six pena (the pena was a contemporary monetary unit). He was under the king's immediate protection from the time he began his first recitation until he had finished his last. He, and he alone, was privileged to take the front of the hall; all mabinogs had to give their tales from the back. His personal benefits were: "A harp from the king, a ring from the queen, cloth and a horse from the king, linen from the queen; and from the court, a man's maintenance."

Until two wars broke the custom, both Welsh and Irish kept their bardic festivals. Once during the year men, women, and even children came from every corner of the two countries to sing, to chant, to tell ancient stories, to present ancient dramas, to pipe, and to harp. I don't know how it was in Wales but in Ireland many of them wore the ancient Irish dress of the Gael, green or saffron kilts and brata. A band of Irish pipers climbed the hill outside of Dublin on the dawn of the first day and piped the festival in; and at midnight on the third day they climbed the hill again and piped the festival out. I know, for I climbed with them.

Down through the Middle Ages—from the tenth century through the fourteenth—life was precarious: individual preyed on individual, feudal lords on other feudal lords; clan was pitted against clan, kingdom against kingdom. Small wonder then, with living at such odds, that the world snatched savagely at its amusement and diversion. Ladies at their tapestry frames; monks about their refectory tables; entire courts afield, hunting, with falcon on wrist or hound at heel; lords, knights, and squires, snug in their castles, after a day of questing or fighting—whoever they were and whatever they might be doing, ears were always acock for a good story. It was a time of rich harvest for those who had the wit to create, the memory to hold, and the grace of tongue to recount tales that could amuse. The ribald story developed beside the legend of saint and Christ and Virgin; tales of heroes vied with those of rogues in popularity.

Trouvères and troubadours were everywhere, going and coming, thick as starlings. There were the great ones: Raimbaut de Vaqueiras, Sordel, Vidal—all attached to a prince or king, many knighted, with castles of their own, traveling about with a retinue of pages, squires, subordinates, and apprentices, whose indemnity—like the pinkerdd's—was worth a king's ransom. And there were the poor ones who wandered the roads in rags with staff in hand, bundle on back. They wintered in some hole like the foxes, shivering with the cold while they composed a ballad or story with which they hoped to win favor at court on the morrow. Many a young vagabond won a king for his patron by some turn of luck or his own nimble tongue.

I think it is the itinerant storyteller of the Middle Ages who has always enthralled me most; he who traveled the length and breadth of the world, carrying his story from here to there, living by the strength of what he told. With the coming of spring, granted that he survived the winter, he fared forth, his garments freshly patched, a fresh stock of tales at his tongue's end, a brave air put on to meet the crowds. Just such an air as the Juggler, in the legend of Cluny, put on as he came down the road to meet the market-day crowd in the month of Marie.

Think of having to live literally on your art! There is whip-lash for you. Think of what it means to earn a place by the fire, a night's lodging, a hot meal, in return for a tale, or a handful of them. I think I have never told a story that I have not wondered if this were not after all the supreme test of the art. To command attention, not trade on mere willingness of others to listen. To take the center of the market-place, or a table at the inn, and, whether by the sharing of great adventure or taking the gentle road of fancy, be able to lift the soul with exaltation or move it with amazement. To put upon listeners the compulsion of a mood, there is true art. To hold "children from play, and old men from the chimney corner"—nothing short of this, I take it, can be called storytelling.

In the beginning the trouvères alone were the composers, the troubadours the reciters; but before long these terms became confused until a troubadour became synonymous for both. A good troubadour, whose patron was noble, was expected to know perfectly all the current tales, to repeat all the noteworthy theses from the universities, to be well informed on court scandal, to know the healing power of herbs and simples, to be able to compose verses to a lord or lady at a moment's notice, and to play on at least two of the instruments then in favor at court.

Vidal gave the following advice to one of his apprentices:

A troubadour must be as wise as a serpent, as harmless as a dove, pliable as a willow, steadfast as an oak. He must have learning without pedantry, wit without folly, keen insight into character, tact to adapt himself to every disposition, to be amiable without being parasitic, edifying without being tedious, his merriment combined with temperance, a model in dress, expert in all matters, possessing all the qualities of every other class in addition to his own.

It may be interesting to note further what a "model in dress" consisted of. I quote from an old manuscript describing a troubadour in the thirteenth century:

Stockings and breeches of Bruges linen, dark brown and saffron. Robe of dark blue woolen cloth trimmed with gris. The bliaut [frock] of deep crimson taffeta trimmed with bands of gold embroidery, caught under the chin with an agate button and belted with buff leather and a silver buckle weighing one mark. The mantle of dark green, cut in a semicircular pattern of brocade and trimmed in the corners with squares of heavy cloth encrusted with small gems—emeralds and sardonyx—and fastened on the right shoulder by a frog woven out of some lady's hair.

One can picture such a fine fellow on his way to the court of Aragon or Navarre, to sit at meat with the king. One can picture further the king in his carven chair before the table, raised on a dais or platform. The hall would be rough-hewn, with ceiling sloping upward toward the center and the smoke hole. About the walls would be narrow embrasures, barred with crossings of iron, the hangings drawn to keep out the night's chill. On the walls would be tapestry; weapons of war and hunting trophies as well. At one end, mounting out of the hall or behind a stone enclosure, would be the narrow winding stairs leading to the women's quarters. A great fire would burn in the center; around it, benches and tables for the men-at-arms and the squires; and everywhere pages scuttling to bring basins for the laving of hands, filling goblets; stewards or constables hurrying in with filled trenchers. There would be venison and boar's meat, fish and green herbs, pasties and boiled puddings; and a steady procession of pages with flagons of ale and wine.

Above the clatter of tongues and platters would sound the clang of the drawbridge, the metal ring of hoofs against flagging, the voice of a squire or herald calling admittance for the newcomer. Then would our fine fellow enter with his retinue: a motleyed buffoon to bring laughter after the solemn telling of a crusader's tale, a tumbler to bring diversion, a page or two to carry a viol, lute, or tympan to make accompaniment for a story of love and intrigue, two or three apprentices to fill in after the king had wearied and gone to his bed. All these would make such a company as later became strolling players and mummers. In the old MS. of Saint-Palaye we find this quaintly written: "The troubadours animated the minds of men; by amusing them they led them to think, to reflect, to judge."

It is possible to go on indefinitely with these storytellers of the Middle Ages; their history is interwoven with the history of Europe and the men who made it. In "The Legend of Saint Elizabeth," which I give later in the book, there is the merest breath of a picture of the minnesingers. If there were space I should like to show the monks at their storytelling and the masters of the guilds exchanging tales of their patron saints and certain miracles of their several crafts.

Like the ollamhs of the Gael, the troubadours grew in

time arrogant and insufferable. They became quibblers over form; they soiled their tongues with too much scandal; in the end they fell into disfavor and their benefits were taken from them. Like the blind Homer and the itinerant storyteller, they became wandering beggars, trading their stories for a flagon of ale, a loaf-end, and a place by the fire.

There are two isolated pictures of storytellers I think may interest. This one is from Sir Richard Burton's translation of *The Arabian Nights* and tells of a storyteller in a bazaar in Tangiers:

The market people form a ring about the reciter, who affects little raiment besides a broad belt into which his lower chiffons are tucked. He usually handles a short stick and when drummer and piper are absent he carries a tiny tom-tom, shaped like an hour-glass, upon which he taps his periods. He opens with an extempore prayer. He speaks slowly and with emphasis, varying the diction with abundant action and most comical grimace. He advances, retires, wheels about, illustrating every point with pantomime. And his features, voice, and gestures are so expressive that even Europe, who cannot understand a word of Arabic, divines the meaning of the tales.

John Francis Campbell in his *Popular Tales of the West Highlands* gives this terse but effective picture in a Breton cabin:

The evening meal is over; the life of the saint of the day is read, fagots are brought, the women spin, the men gossip, the children play. At last all grow tired; the children clamor for a story as a certain blind beggar in wooden shoes comes down the road. He knows many stories and ballads; he knows that wherever he goes he is welcome. He can stay as long as he likes; his mug of cider is kept filled; the cabin that houses him is honored; the children are happy.

Ballads: here is a type of metrical story about which I have said little. Here is rich source of material for those searching for it. The Spanish were past masters at balladry. Through the sixteenth and seventeenth centuries *juglares de boca*—jugglers of the mouth—traveled everywhere making popular those heroes so beloved: Mío Cid el Campeador, Bernardo del Carpio, the Infantes de Lara; and incorporating much of *The Song of Roland* in their own ballads. *Cantares de gesta, romanceros,* these tales were called. They vied in popularity with the picaresque story.

Svend Grundtvig, folk-lorist of Denmark, who has gathered his own Scandinavian ballads and helped James Francis Child, late professor of Harvard, in his invaluable collection of English and Scottish popular ballads, gives ballads the following classification which, although it may not satisfy the scholar, is very helpful to the average student. They might well serve as a classification for all folk-tales and legends: heroic ballads; ballads of magic and marvel; historical ballads; ballads of chivalry and romance.

There is great diversification in the ballad form; but the common form seems to be the quatrain, often carrying a refrain. The mass of material is anonymous—true folk-lore. Like the *juglar de boca,* the minstrel of the North gave form to what he sang, and in many instances created his hero. So was William Tell born to the Swiss and Robin Hood to the English—pure creation on the part of some ballad muse.

I wish there might be more ballads used by storytellers —sung by those who can sing and with the original airs; otherwise told with a feeling for the art of minstrelsy. It means a tedious piece of work, memorizing, and then forgetting the mechanics of word-commitment and letting the story sing forth, extempore, as its creator first sang it. Ballads so sung, or told with a fine, discriminating sense of rhythm and timing, would provide a good contrast in any story hour. It is unfortunate to allow the metrical story to be forgotten. It is important to keep alive in the children of today an ear for that which has rhyme and rhythm. Ballad may not reach far toward a high standard of poetry, but it is true folk-expression and it does satisfy the ear and heart of childhood—especially those of the eight-to-twelve-year-olds.

I have discovered that something very delightful may take place when a ballad with a refrain is introduced into the story hour. In no time at all the children have caught the refrain and are chanting it with the storyteller. So, as in olden times, the listeners take part. A good thing, too. Take a verse from "The Elfin Knight":

> Can you make me a cambrick shirt,
> > Parsley, sage, rosemary and thyme,
> Without any seam or needle work?
> > And you shall be a true lover of mine.

"Parsley, sage, rosemary and thyme"—words that fit young tongues so pleasantly.

I have a happy memory of ballads. My mother never told me a story but she sang ballads—many of them—which she had from her mother, the first Lucinda Wyman. I never knew my grandmother save through those striking pictures my mother gave me of her. She must have been a wonderful woman. She got most of her schooling listening outside the little schoolhouse in Keene, New Hampshire, where her brothers went to school. In her day New England made no effort to educate its girls. She married my grandfather, of Lexington, Massachusetts. He had been a famous fifer through the war of 1812, and brought his fife home to march around the kitchen playing obbligatos to his bride's singing of ballads while she "did up" the dishes. And what couldn't she sing! All who ever heard her testified to the warm, lovely quality of her voice and the fine dramatic art she showed. Neighbors dropped in to hear them; they must have been the star performers of Lexington in their day—Lucinda and Josiah. They had a collection of broadsides and chapbooks, which gave the early printing of the ballads in England.

I hope this may provide an appetizer for those who are honestly hungry for all that lies at the beginning of this art, for something of what has gone into the most romantic and picturesque period of storytelling, for something that may give us an appreciation of all that has gone into the building of our folk-literature. This seems immensely important to me. It has added substance to my own storytelling, a sense of festival. I think every would-be artist needs to make this effort to link up with the great, towering figures of the past, those who were the true creators of their time.

And so, at long last, where does it bring us? To the starting-point. We are today at that exact spot where storytelling had its inception—every man his own storyteller. For, today, few are chosen. There are no elect among us. But we have a treasure-house of material, stored through these six thousand years, within reach of hand and imagination. As distributors we can do a fine piece of work, remembering always that to tell a story is not enough, remembering to honor what we tell, and to bring to the receptivity of the listener something of the universal appeal, the deep significance of folk-literature—to touch the heart tnat the head may understand.

Experience

Out of your cage,
Come out of your cage
And take your soul on a pilgrimage!
Pease in your shoes, an if you must!
But out and away before you're dust:
Scribe and Stay-at-home,
Saint and Sage,
Out of your cage,
Out of your cage!
—Song from JOSEPHINE PRESTON PEABODY'S
play, *The Piper*

Experience

WE LEARN by experience. All that we ever learn comes out of that everlasting process of taking in, assimilating, and giving out. Much we do unconsciously; much we intend our minds and our wills toward getting, to the end that we may have sound working values for what we may elect to do.

I think this business of getting experience is tremendously interesting when one looks back at the gathering of it. It is like fairy gold: make use of it, and it serves you bountifully; hoard it, and it turns to dust. As with fairy gold, you can never trade it directly over the counter. It must be used with indirection; for who will take another's experience in trade for one's own?

I sat in an Irish cabin one night while a little, small grandmother told me of that Bealtaine time when she got her gold. She was bringing a pot of stir-about to its end of cooking, having kept it stirred well off the pot's bottom so there might be no burning. And then the door opened and two wee fairy men came in, bringing a big-sized firkin between them. They dragged it to the hearth. And while one wee man climbed up the pot, the other waited below to hand him the spoon so that he could spoon out some of the porridge into the firkin. It was as comical a sight as you could wish, according to the grandmother. But the wee man on the pot's rim lost his balance and fell in. And then it wasn't comical. His companion climbed the pot and tried to pull him out, but the thick, heavy porridge held him fast. There was much squealing and lamenting till the old woman got up, reached in, drew him out of the pot, wiped him clean of the stir-about, filled the firkin for them, and placed them both safely outside her door again. A bit of an hour later the tumble-in wee man returned, lifted the latch, came in, and laid a fairy gold-piece on the stool beside the hearth. The old woman took it that very night to the village shop, measured for herself the length of blue print for a dress and apron that she needed, chose a warm, black shawl from the bundle, left the fairy gold on the counter, hidden, for the shopkeeper to discover for himself, and came home.

"The virtue in it lies in exchanging it for another thing you may be wanting or needing. Never give it direct, and never hoard it, or all its virtue will be gone." And then she said a delicious thing: "Faith, the world would be a dreary place were there no passing of fairy gold."

I was sixteen when I had my first experience in telling stories—three nights running. I was visiting in one of the Boston suburbs. So were a handful of professors who had come on from New York and the West for a meeting of the N.E.A. One had brought his little girl, a child of seven. Each day, after breakfast, the house emptied itself of all but the child, the maid, and myself. 1 was to mind the child.

Throughout the day all went well. But the moment daylight left and shadows began to fill the house the child became restless, then nervous, finally frightened. "Light the lamps—light all the lamps!" she demanded, and I would not get the smallest piece of her attention until the house blazed with light. Then she was satisfied and could be coaxed into playing a game.

At bedtime it began again. She wouldn't go to bed; and then she would go if I promised not to leave her and would keep a light burning. For one who had been Johanna's child this fear of the dark was a strange, incomprehensible thing. I wondered what Johanna would have done, and offered a story. The child would have none of it. She hated stories as she hated the dark—especially those with witches and ogres and giants in them. "How about fairies?" I asked.

Night had been fairy-time for Johanna's child. She could hardly wait for lights to go out and the nursery door to close to begin her peopling of the dark. "How about fairies?" I asked again.

"I don't know much about them. I don't think I would like them."

"They're elegant," said I. "Listen," and listen she did, tense and doubting and restless for the first few minutes, then relaxing until the bedclothes, which had been an acute hump, became flat and smoothed down and quiet.

I told about the boy who gathered precious herbs on a fairy rath at the dark of the moon, that his mother might be healed. "It will sound better if I put out the light," I said at long last. There was no frightened outcry this time and the light went out.

The story was told two and a half times before the child went to sleep. The next night fear showed at twilight; but bedtime came without protest. One and a half times the story was told. The third night was warm for early spring. After a daylight supper we put on our coats and climbed a hill to a near-by patch of meadow with woods beyond. Here we played at finding the herbs, at watching the fairies come. An early downy woodpecker was hammering away on an old oak for a last snack before bedtime. "It might be the lepre-chaun," said I. And then we had a tale about Rory O'Don-nel and the wee small cobbler. Dark came gently, with it the stars, the call of the screech owl, and all the little sounds of earth that come with the spring. Together we listened, made words for the sounds, felt the comfortable darkness fold us in.

They left the next morning, the professor and his child. I never saw her again until we met at the Horace Mann cafeteria, I a last-year student at Columbia University, she beginning her eighth grade. Each was uncertain of the other's identity for a moment. Then she cried: "I know who you are! You're the girl who made me like the dark."

"Love and a propensity to it"; not moral persuasion, not a deliberate teaching of anything. There had simply been the passing of fairy gold. From that day in the Horace Mann cafeteria was established that awareness to the power of the spoken word which all storytellers, potential or actual, must come by. And with it must come a feeling for the beauty of words, the delight in using them. After all they are our clay, or the colors on our palette. They have infinite variety, and custom need not stale them.

When I began storytelling in earnest my approach was highly intellectual. I was a third-year student at Columbia University, majoring in folk-lore. All research students were working on source material; and as an additional project we did much rewriting, adapting, and grading of stories to be made into some of those early secondary-school readers. There was often much contention in the class over the right age grouping for certain stories. The only way to settle it seemed to be to carry the stories to the two schools then under the direction of Teachers College: Horace Mann and Speyer. Volunteers were asked for; only two were keen to try. Two afternoons a week, through half a year, we spent in the schools telling Norse and Greek and Eastern stories. I remember the fun I had, and how the research afterward took on a livelier aspect.

The next fall I was offered a place on the New York Public Lecture Bureau. It sounded terrific. Dr. Henry Leipziger, the director, had been trying out folk-music among their highly heterogeneous groups with considerable success, and he wanted to try out folk-tales. So I began my rounds of schools, churches, missions, reformatories, asylums, and back to schools again.

Ghastly is the word for the performances of those two years. Two years of floundering, of giving stories instead of fairy gold. I had made a careful analysis of my material. With intelligence I had gauged the educational capacity of each group. I had prepared my stories with meticulous care. I had brought to the storytelling all the intellectual capacity that was mine; and I felt like a pygmy trying to move the Giant's Causeway.

The second summer I went to Ireland. Three months were spent listening to traditional storytellers, tinkers, tailors, stonebreakers, with a grandda or a grandmother thrown in. I heard John Hegarty for the first time; heard him chant the old loidhes of Oisin, Duirmuid, and Fionn. Very slowly, but never to be forgotten, the full significance of Johanna's art came to me. When I came back to the lecture bureau that fall I at least knew what the matter had been with my storytelling. I was going about it the wrong way. One could not acquire a folk-art by means of a college education. One could not really tell stories, if one learned them by rote. Traditional storytellers got theirs by assimilation, by repeated telling, by living with them and absorbing them until they had become so much an unconscious part of them that the telling was as involuntary and spontaneous as their Gaelic greeting: "God and Mary with you!"

This was not all. Traditional storytellers had vital pride in what they had to tell, a deep sense of belonging. Back to me ran the voices of half a dozen I had listened to: "Here's a tale that will bide long with ye. 'Tis proud I am to tell it." . . . "Did ye ever hear about Rory, the robber? I had the tale from my grandda, and he from his." . . . "Hearken to this one. 'Tis about Hughie, the smith of Inver. 'Tis as gentle a tale as any ye'll be after hearing." Pride in the telling, a strong sense of kinship with everything they had to tell, an easy, effortless flowing of words. And still there was something I lacked—an established friendliness with the listeners, and a kind of jubilation at the sharing of it. Fairy gold. Something one keeps and yet gives away. Something that is mine, is yours, is everybody's—a spiritual legacy in perpetuity.

The realization of this came slowly at first; in the end it flooded and pretty nearly sank me. I had no background for that kind of storytelling. I had no direct folk-inheritance. I had never heard my Grandmother Wyman sing ballads to Grandfather's piping. But I had heard Johanna, and the storytellers of Ireland. New York City was full of foreign-born; among them, somewhere, for me to discover, there must be many who were instinctive storytellers, who had brought stories with them from the old country as they had brought their goosefeather beds, their hand-loomed blankets and linen.

That year was a rich year, albeit a down-daunted one. I told stories at the Clarke Neighborhood House, invited the mothers and grandmothers to come with the children to listen; and then got them to tell their own stories. "Here is a story about a widow's lazy daughter." Then the Irish version of Cinderella would be told and finally: "Has anybody got a story like that from her country?" Somebody usually had. I told type stories and almost always got back some variant. With each story offered by a Polish or Italian or German mother I marked again the deep quality of joy, of grace, of fellowship in the telling. Later I went to Boston. There in the Italian quarter, near the old North Church, for which my English great-grandfather had brought over the first bells, I got the story of "The Magic Box" from an Italian baker, in exchange for a small bottle of argyrol to cure his pink-eye.

My first assignment that fall from the lecture bureau was to the Five Points Mission. It lay over on the East Side of New York, in one of the worst sections of the city. The hall was crowded with sailors, longshoremen, draymen, and bums. Some of them slept, many were drunk; more were in that heavy stupor which overtakes human beings exhausted by hard work, over-full of food and drink, coming to rest in a hot room. I remember the janitor's saying: "They may do a bit of quarreling among themselves; but don't you mind. It never comes to anything."

The stories were broken into fragments by bursts of shouting, one man across the hall to another; this to be followed by a general avalanche of burly laughter. It was a tough ordeal. But I discovered that something rather amazing was happening. In the process of the story's leaving my lips and reaching across the hall to the men out in the darkness it had become, by the grace of God and the power of imagination, living substance; it was feeble, limping substance, but life was in it.

Something happened to my voice that night. I remembered all the things John Denis Meehan had taught me about reality of tone: that no honest, convincing sound came out of a human being short of the diaphragm and the abdominal muscles. For the first time that night I brought my stories up from below my belt-line. Every word was spoken with physical vigor and a faith that could almost have moved mountains.

I remember the stories: "Rory, the Robber," "The Widow's Lazy Daughter," "Hughie, the Smith of Inver," and "The King Who Was a Gentleman." I remember two responses to the stories, one coming after the first and putting heart back into me again. A man shook his sleeping neighbor and shouted for the whole hall to hear: "Wake up, man! You're missing the night of your blasted life." And at the end an Irish sailor—from County Wicklow, I discovered afterward—sprang up and bellowed: "I've been away from Ireland for forty years, but, Glory be to God, I'm back there ag'in the night."

"You did well," said the janitor, seeing me out; and I think no praise has ever come to me on so silver a tongue.

I had far more of discouragement than praise that winter; and a good thing, too. There was the Catholic Asylum where the children made their reverences every quarter of an hour and the stories and I became so detached that they might have been my astral body, floating in ether. Afterward a gentle sister came up and patted my hand. "You're still young. Some day you'll do better." Far better this than the damning by faint praise.

I had begun to think of storytelling as a folk-art; but it took the coming of Marie Shedlock to Teachers College that winter to make me know it as a living and a creative art. The name Marie Shedlock meant nothing; but the fact that she was telling stories from Hans Christian Andersen meant a great deal. I had lived for years in and by the Danish fairy man's book. I can see it now—a very grub of a book, with dingy covers, small print, narrow margins, no pictures but a frontispiece for "Little Ida's Flowers"—nothing to charm the eye of a child. It had traveled back and forth to Maine with me every summer on the old Boston and Bangor steamer. Andersen, the Brothers Grimm, Hawthorne's *Tanglewood Tales,* Joel Chandler Harris's *Uncle Remus,* and Irving's *Tales from the Alhambra*—these had been my folk-literature during childhood, but of them all I loved Andersen most. Marie Shedlock told first "The Tin Soldier," and all that Andersen had meant to an eight-to-ten-year-old took living form. Here was no Andersen recitation. She might have been the Danish fairy man himself, telling his own stories for the first time to a group of children. The words were Andersen's, but so were they Miss Shedlock's; the story might have been a figment of her imagination made manifest. In Ireland storytelling had seemed a natural, comparatively easy art to accomplish; Miss Shedlock's brought to me consciously and for the first time some awareness of the long, hard way ahead. Here was an art whose seeming simplicity and directness only hid for a novice the difficulties of its accomplishment. It must have taken Marie Shedlock years to become the artist I knew her then to be. Here was nothing to be taught, save what one could teach oneself by that oldest of all methods—trial and error.

That experience reconciled me to what seemed a lifetime of failures. I was ready to go on and have more failures, holding hard to the faith that something good might grow out of them. Dr. Leipziger was blessed devoutly, but silently, for not sacking me; and more orphan asylums, reformatories, churches, and schools were attacked. If I could fuse together what Johanna had given me and what I had learned that afternoon in the college chapel from Marie Shedlock, I might, given time and dogged effort, reach my goal.

The second event of that year was Anne Carroll Moore. She had but recently come from Pratt Institute to take up her work in the New York Public Library. I had a letter of introduction to her. I remember nothing of the interview but Miss Moore herself. But I must have been able to make her feel how deep went my urge to tell stories, for she gave me my chance. Just before Christmas, at Hudson Park, I told for the first time the Christmas story I had heard in Ireland from the drab and dirty tinker, about a tight-fisted man by the name of Teig and his voyage with the fairy wee red cap.

I shall always remember the faces of the American-born Irish boys who came over from a near-by parochial school. I shall always remember Miss Moore's lighting of candles; and the Christmas wishes which came out of that first library story hour. Those candles have never gone out for me; they still burn and always will. And there—also for the first time —I discovered Miss Moore's gift for making a festival, a gift she shared through the years with her own librarians, with storytellers, with authors and artists and all who, lacking the gift themselves, have come that they might light their candles from hers.

As Marie Shedlock and Johanna had made actual this art of storytelling for me, so did Anne Carroll Moore give grounding in appreciation and a clear evaluation of the stories. These have served me through my years of apprenticeship as bell and book. Fortunate are all those who came to be in true literary fellowship with Miss Moore. To know that no compromise can be made with what is trivial, mediocre, cast-in-the-mold. To know the attitude of the explorer over unmapped roads. To know something of the vigorous, critical mind that can purge, stimulate, and invite. Though she was never a storyteller herself, there has been no one who has given so generously and vitally to those who were. She held no brief for the easy-and-make pleasant school of training; she had no patience with the slipshod and the lazy. Her interest, her unfailing zeal to make storytelling a part of the library's gift to youth made possible the story hour in the children's rooms throughout this entire United States. There should be a candle for that—to burn high and clear in every room on Saint Nicholas' Eve.

Storytelling in hospitals—that for the Ruptured and Crippled, Saint Mary's, the Chapin Home for Incurables— besides bringing me much experience and happiness, gave substance for my first book, *The Primrose Ring*. I can still feel that glow of delight which came with a letter from Anna Cogswell Tyler, telling me she was using it as story material for her Girls' Club. And how much they liked it.

Back to Ireland, and a summer in Brittany; my own children and neighbors' children to tell to—on Sunday nights, around the fire, over bowls of popcorn and milk. Then throughout the state, serving on the Extension Service of

Cornell University. These were rare, good experiences. So much to bring, so short a time to share it all! Here for the first time I used much out of the Bible—some of the Psalms, Jonah under his gourd vine, the Christmas story from Luke, a little of the parables, Joshua, the trees choosing their king. Always trying out with others something that had moved me deeply; always finding out that what had been for me a spiritual feast usually fed others. This came back to me years later when I was in Spain and was told by a peasant from Toledo the tale "Where One Is Fed a Hundred Can Dine."

I remember the pink-cheeked boy and girl who arrived at one county meeting, bringing between them a clothes-basket with a three-month-old baby in it—their first. They sat in the front row; the baby slept, peacefully as a little rabbit. I would like to have a sleeping baby at every story hour. Afterward everybody crowded up to see; and the young and proud parents explained they wanted to start the baby right and they were sure this made a fine beginning. To me the mother said: "I'll remember every one of those stories—put them away on the cupboard shelf till Johnny is big enough to reach them." "She will, too," said the husband. And then they brought out paper and pencil and wrote down the names of picture books, story books, and books to grow to. I am still telling stories at Farm and Home Week at Cornell. Some who were babies in baskets at the beginning are now coming back on their own sturdy twelve-to-sixteen-year-old legs.

Name me any city, town, or crossroads settlement that

would not eagerly reach out for stories, told; stories that have the confirmation of centuries and the heart of the people. There are few groups of adults that do not take them in with refreshment, feel the spiritual bond which comes from an hour of storytelling. Women's clubs, university students, even Rotary Clubs can go back to their childhood and "eat it up," as one Rotarian put it. Once I swapped stories with three Rotary Clubs in different parts of the state in return for gifts to our Girl Scout Camp.

And here is a need. I find that the campfire period in so many scout camps has the tendency to sag at times into very commonplace performances, stunts, and wisecracking. A sharing of good stories round the fire often provides suggestion, if not material itself, for better programs. Stories can be dramatized. Long ago we made out of a summer's storytelling of "Robin Hood" one of the loveliest pageants I have ever had the good joy to take part in.

Experience. There is no lack of opportunity for the apprentice with a stout heart, a few stories in her grasp, and a determination to become. Fairy gold! Give and give and give—to schools, to scouts, to hospitals and other institutions. There are so many doorways which have never been lighted by a storyteller. And the wonder of it is that along the way so much more than experience in storytelling is gathered. To know people, of every kind and nationality; for you do know them after the bond is laid. Often stories are given back to you in fair exchange. But there is more to it than this. You get an appraisal, straight from the heart, that is invaluable. You get humanity at its fountainhead.

I have one more experience I feel impelled to share. During the days in New York I went often to the boy's reformatory in Fordham. I have never forgotten the mounting eagerness of those five or six hundred boys. It rose almost visibly and filled the room like the jinni out of the deep-sea bottle. When I was asked to go down to the women's federal prison in West Virginia I went, almost without packing a bag.

It was a lovely place to spend a month telling stories, cupped as it was in a valley among the Alleghenies, with the Greenbrier flowing beside it. Storytelling came at night, in the cottages. It was winter, so there was always an open fire. The girls—they are all girls, seventeen to seventy—brought their work; often they were sewing or knitting for a baby just born in the prison. Afterward they sang, or made candy, or did something by way of saying "Thank you." I felt out gingerly at first for what I should tell. But Beatrice set me right in no uncertain terms. The first week I was there they showed the film of *Romeo and Juliet*, with Shearer and Howard in it. The next evening I went to Beatrice's cottage and before beginning I said, so sure of the answer: "You all enjoyed the movie last night, didn't you?"

"I didn't," said Beatrice. "Call that stuff literature! Two get killed—a guy steals his bride—and she only fourteen. When the family marry her off to another guy she takes dope. Then they kill themselves. Gangster stuff, just dressed up in fancy clothes."

The prison liked storytelling. I had such a wonderful time that I have gone back every year. One of the byproducts was going out with the prison guard into the mountains to tell stories at one of the schools. Hungry young robins—who eat their weight three times over in food every day—that was as hungry as those mountain children were. No hookworm or pellagra here; the children were as bright and wide awake as children anywhere—at their best. But there were no books in the school. West Virginia supplies no textbooks; there were none here, either to be read or studied out of, save those few the teachers had bought and brought. Most of the children had never owned a book. Not one of them had ever heard a story told before. To this day I do not think they took me for real flesh and blood. I would not be surprised if they lumped me in with the Easter Rabbit, a fairy, or the leprechaun himself. For at the last a little boy sang out: "If you're real, you'll come back some day."

And so I must.

The Building of Background

You never enjoy the world aright till the Sea itself floweth in your veins, till you are clothed
with the heavens, and crowned with the stars.
—*Centuries of Meditation* by THOMAS TRAHERNE,
   Welsh clergyman of the seventeenth century

The Building of Background

THE old chroniclers tell of Fionn MacCumhal that he had the wisdom that comes from the nuts of the nine hazel trees that grow beside the well that is below the sea. George Russell, known better in this country as the poet A.E., had this wisdom. He knew the science as well as the love of the earth—he was an agronomist. He had the theory of bettering the world; he had the will to better his own Irish at close hand; he was both an economist and one who served on the Congested Districts Board and worked untiringly to organize the Cottage Industries, the Co-operative Dairies. He was the editor of the *Irish Statesman*. He answered in his own hand many of the letters that came to him from what he would have called the small, little parts of Ireland, the barren parts—letters written in Gaelic, written in English, asking everything, from questions about schooling to who was the queen of the Connaught fairies.

Not only did George Russell write several volumes of poetry, plays, and essays; he also encouraged and printed at his own expense the work of young Irish poets. He was a painter. His first exhibit in London brought him the wide acclaim of the critics, and won for him the name of the Irish

Whistler. Seumas O'Sullivan, who knew him well, said that wnen they went together on their long trampings into Galway "to take notice and to take leisure," George Russell could see the presence ot spirits in every manifestation of nature: spirits in the mist, coming out of the green boles of the trees, riding the winds. A blessed pagan was George Russell.

I got to know him well in Dublin. Richard Gilder of the *Century* had commissioned me to bring him over to the United States for a lecture tour, to speak on Irish poetry. "Offer him anything," he said. And yet I waited until almost the end of my summering to put the question to George Russell. His answer was what I had expected. He wouldn't come. He had too much to lose by coming. "I have always to be going out—to be bringing back things and thoughts. This is the land of the sidhe. I have the sight. I must use it or it will be gone from me. I would not be finding much to fill eyes and spirit, walking among your tall buildings."

And when he did come—years later—he came to us an old man and answered this question of his coming: "Do you think that much of the spirit outlasts what the world and Ireland have suffered? We have had a world at war. We have had trials for treason and sedition and spying. We have had a rebellion. We have had a shooting in Mountjoy Prison of those very lads I helped to make their first quatrains. We have had the Black-and-Tans; with families divided, a brother killing a brother. It is all of a half-dozen years now since I have seen the living spirit of water, earth, or the greening trees. I have nothing left to lose by coming, so I come."

We take deep concern over the books we buy, over the collection of stories we read. We check this person and that for intellectual opinion. But I wonder who concerns himself definitely over this gathering of spiritual experience. Is it not among most a matter of hit or miss? Or is it because there is something so deeply personal about it that, being Americans, we avoid drawing attention to it? Yet George Russell felt it to be a matter of such deep concern he talked about it freely, and would not take up a commercial offer to come to this country and lecture because of what he might lose. But then George Russell was Irish and pagan, his folk-inheritance ran stronger than ours.

How does one come by this building of spiritual background? How does one keep enriching it? No one can answer this for another. The Christian priest would answer: prayer; the mystic or metaphysician: meditation; the ascetic: self-denial; the salvationist: human service. Thoreau said: nature. The poet draws on all, God, humanity, and nature; and so must the artist. A poet has written: "Let each be a chalice for the good." Thomson, he of "The City of Dreadful Night," wrote an essay called "Open Secret Societies." In it he gives five: of the saints, of the philosophers, of the heroes, of the poets, and of the mystics. "There is the Open Society of the Poets," he writes. "These are they who feel that the universe is one mighty harmony of beauty and joy, and who are continually listening to the rhythms and cadences of the eternal music whose orchestra comprises all things from the shells to the stars . . . all sounds from the voice of the little bird to the voice of the great ocean."

I think George Russell held fellowship in all five of these Open Secret Societies. I think all who gather stories and pass them on, who become mouthpiece and interpreter for the work of races or the work of writers and poets, need attain to something of this catholic fellowship. That is why I have put before all else the building of spiritual background.

Once you are made conscious of this need, I believe that opportunity comes from everywhere. I had the good fortune to travel. Festivals, weddings, market-days, church and saints' days—I missed none of them. I rode in third-class carriages, in the rural motorbusses, to take part in peasant life everywhere. There was as much of rich storing away in these experiences as in the actual gathering of stories. It built the unforgettable backgrounds for the stories I did hear. I never tell the Spanish one of "The Frog," that back to me does not come that day in the Cathedral of Sevilla when I followed the old grandmother to the Chapel of the Kings and watched her pray. Arms stretched straight from her body to make the sign of the cross, she began her petition to the Virgin for the well-being of the family: good health, good eating, good fortune. And then she spied the new pair of gold shoes which some rich patron had given to the Child; and at once she was on her feet, over to the altar, talking to the Child: "Little Jesus, where did you get those gold shoes? Did your Mother buy them for you? Did the Good God reach down and put them on your little feet? Tell me—where did you get them?" Laughter, excitement in every word. Afterward we sat together on the floor, our backs to one of the great fluted columns, and she told me the story of "The Frog." But all that happened first has gone into making it a living story.

Travel, however, is not necessary to a building of background. I built much through the winter on Rivington Street; and more, helping in the Tyler Street Day Nursery in Boston. And again while working with the Americanization League in Syracuse. Opportunity lies close at hand for all who are looking for it. New York is rich in it; and I have found most of the children's librarians in New York keenly alive to all that the foreign-born there have to give.

From the time the Central Children's Room was opened, Anne Carroll Moore brought into it a wealth of folk-experience. Picture books from all lands, visitors to this country who had something vital and colorful to give, a celebration of holidays and birthdays belonging to the world. Exhibitions of everything under the sun of interest to children that gives of the vigorous, imaginative outflowing art of other countries. There is that essential integrity always in the material gathered that commands one's admiration as well as interest.

Every folk-craft has much to give in feeling and simplicity, not only the finished products arranged for exhibit, but the workers at work. Mexico is a paradise of folk-craft—silversmiths, glassblowers, weavers, potters, tinsmiths, carvers. The craftsmen work today as they have worked for the past three hundred years. They use aniline dyes instead of the vegetable dyes of their forefathers, but this is all the difference I could find. Some of the silversmiths have more modern tools, perhaps; but the potters' wheels are still treadled by foot, the water dropping on them from wooden spigots. Apprentices still serve, although they must go to school now for part of the day. Ask a twelve-year-old tending a furnace in one of the glass *fábricas* what he would like to do more than anything else and he will answer: "Learn to be a blower of beautiful glass—like Manuel or Pedro or Juan. He makes anything to be what he likes."

The little boys working at the looms, those who could work four treadles and were beginning a two-colored pattern, were voluble with pride. They were agog with expectation at what they would do next. Most of them would never be anything but good imitators; but there was always the one or two who could bring into being something new, different, who had the gift of creation and would become one day famous.

This bringing together of a wide variety of materials—sand, silver, clay, tin, wool—combining it with the skill of the craftsman and watching it all come to a satisfying end, is a delight for the soul. This was good, this was worth sharing. I watched a craftsman with delicate touch blow a wine-bottle of the Virgin of Guadalupe in the color of aquamarine, and then make over it the sign of the cross to show he had not forgotten where reverence was due. To live with what one creates, never to let it become monotonized, no matter how many times one repeats, that is what came to me out of Mexico. Pride in all folk-inheritance was born again, as it must be born again many times for us in this country.

Except in my early years I have never been able to play any instrument; and yet I have got more from music than from any other art. I believe there is much to be gained in background for the storyteller from the performance of nearly every form of music. There is much to be drawn out and applied from books about music, carefully selected. For the analogies between music and storytelling are strong, true. From Wagner's writings, from Hans von Bülow's and Paderewski's, I have gained more insight into my own art than I have from any book written about storytelling. Krehbiel, Henry Finck, Deems Taylor have presented an approach to art and artists which I have found invaluable. I think that one can often gain flashes of comprehension from another art, closely akin, that at times are sharper, more defined, than those which come from too restricted a focus on one's own art. And it cannot be denied that more has been written about music, and better written, than anything upon the art of storytelling. Were an apprentice to come to me today and ask what reading I should put above all others for the gaining of a conception of art, its meaning and the creative power which lies within it, I should give him the best books I could find on music.

You will see that I have put feeling for an art before facts and understanding in this building of background. Not that one rides beyond the other in importance but because feeling must come first. "What the heart knows today the head will understand tomorrow."

There cannot be a solid background built for storytelling that does not include source material for stories as well as a feeling for the ancient storytellers themselves. To know from where the mass of folk-literature has sprung, especially those stories which one has elected to tell, this is essential. Poor indeed is the storyteller who knows only collections, edited and published for her convenience. To me it seems as devitalizing as always to be turning the cock on a faucet and drinking from lead-piping and a water-system when natural well-springs may lie close at hand.

All our main public libraries have much to offer in source material. Why miss the delight and satisfaction that comes from digging in and finding that which will bring fresh understanding and illumination to chosen stories? To trace something well known to its original source offers as great a thrill as any that an archaeologist knows when he comes upon a trace of long-hidden civilization. To unearth, to bring to light, to make yours, this makes for kinship with those who first started the story on its long journey of survival. It brings one into fellowship with the story. This is what the building of folk-background should mean. It is no penny-a-week performance. It means to give true interpretation to hero tales, sagas, myths, legends, and with a fair degree of authority. If authority cannot go with the telling, then better not tell.

It is a matter of years, of a lifetime, this building of background for storytelling, for it is a matter of growth. Something one must never hurry through but be continuously aware of and eager for. Something to which one must bring a keen appetite, fresh enthusiasms, an integrity of attitude, a clear-burning zeal. To be ever ready to discard that which one can no longer use with honesty. To put together all one gathers that there may be a final authority in the telling and a dignity and truth in what one has to tell—this is of the utmost importance. For as storytellers we are concerned not alone with amusement, or with education, or with distraction; nor is it enough to give pleasure. We are concerned with letting a single stream of light pass through us as through one facet of the gem or prism that there may be revealed some aspect of the spirit, some beauty and truth that lies hidden within the world and humankind.

To strive for less than this, to be satisfied with the mere skimming of crust from the surface of that which is great and universal literature, seems to me to indicate an impoverished mind and imagination. Although we may at times fool the adults with this sort of performance, we never for a moment fool the children. They know on the instant of hearing that which springs from true art; they can tell the notes of the real nightingale from that of the mechanical bird.

Not one of us can measure all of spiritual struggle, of endurance, of man's groping for the universe, which has gone into the makings and the passing on of the stories of Proserpine and Baldur, of Prometheus and Galahad, of Oisin and Cuchulain. But if we cannot measure, we can at least honor these and bring to the telling an eager and inquiring mind, a spiritual sense tuned up to the pitch of the tale. To do less than this would make of us mere journey-men among storytellers.

For stories slighter than these, for the good folk-tale of humor and charm, there would need to be something of comprehension of that peasant stock which bred the tale, something of the Celtic heart and imagination for the tell-ing of all that has come out of Ireland, something of the robustness of body and soul, and the rigors of winter in the North for the telling of all that has come out of Iceland, Norway, Russia, Finland; to have a friendly regard, an understanding for the gentle people of the earth who have long since turned their swords into plowshares and elected to be at peace—for how else could one give full measure to the stories of the Swiss, the Danes, the Dutch?

Does this sound too fantastic? I think not. For it brings more than authority into the telling; it brings that spiritual conviction which must be shared between storyteller and listener if the story is to live. I have been gathering Christ-mas legends and stories for as many years as I have been writing this book. One such story has come from the Isle of Man. What I got in the beginning was the bare bones of it, without embellishment. I knew little of Man. Beginning to dig I found on the mythical side that the Isle had been discovered by Manannan MacLir, the Celtic sea-god. I knew nothing of Manx customs, so I dug further and found among old documents and letters a diary written by a former gov-ernor of the island in sixteen-something, all that I needed to build up the original skeleton of a legend into a full-bodied tale. I hope this particular story will become a great favorite, for it gives good balance for other Christmas stories —it gives robustness and the Devil.

For general and essential background I think no story-teller can afford not to know her Bulfinch and John Fiske, Petrie, Malory, Frazer, Campbell, Lang and Dasent, Baring-Gould. For a feeling of early literature: *The Book of the Magicians, The Book of the Dead, The Gesta Romanorum, The Pentamerone,* and *The Panchatantra.* For Gaelic tales something of the *Ancient Books of Ireland,* with Lady Gregory, Douglas Hyde, Dr. Sigerson, Jeremiah Curtin, O'Curry, and William Larminie. *The Song of Roland, The Romance of Mio Cid el Campeador, The Ocean of Story*—volumes of them compiled by Somadeva and from which Constance Smedley got many of her best for the *Tales from Timbuktu.* For those who read no Spanish and cannot go further back, the *Tales from the Alhambra* constitute source material. And Washington Irving's *Conquest of Granada* makes admirable background for the telling of all Spanish stories. There are innumerable journals of folk-lore, all rich in source material. Cushing should be known intimately by all who would tell American Indian tales, and Godfrey Leland. For those who read French the original of Charles Perrault; these tales never have been satisfactorily translated. There are Aesop and La Fontaine; "Reynard the Fox" and "Lazarillo of Tormes," for a feeling of the rogue or picaresque tale. *The Golden Ass* and Plutarch's *Lives:*

believe it or not, I adored the *Lives* when I was a child. Shakespeare went to the latter for much of his source material.

Here are only scant suggestions, a few scattered wellsprings that lie close at hand. But keep an index of what you find. Make a few notes so that you can go back at will and put your finger on what you want without too much fumbling. And share with others what you find. That is half the fun. Share it with the children. I have found a story gains much in interest if there is something to tell of the people, the hero, the times, and the country, before beginning. Sometimes it is not enough for you to have the background—the listener needs it for the full flavor of what you are about to tell. Whether background be kept silent or made audible, let it be constantly, untiringly gathered.

The Italian puppeteers have given me much for my storytelling; and so have the opera and the Russian ballet, its pantomime as well as dancing.

In spite of the fact that I have stressed the folk-approach as the natural and inevitable starting-point for all folk-arts. there must be an intellectual understanding and appreciation for that which we use. I see no way of building up a sound critical sense for stories short of an appreciation and understanding for the whole field of literature. One cannot know what is fine in children's books without having an appreciation of literature as a whole. To know good English, good form, good substance; to be familiar with good writers that there may be a basis for judgment, read the best commentators on literature. I give you Bacon and Sir Philip

Sidney, Emerson and Ruskin and Carlyle, Anatole France, Flaubert, Chateaubriand, Powys, Sir Arthur Quiller-Couch. And for that which more definitely gives background for children's reading—Anne Carroll Moore: her three volumes, *The Three Owls, Roads to Childhood,* and *My Roads;* Bertha Mahony and Elinor Whitney's two books, *Five Years of Children's Books* and *Realms of Gold;* Anne Eaton's *Reading with Children.* Much has gone into the making of these books in experience and enthusiasm and broad critical judgment. The contribution Miss Moore made in her continuous and honest recognition of what is fresh, unhackneyed, and vital to the realities of all youth, whether of mind, heart, or spirit, has been a continuous well-spring of inspiration and guiding force to untold storytellers.

Out of this building of spiritual awareness, of folk-sources, out of this knowing of literature and of what others think about literature, should come something concrete. This, if one is to make a lasting and satisfying experience of it, bring it to a good end. Mary Gould Davis of the New York Public Library advised the making of a collection of stories by every apprentice storyteller for her own use, by way of applying whatever background and power of selection she has built. I think this suggestion is invaluable.

I would suggest that this be supplemented with a determined effort to write at least one original story every year, using some folk-source. Claire Huchet Bishop has made two invaluable contributions in her *Five Chinese Brothers* and *The Ferryman.* Pura Belpré has done a lovely thing with her *Perez and Martina,* and Mary Gould Davis did a fine piece of creative work in retelling Italian folk-tales in her *Truce of the Wolf.* It is worth noting that these have all come out of the New York Public Library's work with children.

The Italian philosopher Croce has said that a great work of art is not completed until humanity itself has set its seal upon it. Humanity has set its seal upon that treasure-house of art we call folk-literature. It is from this that storytellers draw by far the greater part of the stories they tell; and it is for these that background most urgently must be built.

The Power of Creative Imagination

In the beginning God created the heaven and the earth. And the earth was without form, and void; and darkness was upon the face of the deep. And the Spirit of God moved upon the face of the waters. And God said, Let there be light: and there was light.

—The beginning of the book of GENESIS

The Power of Creative Imagination

TWENTY-FIVE years ago Charles Morgan gave a lecture before the students of the University of Paris. He spoke on creative art; and he spoke of it as that power to be at times a flash of communication between God and man.

The artist, be he working with clay, with notes, with words or color, brings his imagination so to bear on his material that there is wrought a spiritual change—from something inanimate, without form or meaning, to something of inspiration and stirring reality. Finally, Mr. Morgan says, an artist is in the world to listen as well as to speak, to gather in as well as to give out, that through him mankind may re-create itself.

I believe that creative imagination is a common factor for all mankind, but held in diminishing degrees of consciousness and strength. Children, scientists, artists, and mystics hold it with strength, and use it with freedom and faith. From a child, sitting on the floor, blocks beside him, waiting for that impulse which will start him off building a castle or railway terminal, to Rodin, standing before his mass of clay about to conceive his *Hand of God,* may seem a fantastic distance for a common factor to span. Yet I believe children to be the freest, the most universal creators.

Left unhampered, a child begins very young to put into everyday life a series of masterpieces of creative thinking and doing. He is everlastingly bringing about that spiritual change in each object and idea with which his imagination plays. He works with direction; he strikes at the core of what he would express; he has nothing to discard, for he has accumulated nothing unnecessary. It is as if he were always saying: "This I like. This I will make—sing—play—be."

"Tell me of the strange lands," said Åke [in *Åke and His World* *]. Aja took her fingers from her ears for a moment. "Asch!" she answered. "That is only geography." But for Åke it was not just geography. He didn't know exactly what it was, but it was a journey to fantastic places; a fairyland of beckoning adventures that still was reality. He sat straight as a candle, and his eyes did not move from his father's lips. He traveled from land to land, and from ocean to ocean. He saw the strangest kinds of people. Eskimos being pulled by dogs, and they were dressed in skins clear up to their eyes; and Åke thought that was too much. But at the equator the people didn't have any clothes at all, just a handkerchief; and Åke thought that was too little. He was up on the highest peak of the Himalayas where no man had ever climbed before, and he gasped when he beheld the endless masses of stone; and his father said that it looked precisely like that on the moon. He laughed when he came to the amusing realm of Japan, and in China the whole place smelled like a tea caddy. . . . And so they journeyed around the whole world, father and son, and when the journey came to an end, his father said, "Here we are. Now we are home again." But Åke sat lost in thought.

* By Bertil Malmberg, copyright 1940. This extract reprinted by permission of Farrar & Rinehart, Inc., publishers.

. . . "Papa.". . . "Yes, my son." "Just how big, exactly on the dot, are the strange lands?"

This is from Bertil Malmberg's moving record of a little boy, himself, during those years of intense wondering, of making words, places, people to change under the divine force of his imagination.

The adult, however, works more by indirection. His mind has become cluttered with rubbish, accumulated through those years of ceasing to be a child. Details rush in to fog his intention; his mind is full of extraneous matter, all to be sifted and thrown into the discard before his thought takes clear form again, made free. It is as if he said: "This I no longer like. This I can no longer feel or believe. This still belongs to me; with care and effort I can shape it to my thought."

Whatever this power of creative imagination, whence-soever it comes, this I think we may say for it: that it is potentially a birth-gift, that it comes into the world with the soul which accompanies new life and the new-made body. During childhood it would seem under good conditions to remain familiar, unthwarted and unbound. It is as if the spiritual birth-cord were not cut as soon as the body's, and there were still a great drawing on the Giver of All Things for spiritual sustenance and growth.

But midway in childhood something begins to happen. The cord is cut. There must be adjustment to a factual, material world. Children begin to conform. Adults help the process along, that adjustment may be made as swift and resistless as possible. Children's minds are railroaded from this station to that, all plainly marked on the map called Education. That space, so boundless in babyhood, that heavenly pasture for play and joy unbounded, becomes narrowed down with each year, each grade, until it becomes no wider than your thumb. Those ears, born cocked to celestial tunes, are forced to grow dull, listening to what parents say, what uncles, aunts, and neighbors say, what teachers and older schoolmates say. A few there are whose ears stay cocked; for a few the cord is never cut. The divine relation between the spiritual parent and the child lasts unbroken from birth to death. These I take to be the geniuses of our world. For the rest there are those who, full grown, recognize at last that they must put forth supreme effort if there is to be re-established a spiritual bond that will restore, that will bring them to be in full spiritual fellowship with the Creator. This regaining can come only by discipline, about which I think we must concern ourselves.

There are many whose minds have never known discipline. There are a rare few whose minds work constantly under discipline. For the rank and file there is discipline at times—when specific work must be accomplished, when an emergency must be faced—when the mind must obey without reward of interest, entertainment, or compensation. I believe the disciplined mind is the free mind, for it is the mind which has established its own integrity and responsibility; and until these are undertaken there can be nothing like freedom.

The old English writers of Elizabeth's time used frequently the expression *intend the mind*. It has a pleasanter sound than discipline, and yet they *intended* the same thing. To fix the mind upon something, the object or idea to be thought about; to hold it there by force of will against all inroads of confusion, of conflict, of irrelevant impressions. To keep the mind burning with a steady, clear flame until there shall come complete illumination. Call it meditation, for that is what it amounts to, this thinking through until the very essence of the object or idea is distilled, drawn out, and comprehended. Then, and not until then, can the creative imagination have full play.

I believe that when Charles Morgan urged that there be love working with the creative imagination he was thinking of this very discipline of the mind. Granted love and a propensity for what one would create and there is no longer that feeling of harshness which comes with unmitigated discipline. For where we truly give our hearts we give our capacity to maintain both work and discipline.

As I see discipline it means that power of the will to work long enough at any one effort until the habit be established. It means the aptitude for obeying a higher command. In relation to creative storytelling it means that ability to hold the mind steadily upon a story, and for a long enough time, until everything about the story is known, felt, made actual. Be it a folk-tale, to draw from it all that has gone into the making of it; be it a story by some author, to draw from it all that another has already created. Not until this happens may a storyteller feel herself to be an adequate interpreter. Not until she has shared in perfect accord that which others have created can she hope to re-create it by means of her own imagination and skill.

How does one go about this business of disciplining the mind? Largely by exercise. Both as exercise and as test try suggesting to yourself certain objects or ideas, and see how fully you can portray them. This is what every writer must do; every artist, for that matter. I have tried this out with would-be storytellers, apprentices who could not understand how one's imagination could be exercised.

It is better to shut the eyes—this way brings less distraction. Then suggest to yourself a variety of impressions, some concrete, some abstract. Ask: How does a New England meeting-house look? What do you see in the country in late March? What is the difference between a gull's flight and a swallow's? Picture the house of the Three Bears; a happy country child coming home from school. How does a summer night feel?

The range of capacity for experiencing these things as actual, and for describing them, is as wide as a hundred-and-eighty-degree arc. Results with students have been in this wise. In answer to the first question: "A church," or: "A snug box of a church, white, with tall steeple, one bell, green blinds, and a front porch. People are going in. The organ is playing 'How Firm a Foundation.'" In answer to the question about March I have had: "I don't know"; "I never noticed"; and then: "Trees still bare, a brook still half frozen. But along it the willows show yellow at the tip. I've heard a robin in late March." For the happy country child: "I guess it would be a child laughing or singing."

And: "She's a little girl, wearing a plaid skirt and a dark green sweater. Her hair is dark, in two pigtails with red bows. Her legs are bare, down to socks. She has a snub-nose and a grin. She goes along the road, hop-skip-and-jump. Her mouth's all puckered up, trying to whistle." One more —about the summer night. One answer was: "Hot." Another: "Hot and sticky." Another: "Lonesome." But a homely, wide-eyed student answered: "Full of magic. The patterings on the ground might be anything—fairy feet— anything. The stars feel so close you could reach up and pluck them."

I believe this is a game children would love to play. Students—all those I have tried it on—have found fun in it. But always there has been astonishment.

Those who could see clearly and could put graphically what they saw amazed those who could see so little. But all, I think, saw the value of such testing. Those who experienced it or those who only watched it happen in others felt that spiritual change take place of which Charles Morgan spoke; a word, a group of words was transformed into actual and living substance by the touch of imagination. A kind of anointing in high places.

There is another point here which must not be overlooked. What we observe—what we can best re-create— often depends on our native interests. I remember the student who created a delightful home for the Three Bears was altogether at sea about the gulls and swallows. I know I should do but poorly if asked to embellish the appearance of a modern woman; on the other hand I would do excellently with the wife of a Spanish grandee attached to the court of Philip the Second.

To use, not to waste. To have ready at hand this power of creative imagination, this is too often overlooked by storytellers who would learn a story today and recite it tomorrow, missing entirely that divine gift of using words to see with and to make others see.

I have spoken before of the analogy between the arts of storytelling and music. Let me talk a little more about it, for it holds not only interest but provocative thinking.

Hans von Bülow was an excellent conductor, a teacher of amazing caliber. As a pianist he ranked as one of the best interpreters of music; but there was little to be said for his execution as pure technique. He was never brilliant. It has been said of him that he was so concerned with giving audible form to the meaning and beauty of what others had written that he never thought of his own execution. In his *Letters* he wrote: "An interpreter should be the very opposite of the gravedigger; he should bring to light what is hidden and buried." And again: "In studying anything work with the head, get all you can get out of it. Then put it away for a month and when you come back to it you will find much that you never dreamed of before." He sent a pupil home one day in despair, telling her not to come back until she had learned to play first with her brains, then with her fingers. He tapped his forehead savagely: "It is here—here—that great music is made."

A legend has built itself up about Fritz Kreisler in the heyday of his career. It was believed among his fellow-artists that he rarely practiced. When cornered one day by direct question he agreed that he worked more on his music with mind and feeling than he did with bow and instrument. He said: "It is imperative that I hear and feel first what I am going to play before I play it." There has been no great violinist comparable to Fritz Kreisler, not in my day. I knew him slightly at that time I was trying to understand something of what lay at the bottom of this art of storytelling. What, I think, enchanted me most about his playing was that consummate art with which he played folk-tunes or the simplest of compositions. He never condescended. Rarely did he play in public that somebody in the audience did not get up and demand Dvořák's "Humoresque," a composition so simple that a second-year music pupil can play it.

I knew Paderewski, too, but not as well. One of his great admirers used to say of him that he could dive below the level of his piano keys and bring up something you had no idea was buried under them. I admired his ability to work. I think I never met a great artist who had won such absolute acclaim for himself in every country of the world where civilized music is heard, who had to such an extent that ability for taking infinite pains. Unlike Kreisler, he practiced terrifically, would wear himself out at the piano working for hours over some cadenza until he was satisfied with it.

Henry Finck used to tell of hearing him practice at Morges, his home in Switzerland. Often, early in the morning, he would sit down at the piano and work on some phrase of three or five notes, work on it untiringly. But he never practiced before a recital. Neither did he go out or have guests. He spent the evening alone, with his program. Far into the night he would lie thinking through each composition he was to play. Phrase by phrase he would go over it, feeling with his imagination for every note his fingers were to play on the morrow, drawing from the music every nuance, establishing the quality of tone, the color, the tempo, until he could hear it as he wished himself to play it. Creating it first, clearly, unforgettably in the solitude of the night, that he might re-create it at the piano the next day.

Henry Finck once asked him how he made his musical ideas so absorbingly interesting to all classes of hearers. In his *Success in Music* Finck answers this in a measure—as well as I think it can be answered short of hearing Paderewski answer it for himself, with his own playing. Henry Finck writes:

Paradoxical as it may seem, it may be said that the genius of the musician is revealed most unmistakably in his power over the unmusical. Genius makes extremes meet. Persons who are bored by piano recitals never miss a Paderewski concert because, when he plays, Bach and Beethoven are no longer riddles but sources of pleasure. Never does he resort to clap-trap, trickiness, or sensationalism in order to win applause. As a boy he used to listen to the vibrations that made up a tone, and modify his own touch until he got those vibrations. The creative gift was his from the beginning. He has always played like a composer as well as virtuoso; and therein lies another secret of his success.

Mr. Finck in the same book quotes from James Huneker, a fellow-critic, who wrote in commenting on the Burne-Jones portrait of Paderewski:

It seems to me to be the best and most spiritual interpretation we have had as yet of this spiritual artist. His life has been full of sorrow, of adversity. Nature paints every meanness, every moral weakness with unsparing brush, and I suppose, after all, one of the causes of Paderewski's phenomenal success has been his expressive, poetic personality. His heart is pure, his life clean, his ideals lofty. He is the Beau Seigneur of the keyboard.

Some years ago in Boston, telling stories to the great delight of the boys and girls in the public schools, was the finest traditional storyteller in our civilized world that I know —John Cronan. He had developed this power of creative imagination to that clear, steady point of burning so that everything he told was illuminated by what he felt, by what he knew, by what he could kindle with his imagination.

His range of telling was amazingly wide. His background for what he told was strong, well built. Like the art of Paderewski, his was the very negation of everything mechanical. Better than anyone else I have heard he could take substance from a book, build up what had gone before, and immediately establish a kinship with that part he was telling. So did he gather up his listeners and transport them whither the story beckoned. He lived with and in a book to a degree I have never marked in any other storyteller. He became for the telling an integrated part of the book so that one wondered how one could well go on without the other. He had that same capacity for delight, for being a part of every happening, that the traditional storyteller has. He invited you to join the fun. He shared good food—if it was in the story—he made you taste it. And yet above, below, beyond all this, he had a quality that baffles description. Experience it once and you never forgot it. It was a quality of spirit; it was as well an essential honesty for the work of others, a power to feel to the limit all that had gone into the making of the story he told. Call it what you will, it was the ultimate factor that established him as a true, a great artist.

The first time I heard him I went, I confess, with apprehension. He had offered to tell the beginning of *Toño Antonio*. I frankly could not see it being told. I had tried it myself once and had done none too good or convincing a piece of work. But John Cronan made the little Spanish boy live for me as he had not lived since that just-before Christmas afternoon when I had come upon him outside the pastry-cook's in Málaga. All the charm, the wistfulness, the eager friendliness and courage of the little boy who would be a man and restore the fortunes of his family—all this came into being. And I know that for each Italian child who listened Toño became as real as the boy or girl sitting beside him. I have heard John Cronan tell Irish and French stories with this same sense of divine conviction.

I have been going through that May 1934 issue of the *Horn Book* which was offered as a tribute to Marie Shedlock and her art at the end of her long, fine career. Many who had contributed to the issues, in fact the majority who had, had not heard Marie Shedlock tell stories for a number of years. And yet when they began to write about what they remembered the experience rose up clear-cut, impelling, never-to-be-forgotten.

With such a fine perspective on the art of one storyteller, it seemed worth checking to see just what were the things remembered, the qualities that still had power to excite and hold in thrall after so long a time. I give them without comment. They establish their own significance:

Directness. Simplicity. Elusiveness. Dramatic interpretation. Intonation. Enunciation. Charm. Her voice. Sense of humor. Strong, compelling sympathy between herself and her listeners. Her own enjoyment. Her vitality. Her spontaneity. She was a born artist. She was a painstaking artist. She gave the impression of creating what she told. She created atmosphere. Before she spoke everyone was aware of her. She had imagination. She had a sense of poetry. She shunned the mediocre and the artificial. She had integrity.

I have been reading again Browning's "Death in the Desert." It is John of Patmos who is dying; and, as so often in death, he is letting his life pass before him, those things for which he has striven, those things in which he believes he has failed. He speaks of the three souls of man: the soul that does, which rests with feet on the earth; the soul that knows, which rests upon the shoulders of the first; the soul which is, resting on the two below but reaching to the stars. "What Does, what Knows, what Is, three souls—one man."

It is out of this trinity comes that power of creative imagination.

A Technique to Abolish Technique

Is not a man rich if he is born with the English language in his mouth? What a language! A glorious and imperial mongrel, this great synthesis of the Teutonic, and the French, the Latin, and the Greek, this most hospitable of tongues, this raider of the world's ideas, full of words from the Arabic desert and the Roman Forum and the lists of the Crusades.

—DOROTHY THOMPSON (from "There Was a Man," *Life*, Jan. 27, 1941)

A Technique to Abolish Technique

"WHAT is your technique?" I have been asked this question more than any other. And how does one acquire technique; and how long does it take? These questions might have been asked in Greek, of which language I know nothing. I am conscious of nothing that might be called technique; but there are specific things to be accomplished by every storyteller and definite ways of accomplishing them.

There are two indisputable facts about this art of storytelling that may be considered carefully and with profit: that our instrument is our voice; that we work with, and by means of, the spoken language—words.

I think there are many who are particularly sensitive to all sound, and most particularly to the human voice. I am one of these. Throughout my childhood and youth I sang, studied singing, wanted to be, first, an opera singer, then a church and concert singer. Very early my capacity for listening was acquired. When I began to study music I found that one of the first essentials was to be able to listen to one's own voice. To hear with accuracy and honesty the pitch, the tone, the vibrations, the color. I was fortunate in having good teachers, two of them in college, where I took "voice training" as part of my schedule. I learned the importance of proper breathing and I have never ceased to be grateful for this. I have never forgotten what Jean de Reszke said. He was one of the greatest tenors in what Henry Finck called the "golden age of music," but he stopped early that he might teach. What he said was: "Your breath must be strong enough to sit on it."

Thin voices, voices badly registered, voices without breath support, coming from the throat, monotonous voices, voices that cannot carry, voices sagging with fatigue, reduced to a tremolo, voices pitched too high—all these inadequacies I abominate because I am convinced they are unnecessary. What I gathered of importance while I went to school is rather simple; anyone can get it for herself has she application and patience. But it takes intelligence and practice to acquire a listening ear. It takes both intelligence and practice to learn to breathe properly and to control one's voice with the breath and not with the throat. It takes intelligence and practice and an ear that hears correctly and delicately to get a voice pitched properly, modulated, and used in the proper register. Women's voices for the most part are too high. They would do well to bring their speaking voice down to the lower register.

I can hear many say: This is too much to expect of any storyteller. We work hard enough as it is to get the stories, to get background for them, to get experience in telling them; and now you say voices need to be exercised, trained.

For my part I think it is too much to ask children or

adults to listen, from ten minutes to an hour, to a lazy, imperfect, unpleasant instrument, when something can be done about it.

In our United States we seldom hear any language spoken but English—and almost entirely United States English. There are dialects even in our country—Southern, Middle Western, Hoosier, New York, New England, and the rarefied Bostonese. But these do not catch at our ears with the same degree of compulsion as a foreign tongue. When I have been abroad, especially in some cosmopolitan city, one of the first things I have noticed is that I am waking up again to sound, listening with a degree of acuity to the human voice, foreign tongues, accent. I am once more agog to make out what is Spanish, what is Italian, what part of France or Switzerland the family of the father, mother, little boy have come from? Am I hearing Dutch or German spoken? I may not be able to answer these; but my ear is tuned, alert to sound as it has not been for years. I am no longer the lazy-eared person I have been.

I think what has been an often repeated experience for me is habitual with most North Americans. I think the majority of people in this country are lazy-eared. Otherwise how can it be possible for so many of them to speak with such excruciating and ineffective voices, to enunciate so badly, to slur their words? I beseech all storytellers to cultivate the listening ear, to learn to hear their own voices, to be alert to the voices around them, to compare. And if their own voices do not satisfy them, to do something about it.

Let the first concern be about the breath. Learn to breathe

from below the belt, not superficially from the chest. Learn to control the breath by the abdominal muscles, not the throat muscles. If you are not sure what you do, find out— it is very easy. Speak a few sentences aloud with a hand cupped not too tightly around your throat. If you feel no constriction, nothing but the epiglottis moving slightly up and down, your throat is free from constriction. If you can feel a tightening of any muscle in the throat, no matter how slight it may be, you are not speaking freely or correctly.

Whether one speaks correctly or not, for general health, for keeping one's voice strong, free, and untiring, one should work regularly at this matter of proper breathing.

I have not the time, nor am I sufficiently expert, to go into this with great precision. But there are a few simple directions for breathing that anyone can follow. For all of these one should stand erect, untense, with one's head slightly back. Have a window open, and clothing loose.

Now then: first put your hands above your hips, thumbs to the back. Expel breath with all the positive force you can muster through an open mouth; press in your hands as hard as you can. You are externally making your diaphragm muscles contract. You should be making them contract under their own power. Draw in the breath slowly, through nose and mouth, letting your hands relax and getting the feeling of your muscles taking hold. Repeat this until you begin to feel breath riding upon those muscles. Concentration, the will to try it over and over, does it.

Second: try panting. Not as a human being does, but as a dog pants that has run hard and fast. Open your mouth, let your tongue hang loose, out, if necessary. Then pant. Keep your breath coming and going in quick, staccato breaths. Keep at it until you are tired out. When you can do this with the regular beat a dog has, and without tripping up with your breath, you will have considerable control over the abdominal muscles.

Now begin speaking on your breath. First with the open vowels: A—I—O—U. Put your hand about your throat and watch that your voice comes through freely. Establish a definite rhythm, and keep to it. Do this first on one pitch, your most natural pitch. Then change it, up and down the scale. Try it with M before each vowel, and finally use M with the closed vowel E. The open vowels naturally throw the tone into your chest, using that as a sounding-board. The closed vowel should throw the tone into the nasal cavity, between the eyes, or where the frontal sinus is. In order to establish the tone here, at the beginning exaggerate the nasal quality. You can do this to the point where your head will buzz, your front teeth vibrate; and with practice you can make a goblet of thin glass on a table vibrate. These are your two sounding-boards—chest and head. A chest tone can be modified by a head tone, and vice versa. A careful listening will indicate which you need to develop to make a balanced, well-modulated speaking voice. Experiment, make sounds, make noises. Be primitive, elemental in your sounds until you feel in them body, life, something that rings, that vibrates with resonance. Keep this resonance, whether you speak with full volume, whether you whisper. It is the tone that carries, that makes it possible for anyone to speak for an hour without fatigue, without a dry throat, without irritation.

Try laughter. Most of us laugh superficially. Make yours robust, with the open throat: ha-ha, ho-ho!

Go from vowels to words. Take a line or two of good poetry. Take a verse from the Psalms, something you know so well you need not feel for the words. Speak them on your breath, slowly, with careful articulation. Listen again, and begin to discriminate between a word spoken with a flat tone and a word spoken with roundness. Again set your rhythm and keep to it. Speak first on one note. Then come down the scale, up again. Do it until you begin to feel flexibility in your voice. A cramped range can be widened. You can give your voice play over an octave and a half with very little listening and practice.

One of the most helpful experiences I have had has been going to some synagogue where there was a good cantor and listening to him. Or to a Catholic church where there is good intoning. Here you get a feeling for what the speaking voice can do—its amazing range, degrees of modulation, the suppleness and freedom with which words may be spoken.

Here is a sad paradox: those musical instruments invented on the pattern of the human body, and stringed to produce the most sublime quality of the human voice, have so far outdistanced us in resonance and beauty of tone that now we turn to them to get the quality we would like to hear in our own voices.

I believe the power of imitation becomes valuable here,

in training both the voice and the ear. Many of the best singers were incorrigible mimics. Jean de Reszke could imitate his brother Edouard's basso, so that were the listener off stage he would be completely fooled. At table both brothers would mimic voices, instruments, even vocalize parts of a symphony, produce the sound of half a dozen instruments, until the company were in gales of laughter.

Learn to know your voice, to hear it correctly, to be not afraid to experiment with it, to feel with it for the emotional quality you wish to hear—laughter, wonder, astonishment, reverence. To feel free with it, not constricted by it. Recognize it as the instrument for that art you are developing; and I cannot see how you can possibly allow it to remain ineffective. Much concentration, thinking, a modicum of time, a reasonable amount of practice, and it is amazing what can be accomplished. The tremendous relief and security of having a voice that can be depended on, that can be played on to the point of pleasuring others, to do away with monotony, with strain, this would seem a sufficient reward for any student.

A word more about the breath. The power to breathe deeply, correctly, has a value beyond health and the furtherance of a good voice. It can be used to center and control emotion. It can put down nervousness, and bring a quiet strength to the breather which makes for poise, for self-control, for an easier approach to the ordeal of speaking in public. Few there are, I think, who do not have to live through that period of panic just before meeting an audience. It is a heart-sickening period even for old-timers. One can become completely disintegrated for the moment. Unless one can gather up nerves and scattered potentialities, at least the first five minutes gives but a poor account of itself.

Patanjali, one of the earliest of the Hindu mystics, writes in his *Sutras* that spiritual force may be controlled by the breath, the indrawing and outdrawing of it rightly. Everyone who has made the attempt to do this with patience has discovered it to be true. There will assuredly come a quieting of apprehension, a sense of fresh inspiration and inner force.

Our next concern is with words: the words themselves, and how well they may be spoken. Clear articulation is as necessary as it is rare. Not labored or stilted articulation, but the free, distinct pronouncing of words, down to the last letter. To be able to give words "trippingly, on the tongue" as well as clearly spoken is a divine gift to the listener. Every storyteller should make it. Here again I think it is the ear which has been largely to blame for our slipshod speech. We do not hear ourselves slur and clip words. And, strangely enough, good enunciation is not necessarily the stamp of culture. One can hold several college degrees and still mumble one's words. It is a kind of selfishness I resent. Why should others be put to the strain of making out what you are saying, do the work for you?

A voice resonant, flexible, and pleasant to the ear, well supported by a fundamentally deep breath, words distinctly and easily spoken, and there you have an adequate instrument for your art. Now for the meaning back of the words. It has been the source of constant wonder and disappointment to find the poverty of vocabulary that exists for the average person. In daily speech we use over and over again a small group of words to express a variety of emotions, to qualify many objects, and to describe much of what we do. We overwork these words; we seem to lack the awareness that they should be retired, and new, fresh, invigorating words put into circulation. We possess a rich language, as honey to the tongue, but we are niggardly with it.

I believe that a limited, poverty-stricken vocabulary works toward an equally limited use of ideas and imagination. While on the other side I know that a growing vocabulary, the provocative use of new words, a wide range of that stuff with which our thought must be clothed, leads to a richer world of thought and fancy. It has puzzled me that those who must use words constantly in their work should be unconscious of their greater possibilities. As a child I discovered that the dictionary was a fascinating book. I explored it with the enthusiasm of a Peary or a Nansen. I wish all children might find the fun in such exploration for themselves, for it can never be imposed upon them.

Dr. Harvey Davis, president of Stevens Institute of Technology, had experiments in vocabulary carried on in the institute for several years. He felt that he was handling an organization of highly specialized and limited studies, nearly ninety percent of them purely technical. He talked with many of the graduates and found that they had missed something on the cultural side while in college which few of them had the time or the incentive to acquire afterward. So Dr. Davis put in classes in English, in literature, and started the experiments in vocabulary. Out of some ten or more years of testing, Stevens Institute feels it can claim a definite rise of efficiency and mental acumen in those students who for four years have concentrated on getting a considerably greater range of words and a facility in using them.

It would seem as if for those artists dependent on words alone for the expression of their art, words made audible, there would be both delight and intelligence in acquiring sufficient material to work with freely. The painter works with his colors, mixes them, tries out effects, knows before he begins just what his box and palette can provide him with. He leaves nothing to chance. He does not try to make sepia explain a tree, or a carmine the water of a lake. He feels for a divine relationship between what he wishes to say and the colors in which he wishes to say it. He studies his composition before he puts line or color down, he creates it by imagination first, then with his tools. He knows how lavishly or how prodigally he may work for the best effect. But he does not limit himself to the primary colors and black and white. And that, I think, is what so many storytellers are inclined to do.

Those who have at their command a wide range of words can best fit their tongues to the work of great writers. There is no doubt about this. They feel at home with them. They are not overawed by fine English. They establish at once a sense or fellowship that cannot fail to bring about a better interpretation, a greater freedom in re-creating what a master has already accomplished. For storytellers must concern themselves not only with what has been said, but how it has been said. It is not enough to use the words of another—they must fit one well. Not clumsily or struttingly on the tongue. I would remind you of Hamlet to the players: "I would as lief the town-crier spoke my lines."

Back of a good vocabulary, supporting a free, wide range of words, I think there must be as well that personal awareness of words, that delight in the sound, the color, the variety they afford. To pluck at them as a player plucks at the strings of his harp. To create with them.

Probably the question asked most frequently by all beginners is: How does one go about learning a story? And this brings us to such a sharp crossroads that I can see all storytellers taking either the road from east to west, or the one from north to south. For there can be no compromise on this matter of learning a story. Either you memorize word by word or you do not. And I think the results matter enormously which way you take.

Those who become great actors, who apply a lifetime of study and experience to the stage, seem to have the faculty of memorizing their lines, of growing into them with a familiarity and rightness, to the end that they can speak them on the stage as if they were extemporizing, as if they were giving free expression, not repeating what someone has written for them to speak. There is no highly mechanized technique apparent in the performance of great actors.

But few storytellers can so train themselves. They have not the time, the continued practice day by day; and I would remind you that storytelling is not dramatic art. For this reason, I think to memorize a story is a dangerous thing to do. It is extremely improbable that anyone who memorizes will be able so to abandon word-by-word commitment as to lose all evidence of it, and be able to give back the story with that perfect art of seeming improvisation. Marie Shedlock could do this, so could Anna Cogswell Tyler; but they were both artists, of drama as well as stories. They are the only two I know who go to prove the rule of exceptions. For a traditional art I am convinced that memorizing is wrong; just as I am sure that imitation is not enough for a folk-craft. There must be fresh ideas, a fresh spontaneous power of creating, brought to every art and craft or these would surely retrogress, and those who worked with and by them would retrogress too.

I think stories must be acquired by long contemplation, by bringing the imagination to work, constantly, intelligently upon them. And finally by that power to blow the breath of life into them. And the method? That of learning incident by incident, or picture by picture. Never word by word.

By contemplation I mean bringing your mind to work on it. To read a story slowly, with your mind intended hard to it. To think intensely as you read until each detail of the story becomes shaped in your mind. If your imagination works better with incident you will make a series of incidents out of the story. If it works better with pictures you will create a series of pictures as you read, pictures which will pass before the inner eye with the sharp insistence and reality of a motion picture. Read the story over several times, letting the words associate themselves with picture or incident. Each time this is repeated the pictures become more a living performance; and the words become more inseparably bound to them. Put the story aside just as soon as you see this happen. When you are ready to take it up again work with the pictures, let the words fit themselves aloud to them as you recall each picture in continuity. At the first attempt the words will break off. You will have to go back to your book and try again. It is like watching the film break in a motion-picture house, and the machine grind on with no picture showing.

In the beginning this may seem discouraging and a far more irksome way of getting to know a story. Very likely it may require more initial effort, harder concentration, for you are disciplining your mind, making it work for you; and this is no easy affair. But once make this way yours and it becomes both simple and vastly enjoyable. There is no drudgery in learning with the imagination. And—here is the crux of the whole performance—you have nothing to unlearn, nothing to get rid of as you have when you learn by rote. You are left free of all the mechanics that otherwise fasten onto you as the Old Man of the Sea fastened onto Sindbad.

Two folk-crafts have provided figures of speech for traditional storytelling: to spin a yarn—to weave a tale. These are good words to keep in one's mind. They provide better pictures for the real art of storytelling than that process of stamping on the memory, word repeated after word. To draw out the fine thread of a story until the spindle is wound full, to throw the shuttle back and forth between the threads of the woof until the pattern or the tale is laid—this is what traditional storytelling must be if it is to bring teller and listener together in that bond of spiritual heritage. To have the power of seeming improvisation that there may be no distraction of revealed technique.

I have heard two significant comments by children after a story hour, one from the East, one West. "She must have made it up—let's ask her." This after a telling of Charles Finger's "Killing of Cabrakan" from *Tales from Silver Lands*. And the other after a telling of Louis Untermeyer's *Fat of the Cat:* "She must have worked awful hard to learn all that by heart."

Learning by heart is a mechanical effort; and afterward to unmechanize a story so that it comes forth with that spontaneity which must accompany the expression of all folk-art is well-nigh impossible. Think of it in terms of music. Who enjoys the playing of a Brahms concerto when the player's attention is definitely concerned over the correct movement of his fingers on the keyboard? How much can one be carried away by the Russian ballet from *Prince Igor* if the dancers give evidence of all the gymnastics that have gone into their preparation? No matter how perfectly memorized, no matter how fluently told, there remains that implication of something mechanically acquired that stands out in marked contrast in the art of the traditional storyteller.

Therefore I do beseech all would-be storytellers to work by the instinctive method of seeing your story first, of making it live for you to the point that you can make it live for others. And in this process of making it live, to fit the words, whether your own or another's, to each movement of life as you see it come to pass before that inner eye.

I knew an elderly man once who took his small grandson to see his friend Joseph Jefferson in a performance of *Rip Van Winkle*. It was toward the end of Jefferson's life and he must have given more than a thousand performances of that one part. The following Sunday Mr. Jefferson was invited to the family dinner that the little boy might never forget this truly great artist. "What night did you see the play?" Mr. Jefferson asked. And the answer provided the old actor with one of the greatest tributes of his career: "I saw you on the night you went to sleep on the mountains and woke up after twenty years, a very old man."

To the little boy that was the one night that particular incident could have happened. On other nights the play must have been quite different.

One thing of which I believe storytellers to be unmindful is the matter of timing. There are few stories which can be timed alike. For musicians there is at least a notation of time on every composition; but unfortunately we do not get our stories marked "4-4 time" or "3-4 time."

Do not take me too much in earnest when I say, unfortunately stories are not timed for us—except in a strictly figurative sense. We carry no regular beat of words through any story; although there are moments when there is repetition. or a special majesty of phrasing, when a suggested beat is called for, when the words themselves gain by it. Put your mind to it and you will see how definitely certain stories call for a marked timing. Some stories, heroic ones, march from beginning to end. Other stories go quickly, on light feet; they call for the suggested rhythm, the delicacy of touch of a Strauss waltz. Some stories go clumsily; and you would not have them go otherwise, for they would lose an elemental strength, a firm groping, that is necessary. Many stories go on bated breath and call for hesitation, that holding of suspense, which taken away leaves but half a story.

To recognize the value of a pause, to know to the smallest fraction of time how long it may held. To appreciate crescendo—the hurrying of both time and intensity. To know, when substance is of great import, how to carry it through on slow, well-marked time, as if the story could not lose one word spoken during those seconds. What timing can do to the emotions is of vast importance. Who does not remember the impact of the beaten tom-tom on the Emperor Jones, in the play of that name? The impact was tremendous. It changed a Pullman car porter for the duration of a held breath into a terrified savage.

I have heard music critics score a performance because a conductor, a singer, a pianist has shown a poor sense of timing. Without it one cannot escape monotony. This can be most apparent when a storyteller tells two stories, one directly after another, and gives no thought to the timing of either story. Some, I think, come by this sense naturally; but even then it can and must be carefully watched, developed. For the rest it means giving careful thought with the preparation of each new story. When to hurry, when to go with slow deliberation; when to pause, to hold the word, that that which comes after may make its imprint of beauty, of wonder, of strength felt, in the minds of the listeners. I rather think that this sense of timing is to those who work with a living art what a sense of design is to a painter: it gives proportion and balance, it makes things to be in the right relationship, one with the other.

It has been a matter of common disturbance among story-tellers in libraries or schools, of whom much is demanded, that there is never enough time to prepare new stories well. I think there is only one answer to that. Why not read some-times? Reading can be made as delightful as storytelling, if the reader makes of it an art. Anyone who ever heard Miss Moore read *Knickerbocker* knows what I mean. Here was an experience as enchanting as any that may come out of a library story hour. Why should not one include part of a book or read some poetry? It makes for contrast; it irons out what could so easily become a rumpled bit of telling. How much better to tell only the stories that have had ade-quate preparation and can be well and happily told, and to fill in what more time is necessary with something read well?

The children know to a fraction what your performance is worth. They can so easily have a good story ruined for them by association with slipshod telling. And the effect upon the storyteller is one of unnecessary discouragement, and often a dislike of the story itself, and a fear of telling it again. Why should not beginners be encouraged to read aloud more? I have another point to make which seems

to me of great value to the storyteller, and right if we are to
encourage good storytelling. In both schools and libraries,
where there may be a possible selection of children to listen
to a story hour, why not have two distinct groups, one a
regular and probably generally assorted group to listen to
what has been tried out and long prepared; and the second,
a laboratory group of children well adapted by experience
to listen to stories told for the first time, stories to be tested
for their excellence and their appeal? One never quite dares
to experiment with stories before an untrained, restless
group of varying ages. And yet the experience of trying out
stories, of getting the children's reaction to them, is something that cannot be neglected.

To be able to create a story, to make it live during the
moment of the telling, to arouse emotions—wonder, laughter, joy, amazement—this is the only goal a storyteller may
have. To honor one's art. To hold for it an integrity of mind,
a love and propensity for it. To build richly of experience
into one's life that there may be more to give out in the
telling. To establish one's place in the fellowship of spirit
that there may be spiritual substance as well as intellectual
enjoyment in what is shared. To keep step with a child's
fancy, to abide for a little space in the Land of Faery, to
know joy unrestrained and those tender secret longings
that belong at the heart of childhood—these are some of
the markers along the way of the storyteller.

The Art of Selection

And yet there is no stone fragment, there is no human hieroglyph without secrets to which the heart of men must forever be returning, lest in its struggle towards new points in the circumference it loses touch with the center. The present is not enough; and the present and the future together are not enough. The past also hath its absolute; for the timeless underlies at every point the flowing of the mystery of time. . . . Books are man's rational protest against the irrational, man's pitiful protest against the implacable, man's ideal against the world's real, man's word against the cosmic dumbness, man's life against the planetary death, man's revelation of the God within him. . . . If the first Prometheus brought fire from heaven in a fennel-stalk, the last will take it back—*in a book.*

—JOHN COWPER POWYS, *The Enjoyment of Literature*

The Art of Selection

UNQUESTIONABLY a large measure of the success
of the storyteller depends on his selection of stories,
his power to discriminate, his growing ability to evaluate.
I think an instinct for selection goes with the art of storytelling. One may base one's choice of good stories on a fair
proportion of appreciation, on familiarity with a wide
range and diversity of literature as well as on a building of
the critical sense. But there seems to be a higher, a hidden
and a silent court that sits in judgment and is usually right.
All storytellers, I think, have discovered this, by the only in-
fallible method of trying a story out on several groups, trying it out so many times that the findings speak with finality
for the story. Thumbs up—thumbs down.

There is as well that very personal relationship that exists
between all storytellers and the stories they tell which must
be taken into consideration. In spite of the fact that one
may like a story immensely, be acutely aware of its fine
points, its quality of appeal, I am firmly convinced that certain storytellers are allergic to specific stories. In other
words, there are stories that are not for you or for me, and
personal liking has nothing whatsoever to do about it.

There are many storytellers who have not the essential delicacy or humor to tell Andersen. There are others who fail utterly, and will always fail, to bring out the true majesty and splendor of the hero tale or saga. Herein lies a part of the storyteller's integrity, to be honestly aware of this and say: This story is not mine. As in the days of the ancient storytellers of Ireland, by some spiritual right we may own certain stories and we may not tell those owned by others.

I have always wanted to tell the *Just So Stories*. I have tried them repeatedly but I lack something that the stories demand. I have always wanted to tell "Toomai of the Elephants" and always failed to draw from it what the story holds. In spite of the fact that I have lived with and adored Andersen all my life I have proved but a poor interpreter for him, and have abandoned the stories to the art of other storytellers.

This intimate relationship between story and teller must be reckoned with. It is as personal a matter as the clothes one wears. Some become one, and some do not; and what storyteller, her personal liking to the contrary, would present herself to any group of listeners with an unbecoming story?

These two points, one of instinctive choice and one of possible allergy, must be taken into account in the matter of selection. I give these before I go on with more specific points which make a story either good or bad for telling. The moment one begins to be more or less prescribed in the choice of stories the whole matter is apt to bog down in a deplorable way. There must be left to every storyteller a great latitude and flexibility in choice. To put stories into a narrow runway, with gates at each end, and let only certain ones out, makes of this matter of selection not an art but a kind of literary conscription.

I believe every storyteller should work through three mediums for her own benefit and the pleasure that a variety of material always affords. She should work with folk-literature, with stories by individual writers, and with selections from a full-sized book. The telling of folk-tales is by far the easiest. The beginner will do well to make these the major part of her choice until that time when she has grown perceptibly in creative power. And for another reason a folk-tale is by far the easiest to apprehend. It has a universal structure, the language is simple and strong. It holds an unquestioned appeal. By the very fact of its universal character, to learn it, to interpret it, comes naturally to most of us. What the race has created we, as individuals, re-create easily. The only danger lies in a patronizing attitude undervaluing the art hidden within.

What must be remembered is that folk-tales have as wide a range as the human imagination which created them. The idiom, the flavor, and the very psychology back of them differ as much as the peoples who gave them tongue. A teller may do excellently with one type of folk-tale and not so well with another. This is to be remembered.

After the folk-tales, the myth tales—of Odin and Thor, of Zeus and Hermes—and all the lesser tales that have come out of mythology. The hero tales are by far the hardest. They demand a type of language that does not sit comfortably on all lips. They demand a tempo that is not easy for all to master. All this must be reckoned with in selecting stories to tell.

The structure of the story told must be taken into account. It is largely because of the firmly knit, universal form of the folk-tale that it is both easy to tell and easy to listen to. It begins with an introduction or preparation so short that often one is hardly aware of it. "A king had three sons." . . . "There was once a widow who had one lazy daughter." . . . "Once there was and was not a king of Spain. He loved to laugh." The longer the preparation, the greater the skill needed; for the listener is concerned with what is about to happen. The development of the folk-tale is direct and usually in sequence: because of this, this happened—a series of natural consequences which the mind follows with little effort. The development is cumulative, it builds up to the climax. What explanation follows the climax is usually as brief as the introduction. It may be summed up in a single paragraph. What happens must be inevitable—it must follow a kind of divine logic, be acceptable to all. It must leave the listeners with a complete sense of satisfaction.

I think, in the main, with a reasonable tolerance for exception, that all stories successful for telling must be built on this form, especially when the stories are told to young children. The matter of description must be marked carefully. In a book time may be taken for considerable description. Castles and countries, gardens and princesses, heroes and dragons may merit having a good deal said about them; but when these are put into a told story one must watch out for that which might throw the story out of balance. Stockton's *Ting-a-Ling* tales makes a good example. The delight of the writer in his delicate shadings, in how this certain thing looked and what happened in the past to bring this about, is amusing enough for the reader but apt to be tedious for the young listener who wants to get on with the story.

Any story loosely put together is a difficult story to tell no matter how amusing it may be. I think there must not be too much digression in a story that is good for telling. If the writer goes steaming off on a happy bypath, as many do, and the main road is forgotten for the moment, the reader may always turn back to the page before and make himself right with the story again. But not so the listener. Stories that confuse had better be left inside their covers, to be read, especially for the untried.

Intricate stories, involving many characters, a main plot, and a subsidiary plot, are difficult to tell. A play within a play may be presented admirably upon the stage; but this likewise tries the art of the storyteller and the capacity of the listener. For this reason I have left out in the story of "The Juggler of Notre Dame" that very lovely and touching legend of the sagebush which Brother Boniface tells to Jean that he may see how even the lowliest thing may serve Our Lady. However, this objection applies to a story I have included here, "The Bird Who Spoke Three Times." Merely the business of keeping the characters apart in the two stories and not confusing the names of the two heroines, I have found tricky. Yet my reason for including the one and abandoning the other provides a good point in this matter of selection. In the story of the Juggler the legend Boniface tells is not necessary to the enjoyment and understanding of the story. It is extraneous matter. In "The Bird Who Spoke Three Times" the story the bird tells is necessary. The main story is built largely on the suspense the secondary story creates—everyone is waiting expectantly to see if the bird will go on. The action of the main story depends on this. Also the story within the story, which the bird tells, is simple and so easy to follow that it does not put too great a strain on the listener. I have found that making a definite change in pitch and timing, and telling the bird's tale in a thin, bird-like voice, keeps the two stories definitely separated in the listener's mind. Yet I will contend this is a difficult kind of story to tell, and the beginner would do well to think twice before attempting it.

A story good in substance may be poor in form and language. Our children hear enough poor English spoken everywhere. We should discard the use of what is bad when we tell stories. I believe that strong, simple, vigorous language adds a story's weight in substance to the telling. I think that multiplication of words should be watched for; often one adjective will serve where two are used. The very beauty of the princess, the terror of the giant, the courage of the hero can be enfeebled by too much or too weak wordage.

In the stories we tell let the spoken word be strong in itself, of a compelling and imaginative nature. Let it be put with other words in a manner to charm the ear and arrest the mind, to build with perfection and delight that story which in itself is worth remembering. But let there be substance equally good.

Stories that make for wonder. Stories that make for laughter. Stories that stir one within with an understanding of the true nature of courage, of love, of beauty. Stories that make one tingle with high adventure, with daring, with grim determination, with the capacity of seeing danger through to the end. Stories that bring our minds to kneel in reverence; stories that show the tenderness of true mercy, the strength of loyalty, the unmawkish respect for what is good. I stress these above the merely clever story, the rogue story, the story that amuses with what is sly, tricky, and successful. There are far too many of these sly, tricky, and successful ones in real life for us to put our stamp of approval too constantly upon them. Alas and alack, they are amusing. It is fun to tell them; and far better to do so than to allow ourselves to take them too seriously.

Let us watch out for unity in the story selected; that the form, the subject matter, the emotions which inspire it and the words which clothe it shall stand in good fellowship, each with the other. In folk literature this unity need never be questioned. Perhaps because of the centuries it has taken to shape it, nearly every folk-tale, well rounded as a pebble in a stream bed under the constant movement of the water, comes to us perfectly unified. There it is: the form simple, complete; the subject matter universal; the language forceful, pictorial.

Unity in a modern story is somewhat more complex. But we demand the same relationship between substance, form, and language that we do in the folk-tale. They must belong together. Otherwise the essence of the story is clouded; and then how can the storyteller draw out, clear as crystal, the essence of what she tells so that it may be passed on, clear, to the listeners.

A Biblical story should go clothed in a majesty of words; a medieval story told in the vernacular of today should be challenged. One does not paint fairies with the broad heavy strokes one would give to painting a house; nor are Ariels molded with the lumpishness Rodin gives his *Thinker.*

As for qualities to beware of in all stories: there is cheapness, mediocrity in substance, form, or language; smugness; an overstress of certain attitudes. Let us not have stories which overexercise virtue, godliness, moral values. Honest souls, be they young or old, react violently to these. There is that noteworthy young Quaker theological student who, after a lecture on the province of the church delivered by a very righteous man, was heard to say: "Almost thou persuadest me *not* to be a minister of God."

Storytellers are often faced with situations where any right and reasonable choice must be abandoned on the moment, and something entirely foreign to the usual story-hour program must be snatched for ana used. Herein lies a point not to be treated lightly. A story hour is a fluid thing—it may take on anything that is good, with color, emotional appeal, and living interest. It may include almost anything that has a bearing on what young people are thinking about, curious about, actually doing or merely dreaming about. It is not right that a story hour should become

static; on the other hand it would be deplorable if a story
hour should become commonplace.

I have already spoken of my boys' club in Greenwich.
They were a group of eighty, aged twelve to sixteen. They
provided one of the problems of truancy, petty misde-
meanors, and vagrancy for the neighborhood police. The
college settlement could hold them on two interests—man-
ual training and baseball. I think none of the boys had gone
beyond the seventh grade, yet most of them were bright,
sharp as gimlets. The head of the house warned me beforehand of what I might expect. They might hoot me out.
They might raise particular Hell; or, at a sign from their
leader, they might simply walk out.

I came, as I thought, prepared for the first night, all
ready with stories which I believed forceful and exciting
enough to hold them: a good adventure story, a good ghost
story—it was not far from Halloween—and one hero story.
But the moment I looked at the boys I knew I could not
begin with any story, nothing that had a fixed form, that
might savor of what "teacher" might do. And so I told of
the circus, told of the few days I had spent some summers
before on the road with the Ringling Brothers. They listened for the hour. The next week when I felt my way by
asking what kind of story they would like the shout went
up: "Tell us more about the circus!" I told about it for
three weeks; told about the daily run of life with any circus:
now the tents were put up, the parade started, the animals
trained; how long it took, how long to load it back again
on a train and get going to the next town. When they were

finally ready to listen to stories we got along famously. Luckily for me, the leader had a weakness for stories and it there had been any inclinations toward delinquency, in favor of the poolroom, the leader saw to it that no one slipped.

Before the year was out I was telling them the best stories I knew, straight literature. They not only liked them but they began to use the town library; and the last evening the club met we had a round-up of all who had taken out library cards—more than thirty of them. Not bad.

With such an experience as this a wide vocabulary, a feeling of at-home-ness with words, provides that final weight that swings the balance in favor of the storyteller. Had I only had that which I had learned by rote, no matter how well I had learned it, the club's first meeting would have been its last.

With a boys' club in Syracuse I had as complete an opposite in experience as was possible. Here were Jewish boys, some fifty of them. When I asked what they liked best, they said literature. Many of them worked; many had left school earlier than they had wanted to. They looked upon the story hour as a means of going on with their education, or at least one part of it. And so I told stories from the *Odyssey*, from mythology, from *The Arabian Nights' Entertainments*—those especially which gave the judgment of the caliph as administered to certain criminals. These points of oriental law and wit delighted them tremendously. I told of Fionn and Cuchulain; and later in the winter the boys brought in stories themselves. It was these Jewish boys

who first introduced me to the books of the Apocrypha,
which the Jews consider spurious. Incidentally, those who
told the stories told them exceedingly well. I think they too
had borrowed something of the cantor's voice and power
for their telling.

The stories I have included in the book have been proved
by long years of use. I have tried them out before every
grade of society and every age. They have been chosen to
give contrast, to show the influence of a people on what
they created. I think only a Latin could have brought forth
"The Magic Box." I know only a Latin could have con-
ceived "The Bird Who Spoke Three Times." No one but
the Irish could have given form to "Wee Meg" or "A Matter
of Brogues"; but "The Princess and the Vagabone" and
"The Peddler" are cosmopolitan material and might have
had their origin in any country in Europe. I have given no
oriental stories; and none from *Uncle Remus* or the South.
I have a firm conviction that no Yankee can do justice to
these last.

I have found in the many years of telling stories that
while some may offer a background too foreign or for-
midable for some groups, thereby demanding too many
explanations beforehand to make the telling practical, there
was no story too good, too fine in its appeal, to reach the
imaginations of any group—be they boys in reformatories,
women in prison, families gathered at some rural crossroads, children in asylums, men in Kiwanis and Rotary,
students in university or library, women in their federated
clubs. A good story never fails to kindle something that

may not have burned for years—laughter for those who have forgotten how to laugh, excitement for those whose lives have dulled down to monotony, awe for those who have forgotten what wonder was, and reverence again for those who have abandoned churches. It is the ordinary, the mediocre story that one cannot afford to tell.

"Creative art is the power to be for the moment a flash of communication between God and man."

Storytelling as an Approach to Children's Books and Reading

We are tired of substitutes for reality in writing for children . . . of sham efficiency, mock heroics and cheap optimism, above all—with the commonplace.

We have felt uneasy ever since the publication of children's books has become profitable. There is grave danger lest American children's books become a commodity rather than a contribution to the literature of all countries.

—ANNE CARROLL MOORE

Storytelling as an Approach to Children's Books and Reading

I T IS most fitting that Anne Carroll Moore should intro-
duce this chapter on storytelling. Never in her long
years of vigorous and vital service to children's books and
those who have published, edited, distributed, and read
them—as well as those who have written and illustrated
them—has she failed to hold their standards high and
their values clear. Her books *Roads to Childhood* and
The Three Owls remain today as alert to those values, as
wise and uncompromising, as the day they were written.
As Walter de la Mare said not long before he died: "The
children of the world owe a debt to Anne Carroll Moore
they can never repay." And no one has more zealously
supported the need of storytelling in libraries, schools,
playgrounds—everywhere children may gather; and no
one has more compellingly upheld the quality of the
stories told and the manner of their telling.

So far I have spoken of storytelling as an art, a traditional art, sufficient unto itself. But that is not the whole
picture. Storytelling can be used both wisely and help-
fully as an approach to books—old familiar books, too

often forgotten, and new books, too often lost in the welter of each year's publication. It may be used more often than one realizes to arouse the enthusiasms of the slow, the lazy, the indifferent reader—that boy or girl who would rather do almost anything else than read a book. These lazy, indifferent readers should not grow up missing the rich heritage of books. Not when some timely urging, an exciting whetting of fundamental childhood interests, can send them on to explore books for themselves.

Since I first wrote of storytelling, publishers have more than trebled their yearly output. There are now more than forty publishing houses advertising in *The Horn Book,* where there were originally four or five. What Anne Carroll Moore prophesied over thirty years ago has come all too true; children's books have become both profitable and a commodity. All who buy, who read, who use these books need guidance today in selecting the best. All central libraries in large cities have young-readers' guides. The schools in large cities have libraries and excellent librarians to invite and direct good reading. There are bookshops to browse in. But what of the smaller communities? What of the parents and teachers who bumble along, wanting books for their children and having no idea what to choose; and the children themselves, wholly bewildered by the enormous number of books that confront them?

I think here we find an answer in the story hour. Here there is an intimate group that gathers for the sharing of a good story; there are expectancy, curiosity, laughter, and a sense of trusting what one hears, like an invitation to reach out beyond the told story to the books that may also invite, hold curiosity, and adventure into a farther-away world. Herein lies a sense of reality, of wider interests, that may well catch the lazy, indifferent reader unaware.

A few years ago when I took over much of the story-telling in greater Boston, its branch libraries and schools, I learned much; learned the great need for using books as part of the story hours—the need for bringing to the listeners some of the books left forgotten on the shelves, and for bringing some of the most worth-while of the new books. I rarely spent more than a few moments on any book. I always held the book in my hand, a visible sign and symbol of what I was telling. I always began: "Here is a book I like. Would you like to hear about it?" The answer was nearly always a unanimous "Yes." The results were amazingly immediate and rich. It was good to hear afterward a young voice ringing out across the school yard: "Listen, kids, I've got a terrific book to read."

This whetting of young appetites, this giving of a wider vision of the world and of youth itself, I feel, should place a well-defined marker on the way of every storyteller. Insecurity, disturbance, apathy, national distrust are everywhere today. If we can make the art of storytelling an applied art, by which we may bring the rich heritage of good books into the lives of children throughout our country, that they may find a universal eagerness toward life and an abiding trust, then I think we may truly help build for the future. Underlying all childhood is a sense of eternity. Children are far less likely than adults to think in terms of yesterday, today, and tomorrow. Let me quote Anne Carroll Moore again:

We should by no means limit the reading of any boy or girl . . . to any list. We should see to it that early connections with adult books of travel, exploration of natural history, science and the arts are made. Allowance must be made for the wide variety of tastes among child readers. . . . The recent published letters of well-known authors concerning books they have read as children leave us with a stronger conviction than ever that the crucial point in the guidance of children's reading lies in having certain books at hand at the psychological moment.

I know of nothing that provides that psychological moment better than the story hour.

One of these adult books I have brought with me often into a story hour when the group has been upper-graders. It came out at the end of the last war. It is called *The Raft* by Robert Trumbull, and it is a story of what actually happened when a bomber with a crew of three crashed into the mid-Pacific. The plane sank before the crew could inflate their life-raft and gather supplies. They managed, while keeping themselves afloat, to inflate the raft and climb aboard. But they saved nothing—no food, water, compass, oars, or sail. Nothing! They kept alive thirty-four days, until they were rescued on a small island whither they had drifted. But during that time they suffered intensely. Rain brought some water they could drink, chance brought a small amount of raw food. They burned under a hot sun by day; they huddled, cold, at night, full of despair and with little hope. The pilot, who had gone to Sunday school as a boy, vaguely remembered a few Bible stories he had heard there. These he told, over and over again, to keep up their courage, keep their minds off their misery. Here were three men, all from different parts of the country, all with widely differing backgrounds, no one of whom had ever read books as a boy. As one reads one becomes increasingly aware of how poverty-poor they were in those many things books and reading might have given them. The listeners become aware of this—even while they welcome the story as one of good adventure. Often at the end of the story hour both boys and girls make suggestions of what there might have been to share had the men known *Treasure Island, Captains Courageous, Moby Dick*—and so on and on.

I often took James Ramsey Ullman's *Banner in the Sky*. This always proved a wonderful success, even among indifferent readers. Around Boston there were many abandoned quarries where potential rock-climbers could try out their prowess. The story about young Rudi Matt, his courage and determination to prove his father right about the only ascent possible up the great mountain—which is actually the Matterhorn—by finding it himself and fastening his father's red shirt to the summit, never fails to ring true and memorable to all who hear it. I had an amusing sequel to one story hour when—a year later—I heard a young voice ring out across Copley Square: "Hi, Miss

Sawyer! Do you know there is a grand movie down at the Beacon about the book you told us. Only it is called *Third Man on the Mountain*."

Dr. Sydney Rosen has written two books that have gathered in many enthusiastic readers after a short telling: *Galileo and the Magic Numbers* and *Doctor Paracelsus*, these especially for the potential mathematician, physician, or chemist. There is no need to offer books about outer space or space fiction; these easily establish themselves among young readers.

Among the adult books, I feel that *Endurance* by Alfred Lansing should not be missed. Here is an amazing saga of endurance, fortitude, and leadership by the explorer Shackleton. *Ring of Bright Water* by Gavin Maxwell is a more gentle book with a background of the lovely West Highlands of Scotland and a delightful story of the taming of two otters. *The Incredible Journey* by Sheila Burnford is an exciting animal story. And for sheer fun and a close-up of many small jungle creatures little known, I have found *A Zoo in My Luggage* by Gerald Durrell makes wonderful telling.

There are three books that are neither old nor very recent, which I feel have a place among the young readers of today—and which I use repeatedly. The first is Eleanore Jewett's *Told on the King's Highway*. This unfortunately is out of print. It is by far the best collection of medieval tales I know. They should not be forgotten. From them I have two favorites—although I have told nearly all of them with never-failing success: "Will o' the Griskin" and

"The Knight of the Bucket." Any storyteller can have fun with "The Good Little Devil," and "The Forge in the Fen" makes a classic for Halloween. I wish the book might be brought back into print. These old tales of saints, miracles, devils, and holy ones need to be remembered.

My second book is James Daugherty's *Daniel Boone*. Because of its format, fine as it is, it has been too often overlooked by the older boys and girls. Young people are apt to class it as a picture book and pass it by. It has been exciting always to bring this book to a story hour and watch what happens. There is always a steady growth of interest, of realization of the vastness and challenge of those pioneer days, of what it meant for Boone and others to open new country for the generations to come after. I like to begin with what the author says to Boone:

You were a free, singing rider in a lost dream. Your name still echoes in the mountain passes and is a whisper and a heart-beat along the old trail.

And then on—to where Boone speaks for himself to the youth of America, the youth of today:

Rise up, you lanky sons of democracy, of Tennessee, of Texas, Vermont, New Hampshire, Mississippi, Ohio, Oregon, and the rest of the glorious brotherhood of states. . . . Pray to the God of your fathers that their spirit be upon you. That you may have the enduring courage to cut a clean straight path . . . through the wilderness against oppression for generations marching on to higher freedoms, riding toward the sun, singing in the canebrakes, singing in the tough spots, chanting: Democracy, here we come! . . . Shouting to the bullies, the tyrannies . . .

Great words; words to stir young hearts and imaginations. Words that need to be spoken today. *Daniel Boone* makes a "terrific" book for all our young people.

My third book is *Amos Fortune, Free Man* by Elizabeth Yates. Here is another book we cannot afford to forget—not from Arkansas to Harlem. I begin with the epitaph in the churchyard in Jaffrey, New Hampshire:

> Sacred to the memory of Amos Fortune.
> Who was born free in Africa,
> a slave in America.
> He purchased his liberty,
> Professed Christianity,
> Lived reputably,
> Died hopefully.

This may seem a strange beginning, by way of giving to young people an invitation to read a book; but it grips the interest at once; it establishes an immediate sense of reality. Then I go forward to the beginning of the story, to equatorial Africa and the season for planting the corn. Here the author gives a sharp-drawn background for the rest of the story in words strong and sure:

Night came down swiftly over the forest; after the snuffing out of the sun, darkness, the bright appearing stars. No silence came with the darkness, for this was alive with song and movement. . . . Time for planting, when the earth was about to be reborn.

The great drums set the rhythm, small drums follow, voices chant:

> Earth, our Mother, Sun, our Father,
> Watch while we plant.
> Moon, our Sister, Rain, our Brother,
> Aid the seeds to bear fruit.

And then the slavers come and put chains on the young prince who became Amos Fortune. Truly here is the stuff for the making of a hero tale.

I like to follow Amos Fortune with the book about Harriet Tubman: *Railroad to Freedom* by Mrs. Hildegard Swift. It has not the fine writing or the appeal of the first book, but it supplements it, giving a vivid and far-reaching picture of those days preceding the Civil War. It tells of the establishing of the underground railroad to freedom for those slaves of the South by men like William Lloyd Garrison.

Much space fiction among our middle-aged children is taking the place of the "once-upon-a-time" folk, fairy, and hero tales. Underlying these traditional tales, there are those universal truths and wisdom childhood today cannot afford to miss. There is a simple justice, a pattern of reward, a confirmation that it is often the simpleton, the youngest brother, the disregarded member of the family who succeeds by virtue of patience and kindness—these are things lost in the modern science fiction. I have found undeniably how much beloved the Greek myths become when told with careful selection, some adaptation, and much enthusiasm. Let me repeat here, however, what I have said in the beginning: do not use these myths if they are not yours to tell.

I usually begin by telling about Pegasus and the Chimera. Here is a myth that never fails to arouse both delight and enthusiam. I have made a version of my own from Hawthorne's *Tanglewood Tales*. I like the gentle beginning and the sense of reality that is immediately evoked with the telling of the Fountain of Pirene and the four that are gathered there: the farmer, the maiden, the old man, and the boy. When the stranger joins them, the enchanted bridle in his hand, then does expectancy soar. From the moment the stranger asks if any of them have heard of a winged horse, and all but the boy deny him, and they leave—all but the boy—one inevitably expects what happens to young listeners. How right it is that the boy is the only one who has seen the winged horse—who else could? And from then on the story mounts on wings of its own to a wholly satisfying end.

My faith in this myth is absolute. Let me give two incidents in the telling of it, each remote from the other. I shall never forget the day I went down to tell stories for an assembly for upper-graders in a school at the North End of Boston. It was widely known as a "problem school." It was overcrowded; the teachers were tired and harassed; there were many delinquents and truants among both boys and girls. Before I began, I could see, writ plainly on nearly every face, open contempt for what I might bring them. School authority would keep them in their seats until assembly was over, but I need expect nothing more from them. It looked as if I might as well give up and go home.

It was the day before Lincoln's Birthday. I began with Lincoln. I tried to make him a boy such as any boy there might be. I tried to bring out his eagerness for books and what education he could get through books. I told the best Civil War story I knew with Lincoln in it. With a show of interest on the faces in front of me, I even finished with "Nancy Hanks" from the Benét *Book of Americans*. They openly liked that. Next I gave them the story of Lou Gehrig, knowing full well there would be plenty of baseball fans among the students. And then, by way of utmost daring and experiment, I finished with Pegasus. It was incredible how that story sprang from Nathaniel Hawthorne to those boys and girls. Afterward many asked where they could find the book it came from. The branch library, not far away, reported a veritable epidemic of new cards taken out that week.

The second well-remembered telling came in the mountains of North Carolina. I was there for a workshop in storytelling, which drew from the Appalachian States teachers, librarians, and some parents. There were many teachers from among the mountain folk, and their background for stories was limited to the "Jack-Tales." Greek myths seemed as far removed from them as from my students at the North End. So I tried Pegasus. It caught the imagination—like a spark on dry kindling. After that, three of my mountaineer teachers told only Greek myths, told them in the vernacular, to be sure, but told them with great enthusiasm and much faith. It was good to leave North Carolina and know that at least some of those children in school along the Blue Ridge would be listening to the stories of Pegasus, King Midas, Perseus and the Gorgon's Head, and Jason and the Golden Fleece—also Hercules and his labors.

Tales of Thor, Loki, and Baldur from Norse mythology are, perhaps, not quite so quick to catch at the imaginations; but I have found that the older boys and girls delight mightily in those stories from the *Arabian Nights* which deal with the justice dispensed by those old caliphs.

I still feel, and use, the stories from Howard Pyle's *Wonder Clock* more than those from any general collection. But we are most fortunate today to have a series of *Favorite Fairy Tales* by Virginia Haviland, six of them, from Germany, France, England, Ireland, Norway, and Russia. I have no idea whether Miss Haviland selected these stories with storytellers in mind, but they are nearly all excellent for telling.

Before leaving behind those long-ago authors who belong to our heritage of children's books—what of Washington Irving? He is seldom read, in spite of the fine collection made by Anne Carroll Moore: *The Bold Dragoon.* I still think his *Tales of the Alhambra* offer first-rate material for any storyteller willing to put a little time on them. As an eight- to ten-year-old I spent long, foggy mornings in Maine, on my stomach in front of a roaring fire, reading "The Moor's Legacy" and all the rest of them. They carried me as an adult into Spain, to Granada, where I sat at dusk in the "Moor's Seat" watching the water-carriers and their donkeys climb the road to the Alhambra. Irving's *Rip Van Winkle* I told all over Ireland. It made a never-failing springboard from which an Irish storyteller would take off for the telling of one of his own tales of fairy and fancy. I have the Scribner edition, with pictures by Arthur Rackham—and I defy anyone to read it with the accompaniment of those pictures and not have an urge to tell it.

It is regrettable how much *Treasure Island* is read but how little known are *The Black Arrow* and *Kidnapped*. Here is elegant material for any story hour. I hope there may come soon and bountifully the urge of many story-tellers to bring Robert Louis Stevenson back to our present-day young people. It is time, as well, to bring Kipling's two *Jungle Books* back—to be better known. His *Just So Stories* are more widely read—but think of the loss, especially to the middle-aged children who have never followed the small Mowgli as he takes shelter in the cave of Father and Mother Wolf; and the growing of expectancy as they wait to hear whether he will be given sanctuary against the coming of Shere Khan, the crippled tiger. I have found the telling of a single tale from *The Second Jungle Book* enough to send even lazy readers to the rest of the book.

I have spoken already of the enduring value of building background. May I again give urgency to this building. I have found some of the most unlikely experiences have led to much good experience in a story hour. I should never have succeeded with my boys' club in Greenwich had I not first gone trouping off with the Ringling Brothers' Circus for three days. And as a beginning for *The Jungle Books* I have retold about the day I spent at the zoo in Dublin. My press card gave me entrance on a day closed to the public. With the keepers, we had the whole zoo to ourselves. In a cage in the monkey house I saw for the first time a mongoose. I asked the keepers if they had ever read Kipling's story of a mongoose, and when they said they had not, I went on to tell what Kipling had written about the mongoose—its friendliness, its curiosity, etc. "Let's take this one out and see what he does," said the head keeper. So we did. It was fun to watch him snuffing, feeling his way out of the cage to the floor, then to us. He sniffed all our shoes, and chose mine. He climbed up until he reached the pockets of my coat, then he explored them, then the cuffs, then down my collar and under my hat. Finally he went back to the pockets and helped himself to peanuts I had brought for the monkeys. It was in the monkey house, with the keepers as listeners, that I first told the story of "Rikki-Tikki-Tavi."

The books of George Macdonald are among those that have been left too long on the shelves. I have never told *At the Back of the North Wind,* but I think it could be told by the right storyteller. Here is a book that would reach the imagination and the heart of only the exceptional child. *The Princess and the Goblin* and *The Princess and Curdie* make easier telling—and will reach more children. And while speaking of Macdonald books, let us not forget that delightful book, *Billy Barnicoat* by Greville Macdonald, George's son. There are three more books, highly imaginative and forgotten, that should be remembered: Charles Kingsley's *Water Babies,* John Ruskin's *King of the Golden River,* and last and most especially, Kenneth Grahame's *The Wind in the Willows.*

I have already spoken of *The Wind in the Willows,* and of how our family every spring read it again, with a neighbor or two listening in, who, like Mole, had abandoned spring-cleaning. Our three generations have shared it with the same delight. It has never staled. It can be told almost entirely in Kenneth Grahame's own words—with some cutting. There is a rare appeal to the fun and absurdities of Mr. Toad, and an honest appreciation of his "little songs." Especially the last one:

The Toad—came—home!
There was panic in the parlour and howling in the hall,
There was crying in the cow-shed and shrieking in the stall,
When the Toad—came—home!

Bang go the drums!
The trumpeters are tooting and the soldiers are saluting,
And the cannon they are shooting and the motor-cars are hoot-
    ing,
As the—Hero—comes!

Begin at the beginning—I do—that the listeners may feel the urge and stir of spring, the renewal of life everywhere:

Mole had been working hard all morning, spring-cleaning his little house. Brooms and dusters, ladders and steps, pails—and whitewash. . . . But spring was moving in the air above and in the earth below. Was it a wonder that he threw down his brush and said: "Bother!" and "Oh, blow!" and "Hang spring-cleaning!" So he made for his little tunnel and scraped and scratched and scratched and scrooged, muttering, "Up we go!" until at last his snout came into the daylight and he found himself rolling in the grass.

One does not attempt to tell the whole book—but urgently comes the need of telling of Mole's meeting with Water Rat, of the picnic up the river, of the happenings in the Wild Wood, of the finding of Little Portly at the Gates of Dawn. The children enjoy to full measure the poetry throughout, especially the carol the fieldmice sing on Christmas Eve outside Mole's little house, which he hasn't seen since he escaped from his spring-cleaning:

> Villagers all, this frosty tide,
> Let your doors swing open wide,
> Though wind may follow, and snow beside,
> Yet draw us in by your fire to bide:
>   Joy shall be yours in the morning!
>
> Goodman Joseph toiled through the snow—
> Saw a star o'er a stable low:
> Mary she might not further go—
> Welcome thatch and litter below!
>   Joy was hers in the morning!

So much more can be said of the value of storytelling as an approach to books and reading; so many more books may well be given. My hope is that what has been said may rouse more to look for forgotten books as well as to search carefully for the new ones—both those written for young people and those for adults—that story hours may be made richer withal.

But before I go on to another subject that concerns me mightily, I would like to remind you that reading habits are established very early, if they are to be established at all. And the place to begin this bringing of books to a story hour is in the picture-book years. It was a great joy to watch our first granddaughter, Sally McCloskey, at the age of two, show her delight in books. The first sentence she put together was: "Read a book." Picture books were coming in plentifully sixteen years ago. Robert McCloskey had done his *Lentil* and *Make Way for Ducklings*. Wanda Gag's *Millions of Cats* has never failed to reach eager young hands and imaginations. Her *Gone Is Gone* has become a dearly loved classic for all ages. All these and many more Sally has passed on to our third granddaughter, Marie Durand, and it has been good to watch her at two years old reach eagerly for books. Marie's vocabulary at two-plus far exceeds that allotted by educators, editors, and publishers to four- and five-year-olds—and not only a richness in words used but in putting sentences together and a discovery of synonyms. Marie delights in finding more than one word to describe the things in her own small world, saying: "A story is a tale, a book, something to read." Why are so many limiting a child's vocabulary in those early years when words come bountifully and bring wonder and understanding with them? All appreciation of the true values in life, and all life holds, begins early and grows slowly. So does an acceptance of all that is mediocre and shoddy. If parents would only remember this. Standards as well as habits are formed early.

Today is rich in picture books—the best—to bring early to story hours. There is only one I can take time to mention, for it is not known and used as much as it should be. Palmer Brown's *Cheerful*, "a story of a mouse, maybe two mice, or four mice." I have never fathomed why small ones love stories and pictures about mice, but they do. It is a story to share throughout the year, but it is especially right at Easter time, and there are so few stories for Easter.

After many years, Marie Ets has done another book about Mister Penny—*Mister Penny's Circus*. Here is a new picture book that will be welcomed by small ones and grown-ups. With so many delightful picture books to choose from, it is bewildering to those of us who have tested the value of good books throughout the growing years of children to find so many parents willing to buy books with retold stories of little value and with cheap pictures—just because they can buy them for less than fifty cents. Too often we have been asked by parents: "Why is it important to give the youngest children nice books when they are perfectly satisfied with cheap ones?" Alas and alack—if they wait until their children are older it may be too late for them to choose for themselves a good book. And if parents cannot and will not bring good books to their children at the picture-book age, then storytellers must. Here is a time when the small ones gather with eagerness—when they watch and listen to the best—with the book open so all may see. It is a time of closeness, intimacy, complete trust in what is shared—a time of wonder and remembering.

It is easy for all of us—whether we be storytellers, librarians, teachers, or parents—to meet the needs of the ordinary reader: the boy who says he wants a book about baseball, building radios, space exploration; or the girl who asks for a book about Mexico, about shells. But what of those children who are reaching for more? We so rarely know, from what we can read of childhood as it runs so swiftly by us, of those who are needing to have us guide them toward creating beauty, music, poems, cathedrals, pictures. Here are children reaching for the stars. Let us never forget them—let us reach with them.

Shall We Have Poetry in the Story Hour?

Poetry begins with delight and ends with wisdom.

—ROBERT FROST

Shall We Have Poetry in the Story Hour?

IN THE urgent voice of one storyteller I answer, "Yes!" Children are poets, nearly all of them, if you listen carefully while they play—and if you catch them young enough. The world around them sings; it has a rhythm and a picture-making delight that they are continually expressing. How often have I heard a chanting out-of-doors as a child hopped, skipped, and jumped along beside his sober companion!

> I am going for a walk—
> I will see many things—
> There are ducks in the pond waiting to be fed—
> There is a white swan who floats and floats—
> There is my friend, the policeman—
> There is my friend, Alice—
> I will give her one of my cookies—

Thus chanted a two- to three-year-old.

Our son, who early began to make easily recognized things with blocks—castles with moats, bridges, towers and buildings for trucks and engines—sang at his building. I have already, in a previous chapter, given the song of his red engine. The simple things that happen during the ordinary day, children sing about; for the world around them is still full of rhythm, and, having not yet been forced to conform to the school and adult world, they give it unconscious and free expression.

As I have heard Robert Frost say before reading his own poetry, "It begins with delight and ends with wisdom." Would that our children might not lose this singing world somewhere along those years of growing up.

Parents seem to have little time for poetry themselves, much less time to share it with their children. Teachers seem to be too often embarrassed by it—they do not trust themselves, or poetry. Some poetry is included in the early grades—in an elementary class in English, as recitation during oral English periods. Sometimes it is good poetry; often it is hackneyed. If a librarian likes poetry herself, she usually shares it with her children. But I think there should be more sharing—a wider sharing—that more children should hear it before they lose that first instinctive love of rhythm, of what makes words sing. Let me give you what Eleanor Farjeon says of poetry:

> What is poetry? Who knows?
> Not the rose, but the scent of the rose;
> Not the sky, but the light of the sky;
> Not the fly, but the gleam of the fly;
> Not the sea, but the sound of the sea;
> Not myself, but something that makes me
> See, hear, and feel, something that prose
> Cannot. What is it?—Who knows?

Take the youngsters interested in factual things—what really is! They want to be told, or read what is signed and sealed for its accuracy—what is written with knowledge and authority. When we bring that which appeals to the imaginative, creative mind and spirit of the child, it appeals to the subconscious as well as to the conscious—to the emotions. These children want to feel, to gather in the beauty, the sense of something hidden, to be revealed later. First delight—then wisdom.

As a family we were fortunate in having a neighbor who not only loved and knew poetry but could read it better than I have ever heard poets read their own poems. He came often, early in the evenings. It is a remembered time for all of us—from the head of the family down to our four-year-old. When our neighbor came, pockets always bulging with books, bedtime was put off an hour. We listened to Matthew Arnold's "The Forsaken Merman," to Vachel Lindsay's "The Ghosts of the Buffaloes," and the little-known "Dirge for a Righteous Kitten." We had much of Robert Frost's *North of Boston* and *A Boy's Will.* We knew all Walter de la Mare's *Peacock Pie* and *Down a Down Derry,* but we shared these aloud. That there might be a time for giggles, we had spots of Edward Lear's nonsense. After one such evening, as the children mounted the stairs to bed, talking, we heard the four-year-old say: "Wasn't it nice!" "You can't understand half of what Professor Davenport reads," said the older. "You don't have to understand poetry. You just like it," was the reply. So there you have Robert Frost again—first delight, then wisdom.

Let us never forget we must trust poetry; we must **never**

try to grade it down to an age level. Good poetry can be enjoyed by all ages and understood—if that is necessary— later. Children are alert early to the picture-making qual- ity in poetry as well as to the rhythm. They like repetition —this you will find in Shakespeare as well as in *Mother Goose*. Deep within them they gather the universal truth, the spiritual appeal that fine poetry holds. And God knows, we need that nowadays!

How may we use poetry effectively in story hours? I have used it often just to break up the monotony of prose stories and to give something fresh and vivid in a short compass of words. I have used it as a forerunner of some story, to set the atmosphere, the feeling for the story. Often a poem may give in essence what to expect next. So I have used the poem from *The Book of Americans* by Rosemary and Stephen Benét about Daniel Boone:

> When Daniel Boone goes by at night
> The phantom deer arise,
> And all lost wild America
> Is burning in their eyes.

Before a sea story I like to give a good sea chanty. Here is one of the best:

> Come all ye young sailormen, listen to me,
> I will sing you a song of the fish in the sea.
>   Then blow ye winds westerly, westerly blow,
>   We're bound to the south'ard so steady we go!
>
> The herring come saying: "I'm king of the seas.
> If ye want any wind, why I'll blow up a breeze."

Then blow ye winds westerly, westerly blow,
We're bound for the south'ard so steady we go!

Boys and girls alike enjoy John Masefield. Before or
after a sea yarn I often use his "Sea Fever":

I must go down to the seas again, to the lonely sea and the sky,
And all I ask is a tall ship and a star to steer her by:
And the wheel's kick and the wind's song and the white sail's
    shaking,
And a grey mist on the sea's face and a grey dawn breaking.

Sometimes the children respond so immediately I give
the whole poem—sometimes only a couple of stanzas.

When Lincoln's Birthday comes, besides "Nancy Hanks"
I like to share with them Vachel Lindsay's "Abraham Lincoln Walks at Midnight":

It is portentous, and a thing of state
That here at midnight, in our little town
A mourning figure walks, and will not rest,
Near the old courthouse, pacing up and down. . . .

A bronzed, lank man! His suit of ancient black,
The famous high top-hat and plain worn shawl
Make him the quaint great figure that men love,
The prairie lawyer, master of us all.

He cannot sleep upon his hillside now,
He is among us—as in times before!
And we who toss and lie awake for long
Breathe deep and start, to see him pass the door. . . .

It breaks his heart that kings must murder still,
That all his hours of travail here for men

Seem yet in vain. And who will bring white peace
That he may sleep upon his hill again?

To break—perhaps—into the solemnity of some story
hour and give a feeling for what Lindsay can do in a lighter
mood, more for younger children, let me give "A Dirge for
a Righteous Kitten":

> Ding dong, ding dong, ding dong!
> Here lies a kitten good who kept
> A kitten's proper place.
> She stole no pantry eatables
> Nor scratched the baby's face.
> Until she died she had not caused
> Her little mistress tears;
> She wore her ribbon prettily,
> She washed behind her ears.
> Ding dong, ding dong, ding dong!

Sometimes when poetry comes in the pauses between
stories, one may see the swing and rhythm of it catch at
young fingers and feet—tapping out in unison—or heads
nod unconsciously their sense of timing and delight. At
some times it is good to think that young people are ready
to reach out for something that strikes deeper than the
beat of jazz and the blues. I have always found that the lilt
of Irish poetry will set feet to tapping gently. At any time
Seumas O'Sullivan's "The Piper" can be shared with the
six- to sixteen-year-olds. I give it because it appeared originally in a small booklet published by The Tower Press of
Dublin and is long out of print. I have failed to find it in
any anthology. Here it is:

A piper in the streets today
Set up, and tuned, and started to play,
And away, away, away on the tide
Of his music we started; on every side
Doors and windows were opened wide,
And men left down their work and came,
And women with petticoats colored like flame,
And little bare feet that were blue with cold,
Went dancing back to the days of gold—
And all the world went gay, went gay,
For half an hour in the street today.

William Butler Yeats—those poems of his early years
when he was still an Irish poet—can be generously shared.
All ages of childhood delight in his "The Lake Isle of Inn-
isfree"; and his "Down by the Salley Gardens." Before an
Irish fairy tale I especially like to share his song of the
Fairy Child from his folk play, *The Land of Heart's Desire:*

The wind blows out of the gates of day,
The wind blows over the lonely heart,
And the lonely of heart is withered away,
While the fairies dance in a place apart,
Shaking their milk-white feet in a ring,
Tossing their milk-white arms in the air:
For they hear the wind laugh, and murmur and sing
Of a land where even the old are fair,
And even the wise are merry of tongue. . . .

I have been surprised that most of the children today
have never heard William Allingham's "Up the airy mountain, down the rushy glen . . ." And none of them know

that short burst of pictures, "Four ducks on a pond." There seems to be more than one version extant. Whenever I share it I am prone to believe that Robert Browning must have known it well before he wrote his poem, "Pippa Passes." I use the one I heard a young Irish poet repeat on a day in spring—on a stretch of water on the Dalky coast, outside of Dublin:

> Four ducks on a pond,
> A green bank beyond,
> A sky full of spring,
> A lark on the wing—
> What a very small thing
> To remember for years—
> To remember with tears!

Before dismissing Irish poetry I would like to remind you of the place Padraic Colum holds both as a poet as well as a writer of prose epic tales. There are many poems, especially for the older children, that are delighted in and asked for again and again. Here is something he calls "An Old Woman of the Roads." I think it could come only out of Ireland—with its lilt and its heart-hunger:

> O, to have a little house!
>   To own the hearth and stool and all!
> The heaped-up sods upon the fire,
>   The pile of turf against the wall!
>
> To have a clock with weights and chains,
>   And pendulum swinging up and down!
> A dresser filled with shining delph
>   Speckled and white and blue and brown!

Och! but I'm weary of mist and dark,
  And roads where there's never a house nor bush,
And tired I am of bog and road,
  And the crying wind and the lonesome hush!

This last makes a good setting for the telling of "The
Wee Christmas Cabin of Carnna-Ween," in my collection
of *The Long Christmas*.

Ballads go with all ages. I find young people like one of
the Robin Hood ballads as a starting point for *The Merry
Adventures of Robin Hood* by Howard Pyle. I have already spoken of them at greater length in a previous chapter—this is a reminder that they belong with poetry as
well as with the beginning of so much folk literature.

I would like here to give some poems by more recent
authors—who have, perhaps, written more directly on the
level of childhood. Here is one I like that gives so delightfully a universal urge and experience of all children. It is
by Rachel Field, called "General Store":

> Someday I'm going to have a store
> With tinkly bells hung by the door,
> With real glass cases and counters wide
> And drawers all spilly with things inside.
> There'll be a little of everything;
> Bolts of calico, balls of string;
> Jars of peppermint, tins of tea,
> Potatoes and kettles and crockery;
> Seeds in packets, scissors bright;
> Kegs of sugar, brown and white;
> Sarsaparilla for picnic lunches;

Bananas and rubber boots in bunches.
I'll fix the window and dust each shelf,
And take the money in all myself.
It will be my store and I will say:
"What can I do for you today?"

The little books of poems and pictures by Harry Behn are much beloved: *The House on the Hill* and *The House Beyond the Meadow,* and for a connected poem of delightful fantasy, *The Wizard in the Well.*

In a speech Harry Behn made in the New York Public Library in 1959, he said some very wise and accurate things about childhood. Let me quote a little of what he said: "I wonder if children in the general category amaze you as they do me. . . . Sometimes it seems as if the only ambassadors all nations hold in common respect are under five." A long time ago it was said that "except ye become as little children ye shall not enter into the kingdom of heaven." In matters of fact and information children are blissfully ignorant, so that is not what is meant. How, then, must we become? I should say, we must be more respectful of mystery, more aware of beauty and wonder.

John Ciardi, that stern critic of other poets, has now begun to write for young people. His poems are, in the main, light, amusing, and the children like them. For sheer fun I like to go back to the first volume of poems David McCord wrote, and share. There is a swing to them, a simplicity, a general gathering of the listener into the experience of the poem. And here you have repetition, from "Five Chants":

Every time I climb a tree
I scrape a leg or skin a knee—
And every time I climb a tree
I find some ants
Or dodge a bee,
And get the ants
All over me;
And every time I climb a tree
Where have you been?
They say to me—
But don't they know that I am free
Every time I climb a tree?

And from that universal bedtime "Conversation":

"Mother, may I stay up tonight?"
"No dear."
Oh, Dear (she always says "No dear")
—"But father says I might."
"No dear."

Christmas brings its own poems. There are so many lovely ones one would like to share, it is hard to choose. I have a little volume of religious poetry written by Sister Maris Stella, who heads the English Department at the College of St. Catherine, *Frost for Saint Bridget*. This holds "The Ox and the Donkey's Carol":

The Christ Child lay in the ox's stall,
the stars shone great and the stars shone small,
but one bright star outshone them all.

The cattle stood in the cleanly straw,
and strange to them was the sight they saw.
The ox and the donkey watched with awe.

The shepherds ran from the uplands wide,
the sheepbells tinkled, the angels cried
—joy to the dreaming countryside. . . .

The kings came last in a lordly throng.
The shepherds ran in the space of a song,
—but the beasts had been there all night long.
    Noel, Noel, Noel.

And here is her "Christmas Carol of the Dog":

This is the carol for the dog
that long ago in Bethlehem
saw shepherds running towards the town
and followed them.

He trotted stiffly at their heels;
he sniffed the lambs that they were bringing;
he heard the herald angels sing,
yet did not know what they were singing. . . .

But only being dog, he knew
—to follow when the Family led
to Egypt or to Nazareth.
And no one said

a word about the sharp-nosed dog
who stuck close to the Family then.
And yet, there must have been a dog.
This is a song for him. Amen.

There is no lack today of poems to share from good an-
thologies or collections. I believe there is nothing more

personal than what one likes in poetry. What I have chosen herein will not be what another might choose. The field is wide and rich. The best I can hope for is to send others to search for themselves, to choose and to share what they have enjoyed deeply. Perhaps more than anything else I hope that this chapter may bring fresh enthusiasm and a deeper trust in good poetry. For we need the delight and the wisdom it holds today.

I repeat the refrain from Coridon's song in *The Compleat Angler:* "Then care away and wend along with me."

A Postscript to the Revised Edition

AFTER a careful checking I can find no reason for re-vising the original eight chapters in the book. Story-telling being a folk art and a traditional art, it has changed very little in the two thousand years that have carried records of both the storytellers and the stories they told.

The storytellers themselves have changed mightily, also the pattern of stories told; but the art behind the telling has been the same—whether it takes the form of prose, ballad, chant, or epic. All storytellers, whether in kings' houses or in public libraries, have been impelled in the telling to create laughter, curiosity, expectation, suspense, and wonder for their listeners. Their primary urge has been to make their art a living art—that their stories might live.

But if storytelling as an art has not changed, our world has. To amuse, to bring excitement, to bring entertain-ment in music and narrative that "poets' fees and patron-age of kings and feudal lords might be assured," is no longer the sole reason or challenge in storytelling. Story-telling has become an applied art as well as a wholly crea-tive one. Strength and continuance of childhood's heritage of books and stories today make more demands on the storyteller and the nature of the story hours. Therefore two chapters have been added: that storytelling may be made an approach to children's books and reading, and that there might be a bringing of more poetry into the story hour.

I believe our young people of today are missing out on poetry. In this modern world of slipshod education, of incessant hurry, of space rockets and of threatened destruction, children need to hear the singing heart of the world. Poetry brings to the growing years something nothing else can bring, whether it be the psalm-poetry of David, the fairy songs of Shakespeare, or the sea poems of John Masefield.

What each of us likes in poetry is a deeply personal thing. May I repeat—what I have chosen in my chapter on the need of poetry in the story hour may not be another storyteller's choice. The urgent point is to share good poetry—to use it to break the steady prose of narrative, or to lead on to the next story, or just to use it for itself alone. So—to establish a moment of singing, of inspiration, of the reassurance that life carries with it something more eternal than atom bombs—let Robert Frost's words stay with you as they have stayed with me down the years: "Poetry begins with delight and ends with wisdom."

It is twenty years since *The Way of the Storyteller* was first published. I earnestly hope that the experience of one storyteller, gathered herein, may be both a signpost and a banner reminding the young librarians, teachers, and parents that stories are needed more than ever—that poetry must not be forgotten.

Many of the original books listed at the back are now out of print. I have left them, for there seem to be no new books to take their places, and they can still be found in city public libraries and university libraries. Many books have been added. These I hope may serve the reader well and profitably. I have found that continual exploring on so many subjects akin to storytelling leads to good finding and an enrichment of background. All research may well lead to fairy gold. Find it, share it, and you will never regret the time you have spent exploring in books.

Wee Meg Barnileg and the Fairies

This is one of Johanna's own stories. I must have listened to it a hundred times beside our nursery fire. I think I loved it almost the best of any, for, like Meg, I too "had a way of my own, and had it entirely." Since I have grown up I have come to believe it is the only story Johanna ever told me for a purpose. I think she always hoped I would take Meg's lesson to heart and improve my manners.

I cannot remember what Johanna sang for the fairies' song, only that she chanted it down the Gaelic minor scale of five notes, and that she made the song whirl dizzily, like the fairy men themselves. It took no effort of imagination to see them ringing about Meg. Nor did it take imagination to see Meg. She wore French lawn pinafores as I did, and her hair was as black and short-cropped as a blackthorn berry.

It was always after Johanna had finished with Meg that I said: "Let's go to Ireland, Johanna. Let's go tomorrow." But when I went I went alone; and carried a token Johanna's daughter had given me to give to the Sisters at Ballyshannon, in that convent to which Johanna had once been promised.

Wee Meg Barnileg and the Fairies

THERE lived once by Lough Erne a rich farmer. He and the wife were a soft good-natured pair; come-easy-go-easy was the way they took the world and the world took them. They had one child, a girl by the name of Meg—Wee Meg Barnileg, they called her. Now there be's childher and childher, as well ye know; and ye might have traveled the world over to find one the match of Meg. She had a way of her own, and she had it entirely.

It was: "Come hither and go yonder. Fetch that and take this," all with a stamp of the foot and a toss of the head and a spoiled look in the eye.

When the pair went anywhere they fetched Meg with them, to fairs and feises, weddings and wakes; and when the neighbors put their eye to the window and saw the three of them coming they'd raise a wail ye could hear clear to Malin Head and say:

"Faith, there comes Meg. Hide the best platter in under the bed, and the new butter crock in the loft. Take the fresh eggs from the hens and put them in the churn, back of the door. Tie the pig in the byre and pray the Holy Virgin that we'll end this day whole."

As her mother said proudly, Meg was a terribly observing child. She'd come into a cabin and stand in the middle of the floor and cast the two eyes about her, and what she didn't see wasn't worth a tinker's damn; and she was one of them pleasant kind that told everything she saw and more that she didn't.

"Mither," she'd say, "they've got the same ragged chintz at the windows and beds that they had when last we came. Wouldn't ye think they'd be getting new?" Or: "The creepy has a broken leg, the dirt's brushed into the corner yonder under the besom." Or: "See, Mither, the handle of this pitcher's been broke and put together again. Being so ugly, would ye think it was worth the trouble?" And like as not, to try the strength of the mending, she'd pull the handle away and the pitcher would crash down on the floor, gone entirely.

At a wake 'twas even pleasanter. She had a way of twitching the sleeve of this one and the skirt of that and asking in one of them far-reaching whispers: "Do ye think it's true, now, what Barney Gallagher said of him afore he died— that he was the tight-fistedest man in Donegal? Sure, I heard my father say, many's the time, that he'd rather bargain with the Divel himself. Didn't ye, Father?"

And when she wasn't pestering other folk in their cabins —dead or alive—she was pestering the creatures. She had a way of tweaking feathers out of the cocks' tails as they went by, and pulling the pigs' bristles behind the ears. And for good measure she'd be feeling for the little hairs in the soft of a dog's mouth and tug quick at them, while the dog, poor creature, would let out such a howl as would curdle the heart of the dead.

She'd eat what she'd like and leave what she liked; and she had that whiny sing-song voice that sounded like a young calf with the spring colic. Ye could tell her by the voice without ever laying eyes on her at all, at all. "Look at me beat the dog. I'm not afeared of him. Look at me— if I don't like the stir-about I can throw it out and eat currant bread instead."

And you'd hear the neighbors say: "The holy saints protect us—there's Meg." And ye'd hear the soft, wheedling voice of the mother after her, "Meg darling, leave the dog be an' put down the new crock afore ye do be breaking it. Eat the bit of porridge like a good child and your da'll buy thruppence worth o' sweeties at the shop."

The neighbors could laugh or cry about it—whichsomever they pleased—and swear they would bar the door fast against her coming next time. But come she would and there was no end to the trouble she could raise. Days of peace in the neighborhood were rarer than saints' days; and before Meg was nine even her mother, who doted on the breath she drew, began to grow poor- and pinched-looking. Not a decent, entire piece of clothing would the child keep on her back. It was a fresh dress mornings, another noontimes, and often another evenings. She tore and she dirtied with as free a hand as if her wee body had been covered just with skin and feathers—same as a creature's. The neighbors would see lights through the windows long after midnight, and they would say:

"Aye, if ye rear an' raise a child like Meg ye can set up nights paying for it. Like as not, the poor soul has a basketful o' rags to mend and wash afore morning."

At last Midsummer Day came, as gentle a time as any in the whole year to be seeing the fairies. Wee Meg Barnileg went out in a neighbor's yard where they had tied the watch dog. She had fetched a bit of currant cake along with her, and by way of teasing him she'd reach out the cake as if to be giving it him, and then snatch it out of reach as he pulled for it at the end of his chain. Well, he jumped hard for it once, and how she laughed at the foolish look on him as his jaws snapped together on nothing at all. He jumped hard twice; he jumped hard the third time. But the chain broke, and failing to get the cake he took a nip of Meg's leg by way of compensation. Ye should have heard the hurly-burly the pair raised the length and breadth of Ireland, Meg crying and the dog howling. The neighbors came running. Some were for killing the dog and burning the leg. They rushed this way and that for a gun and a pair of red-hot tongs, crying and wringing their hands. And so mixed up and muddle-minded did they get that they couldn't tell at the last was it the dog or Meg they'd shoot.

"If it was me ye're asking, I'd say shoot them both and make good work of it," said one of the sour-dispositioned neighbors who had stood more from Meg than most.

" 'Tis a good dog—leave him be. But the child is bad entirely. If ye must shoot one, shoot her," was another's bit of advice.

It was Wee Meg herself who settled it; she took one good look at the hard set faces about her, and then she took to her heels and put distance aplenty atween her and the neighbors.

She ran clear over Binn-Ban and on to the pasture beyond; and she found a field where the men were making hay. By that time she had run the fear out of her, just; and she was ready for new sport. She broke a rake, and got tangled up in the forks. She tossed the cocks and fell off the hay-cart, till the patience of the men was gone entirely and they drove her from the field. She went but a bit of a ways, howsomever, and there in a corner under a blackthorn bush she found the men's tea in a pail with a covered dish of scones to eat with it. She took as much of it as she liked and scattered what she didn't like, and then she lay down in the shade of the last hay-cock in the field; and being a bit worn from the day's doings she went fast asleep.

She slept the day out. The men finished all but that corner of the field where Meg lay, and went home. The cows came back to their byres for the milking, the sun set; the birds called their vespers across the moors, one to another; and the moon came up, making as gentle and lovely a night as ye could be asking for.

Meg woke quick-like, the sound of voices close beside her ear. She cocked one eye in the direction the sound came; and there she saw a crowd of fairies—wee men as high as your hand—in green jerkins and red caps, dragging small rakes.

" 'Tis a poor dancing we'll have this night," said one wee voice. "We'll never get the hay raked tidy after the way Meg's tumbled it."

" 'Tis not the hay I'm minding," said another. " 'Tis the scattering of scones and cold praties and stir-about, cluttering up everything. I'd like to get my hands on that untidy child once."

"Aye, get them and keep them!" The wee voice that spoke this time was full of a terrible anger. "Think of them piles of dirty dresses down below—and the broken crocks and pitchers and whatnots we have to look at. It fair spoils the place and makes an eyesore for honest fairy folk."

"We'll catch her some fine night. Ye'll see," said the weest man of them all, standing just the other side of the hay-cock from Meg. "If not one Midsummer Night, then another," and he chuckled way down to the tips of his wee green brogues.

Now maybe ye are thinking that with such a conversation going on 'twould put a morsel of fear in Meg, and she'd have the sense to lay quiet and keep a still tongue in her head. But ye are no knowing Meg. There was never a conversation yet that she wasn't for getting in the middle of it, and as for fear—she'd seen the small little men and knew it would take fifty of them to make the size of her. She was just going to show them what she thought of them, and more besides. So up she jumps and flicks her skirt and tosses her head and cocks her chin, the way it would look saucy, and over the hay-cock she jumps, landing right in the middle of them.

"Well, here I am!" says she, in her smartest voice. "Here I am! Now what are ye going to do about it?" And she chins them all in turn.

For the time it takes to draw three breaths it was so still ye could have heard the new grass growing. The wee men said never a word but just looked at Meg; quiet, solemn, and steady. Then up speaks one:

"Make the fairy ring, wee men," says he. And with that the fairies drew close in a circle about her and began a weaving dance, and in their small, wee voices they began for to sing:

> Ring, ring in a fairy ring,
> Fairies dance and fairies sing.
> Round, round on the soft green ground—
> Never a sound—never a sound.
> Sway, sway as the grasses sway
> Down by the lough at the dawn of the day;
> Circle about as we leap and spring
> Fairy men in a fairy ring.
> Light on your toe, light on your heel,
> One by one in a merry, merry reel;
> Fingers touching fingers so—
> Round and round and round we go!

The song finished, they clapped their hands and kicked their heels and spun themselves about like a hundred green tops and cried: "Move hand or foot if ye can, Wee Meg Barnileg."

Meg tried with all her might and main but she couldn't stir hand and she couldn't stir foot.

"Open your mouth and make some of those fine courteous remarks that ye're so famous for making," they cried again.

Meg opened her mouth wide to scream but her tongue stuck fast to the roof of her mouth and not so much as a sigh came out of it.

"Look yonder then at the grand substitute we are leaving behind for ye so when they search this way before midnight they will find ye fast asleep beside the hay-cock." And with that they fetched out as ugly a fairy changeling as ye could ask for. They blew the breath of a fairy spell on him and he grew and changed, all in the wink of an eye, until he was the spitten image of Meg—face, dress, and boots. The thing stretched itself out in the very hollow Meg had made in the hay and was fast asleep in a whisk.

"Now," cried the wee men, "we'll pinch Meg below," and with that a hundred strong wee hands pinched her legs and arms till she jumped straight into the hay-cock and fell down a long black hole, landing with a grand tumble at the bottom. Looking all about, she found she was in the very heart of a fairy rath and it all shining like a thousand glowworms, soft and lovely.

"Now look about ye," cried the wee men, who were close on her heels. "See our fine dancing floor littered up with the food ye've been throwing away since ye were weaned. Here's the rake—tidy it up and put it into those creels yonder; and be saving with it, too, for that's all ye'll have in the way of victuals while ye're down here."

So Meg found herself with a rake in her hands and the ground covered as far as she could see with cold praties and crusts of oaten bread and lumps of stir-about, and crumbs of cake and whatnot. Well, it was a slow business. She raked the biggest and swept the smallest and she worked till she was tired and aching in every joint. And hungry! She could feel the sides of her stomach scraping each other. "I'll not eat this mess!" she screamed. "If I work for ye, the least manners ye can have is to bring me a mug of fresh milk and a slice of fresh bread."

But the fairy men only laughed. "There'll be nothing fresh for them that has wasted good food like yourself. And the sooner ye begin to eat it up, the sooner will it be gone. Not a decent morsel will ye get till then."

So the end was that Wee Meg Barnileg was driven by hunger to eat up her own leavings. How many days it took to gather them all up and fetch them away I cannot be telling ye, but gone they were at last, and Meg had her first sup of good fresh milk and her first bite of bread. They tasted sweeter than all the currant cake she had ever stuffed into her poor silly stomach.

After that the fairies took her into another great place cluttered over with torn and dirty dresses. There was every stitch she had ever worn since she'd been big enough to creep about the floor. "I'll never wash them, not if I die in your ugly old rath," said Meg, and she stamped her feet and stuck out her tongue, the full length of it.

"Hoity-toity," said the wee men. "Ye'd better mind your tongue better than that. For after ye've washed and mended ye'll have to pick out all the sharp, ugly words ye've ever spoken; pick them out from the kind ones. We don't be leaving the two mix. And pulling nettles, or picking burrs out of lamb's wool is pleasanter business than sorting the two, as ye'll soon find out."

So Meg closed her mouth tight, and set to on the washing. If raking up the food had been bad, this was worse. An old fairy woman brought her where the washtubs stood; and when the dresses were clean she had then to starch and to iron and to mend. If the first had taken her days, the last took her weeks and months.

"Will I never get by the work!" moaned Meg at last. "Will I never get back to my own dear lovely home and my precious parents?"

"Lovely and precious ye treated them," laughed the old fairy woman. "I'm thinking they've been having a grand rest entirely since ye've been gone. As for the neighbors, they've settled down to enjoying life for the first time."

When the dresses were clean and mended and folded and piled neatly into baskets the way they could be carried off, the wee men took Meg into another place and there, like a great field of nettles, were growing all the ugly, sharp words that had ever fallen from her tongue. Growing in the midst of them, here and there, were a few bits of sweet pretty things like flowers—pink and white and blue—struggling to get their heads up above the crowding thorns.

"Ye can see for yourself that it's time something was done about this," says one of the fairy men. "Give ye a year or two more and there'd not be a thing worth growing in this garden. Ye are to pull the nettles and leave the place cleared to give them poor wee blossoms a chance to multiply."

Meg didn't trust her tongue. She nodded her head, just, got down on her knees, and began pulling. She pulled till her hands were swollen and like two red lumps of burning turf. Her back ached, her knees were rubbed bare. She cried and she wailed but she learned to keep her tongue still, for every time she let an angry word drop, it took root right under her eye and made one more nettle to pull.

But at last the place was cleared and all alone stood those few wee blossoms like shipwrecked sailors on a desert island. "The poor wee sickly things," said Meg to herself. And then she sighed. "If the place was growing full of them what a pretty place it would be!" And because she was through, and she felt for the first time a bit of gladness, she picked up her skirts and began for to dance.

Now the fairies love dancing, and when they saw Meg turning out her toes so nicely, and bending and swaying so like a flower, they clapped their hands and laughed and said: "So, ye can do one pretty thing, Meg. Will ye dance for us tonight, under the moon?"

"Sure and I will," said Meg.

So that night, the fairy men brought Meg back to the top of green earth. She felt the soft grass under her feet, and she felt the soft wind blowing her cheek, and she smelt the sweetness of the new-cut hay and roses blooming far off in the neighbors' gardens. And it came to her suddenly a thing she had heard one of them say: "If a body gets taken by the fairies and she can find a four-leaf shamrock and make a wish, she can be free of them forever."

The minute the fairy pipers began to play, Meg took her

skirts and began to dance. She danced over the field where the new shamrock had begun to grow; and every chance she got she bent low and looked sharp at the bits of green leaves to see could she count four on any one of them. At last as the moon clipped the top of Binn-Ban she saw at her feet a shamrock with four leaves to it; and with a glad bit of a laugh she picked it, holding it high over her head. "I want to be home!" she cried.

And home she was, in her own wee bed. Beside her sat her mother and a great bottle of physic and a spoon to take it with.

"Dear me," said Meg, natural-like, "I hope you didn't shoot the dog. He'd never have nipped me if I hadn't the life plagued out of him."

"Glory be to God!" sobbed her poor mother. " 'Tis the first word ye have spoken in a year."

And from that day till the day she died Meg minded her own business and kept a civil tongue in her head and ate the food that was put before her. She had a wedding of her own one grand day and raised a fine brood of childher. And like as not, if ye went tomorrow to Lough Erne and took notice of a well-bred child, the neighbors would be telling ye: "Aye, that child is the great-great-grandchild of **Wee Meg Barnileg.**"

The Magic Box

Nowhere in print have I found this Italian folk-tale, nor have I found a variant from any other country. It came to me by way of an Italian baker, who keeps a shop in Boston and bakes marvelous cakes almost in the shadow of the Old North Church. It is as perfect in form as any folk-tale I have ever heard. It is rich in color; it has a gentle humor. It moves to its ending with swift, sure feet. For those who search for a moral in their stories here is one, well handled and satisfying.

The Magic Box

IN ONE of the fertile valleys of the Apennines—north in Emilia—long ago there lived a rich farmer. He had much land. His vineyards were the best pruned and yielded the best vintage; his olive grove was watched over with the utmost care and never suffered a frost. His fields of grain harvested more than his neighbors'; his cattle were sleeker and his sheep gave more wool at the spring shearings. Yes, everything prospered with him. On market- and fair-days his neighbors would wag their thumbs at him and say: "There goes Gino Tomba. His sons will be very rich men one of these days."

He had two sons. The older was a daredevil who handled a rapier better than a pruning-knife and could swing a broadsword with steadier aim than a mattock. Tonio, the younger, was an easy-going, pleasure-loving rascal who knew more about fiddling than he did about winnowing grain. "If I had a third son, he might have been a farmer," old Tomba used to say when he came bringing his skins of wine to the inn to sell. "But we must make the most of what the good Virgin provides," and so he let his older son march off to the wars and set about making Tonio ready to look after his lands when he had gone.

"Hearken to me, boy; I am leaving you as fine an inheritance as any here in the north. See that you keep a sharp eye on it and render it back with increase to your brother. Some day he will grow tired of fighting Spain and the French and come marching home."

In less than a twelvemonth old Tomba was dead. Tonio came from the burying, turned himself once about the farm to make sure it was all there, and settled down to easy living. He made what you call good company. It was, Tonio, come to the fair; and Tonio, stay longer at the inn; and Tonio, drink with this one; and Tonio, dance with that. He could step the tarantella as well as any man in the north, and he could fiddle as he danced. So it was here and there and anywhere that a feast was spread or a saint's day kept; and Tonio, the younger son of old Tomba, danced late and drank deep and was the last to stop when the dawn broke. Often he slept until the sun was already throwing late shadows on the foothills.

The time came when his thrifty neighbors took him soundly to task for idling away his days and wasting what his father had saved. Then he would laugh, braggadocio: "Am I a sheep to graze in the pasture or a grain of wheat to get myself planted and stay in my fields all day and every day? The lands have grown rich for my father for fifty years; let them grow rich for me for fifty more. That is all I ask—that and for my neighbors to prune their tongues when next they prune their vineyards."

But Tonio had asked too much. A place with a master is one thing, but without a master it is quite different. The *banditti* came down from the mountains and stole his cattle while the herdsmen slept; wolves ravaged his sheep; the bad little oil-fly came in swarms and spoiled the olives as they ripened; the grapes hung too long, and the wine turned thin and sour. And so it went—a little here, a little there, each year. The laborers took to small thieving—a few lambs from the spring dropping before they were driven in from the pastures for counting, a measure of wheat, a skin of wine, that would never be missed. The barns were not fresh-thatched in time, and the fall rains mildewed much of the harvest; the rats got in and ate their share. So, after years of adding one misfortune to another misfortune, there was a mountain of misfortune—large enough for even Tonio to see.

Over one night he became like a crazy man, for over one night he had remembered his brother. Any day he might be returning. At the inn the day before there had been two soldiers fresh from the wars, drinking and bragging of their adventures. Another night and who might not come? Once home, the older brother would be master. First, he would ask for an accounting. And what then? As master he could have him, Tonio, flogged or flung into prison. More final than that, he could run him through with his clever rapier, and no one would question his right to do it. The more Tonio thought about it, the more his terror grew. He began running about the country like a man with fever in his brain. First he ran to the inn and asked the landlord what he should do, and the landlord laughed aloud. "Sit down, Tonio, and drink some of my good Chianti. Why worry about your brother now, when he may be lying in a strange country, stuck through the ribs like a pig?"

He ran to a neighbor, who laughed louder than the landlord. "Take up your fiddle and see if you cannot play your cattle back into the pasture and the good wine into its skins."

He ran on to his favorite, Lisetta. She cocked her pretty head at him like a saucy macaw. "Let me see," she laughed, "you have forgotten your brother for ten years, yes? Then come to the inn tonight and dance the tarantella with me, and I will make you forget him for another ten years."

After that he ran to the priest, and found him finishing mass. He did not laugh, the priest. Instead he shook his head sorrowfully and told him to burn candles for nine days before the shrine of Saint Anthony of Padua and pray for wisdom. On the way to the shrine he met the half-witted herdboy Zeppo, who laughed foolishly when he saw his master's face and tapped his own forehead knowingly. "Master, you are so frightened it has made you quite mad, like me." Then he put his lips to Tonio's ear. "Hearken, I will tell you what to do. Go to the old tsigane woman of the grotto. She has much wisdom and she makes magic of all kinds—black and white. Go to her, master."

In the end it was the advice of the mad herdboy that Tonio took. He climbed the first spur of the mountain to a deep grotto that time or magic had hollowed out of the

rock, and there he found the tsigane woman. She was ages
old and withered as a dried fig. She listened to all Tonio had
to tell, and left him without a word to go deeper into the
grotto, where she was swallowed up altogether in black-
ness. When she came back at last, she was carrying something in her hand—a small casket bound strongly with
bands of brass, and in the top a hole so small it could hardly
be seen in the pattern of the carving. She put the box into
Tonio's hand and fixed him with eyes, that were piercing as
two rapier points. When she spoke, it was as if her voice
rumbled out, not from her, but from deep in the rocks.

"Every morning, while the dew still lies heaviest, shake
one grain of dust from the box in every corner of your lands
—barns, pastures, and vineyards. See to it that no spot is
left forgotten. Do this, and you will prosper as your father
prospered. But never let one morning pass, and never till
the day you die break the bands or look inside. If you do,
the magic will be gone."

That night Tonio did not fiddle or dance with Lisetta at
the inn. He went to bed when the fowls went to roost, and
was up at the crowing of the first cock. With the magic box
under his arm, he went first to his barns to sprinkle the
precious grains; but he found the men still asleep and the
cattle unfed. Out of their beds he drove them with angry
words. And, still lashing them with his tongue, he watched
while they stumbled sleepily about, beginning the day's
work. From the barns he went to the fields, and found the
grain half cut and none of it stacked. The scythes were left

rusting on the ground and the men still asleep in their huts. Tonio scattered more dust, and then drove the reapers to their work.

And so it was in the olive grove, the vineyards, and the pastures. Everywhere he found men sleeping and the work half done. "Holy Mother, defend us!" the men said among themselves after Tonio had gone. "The master is up early and looking about for himself, even as the old master did. We shall have to keep a sharper watch out on things or he will be packing us off to starve."

After that, every morning Tonio was abroad before the sun, shaking the dust from his magic box into every corner of his lands. And every morning he was seeing something new that was needing care. In a little time the inn and the market-place knew him no more; and Lisetta had to find a new dancing partner. A twelvemonth passed, and the farm of old Gino Tomba was prospering again. When Tonio came to the market-place to sell his grain and wine, his neighbors would wag their thumbs at him as they had wagged them at his father and they would say: "There goes Tonio Tomba. His sons—when he marries and they are born—will be very rich men."

And in the end what happened? The older brother never came home to claim his inheritance. He must have been killed in the wars; at any rate, all the lands were Tonio's for the keeping. He married the daughter of his richest neighbor, and had two sons of his own, even as his father had had. And when the time came for him to die he called them both to his side and commanded young Gino to bring him the casket and break the bands, his hands being too weak for the breaking. Raising the lid he looked in, eager, for all his dying, to discover the magic that the box had held all those years.

What did he find? Under the lid were written these words: "Look you—the master's eye is needed over all." In the bottom were a few grains of sand left, the common kind that any wayfarer can gather up for himself from the road that climbs to the Apennines.

Señora, Will You Snip? Señora, Will You Sew?

I heard Sor Isabel of the Trinitarias tell this legend to the charity children as they worked on a new mantle for one of the Virgins of Sevilla. I had stood with Sor Isabel in the doorway of the *convento,* as she clicked her castanets, two-four time, to call the children back to their sewing; and later as she stood at the big embroidery frame about which the children sat, packed like dominoes in a box. "You must sew quickly and well. Holy Week is almost here," she had said. "Then tell us a story, Sor Isabel," one of the older girls had asked. "The gold thread will pull through with greater ease."

Sor Isabel took that moment to explain that one of the rich *patrones* of the convent had given forty thousand pesetas for the gold and seed pearls to embroider the robe. But, like the charity children, I wanted a story. I was more interested in that than in the forty thousand pesetas.

It took much thought, much careful running over in her mind, before Sor Isabel selected her story from the storehouse of legend which her mind held. "It is," she explained again, "a legend of Sevilla, of the old *convento* of the Dominican Friars. It still stands, like an empty turtle-shell close by the Roman walls of the city." And with that she began.

Señora, Will You Snip? Señora, Will You Sew?

FOR two hundred years the old *convento* had housed the Dominican brotherhood; and then the rich *patrones* built them a new one. There was a new chapel, new altars, saints, and a new Virgin. They made it a day of fiesta when they left the old convent behind and moved into the new one. All the brotherhood rejoiced except Fray Benito, who could not. He had been porter of the old convent too long. He had grown old with the cloisters and the images. He loved the mellow sound of the bell that summoned him to the wicket a score of times a day. He loved the worn places in the flagging, trod there by the feet of the brotherhood. He loved the orange trees that flanked the cloisters, making the air heavily sweet at blossom time, and the patio golden with their ripening fruit. He loved his own narrow cell, where he had slept through fifty years of tranquil sleep between the hours of *oración* and *maitines*. But more than all these he loved the Virgin who had grown old and battered with the monastery. Therefore, when the brothers moved into their new quarters Fray Benito remained behind.

It was very still when all had gone; and very shabby. Everything that had been worth carrying away had been taken. In the chapel the old Virgin stood in her place over the High Altar; not a chalice, not a cross, not a candlestick remained. For two hundred years that Virgin had watched over the salvations and sinnings of the brotherhood and had grown altogether disreputable doing it. The paint was chipped from her cheeks; the gold was gone from her crown. Her mantle was dropping to pieces and the lace at her throat and wrists was ragged and soiled. All her jewels had been taken from her to adorn the new Virgin.

Fray Benito considered her sorrowfully. "*Perdón*, Santa María, but it is not good for the honor of the old *convento* that you should make such an appearance. There will still be many coming to worship here. We must take counsel together."

Beneath the High Altar Fray Benito knelt and prayed that counsel might come to him. And it did. It lead him straightway to the paint shop of a certain Tío Jacinto, where he begged plaster, paint, and brushes in return for the benefits of prayer. By the light of a candle he worked far into the night, having first lifted the Virgin down from the High Altar.

Santo Domingo himself must have guided his hand, for by daybreak the Virgin's face had become what God had intended it should be. It glowed with beauty, with comprehension, with life; and above it the crown shone with a fresh glory. Fray Benito's soul was burning with exaltation when at last he threw down his brush. He spread his arms worshipfully before her. "My poor hands with your help have performed a miracle, Holy Mother; but they have performed their utmost. What can be done about your robe and mantle? Woman's clothes are beyond a man's contrivance."

So he prayed for further counsel and fell asleep at the foot of the altar. When he awoke he knew perfectly what he must do. Fastening his sandals and tightening the rope at his waist he went out into the city. Straight to the house of a rich *patrón* he went and asked for Her *Excelencia*, the marquesa. "It concerns rich garments for one who must remain nameless, *Excelencia*. If you will procure for me some five or six meters of brocade, some lace and gold thread for embroidery, some velvet that will enrich the brocade, and material such as is proper for undergarments, I myself will see to the fitting and the making of them. In return I can promise your soul many hundred years' indulgences."

Back to the chapel Fray Benito went with his burden of worldly goods. That night he lighted another candle and stood with arms widespread to sing the *saeta* that had been running in his head all day:

> *De rosas, lirios y nardos,*
> *Tengo que hacer una corona,*
> *Para regarla a María,*
> *Hermosísima Paloma,*
> *Reina de Andalucía.*

He made his reverence slowly before her and said: "I have done my part, *Madre Mía*. Here is everything a lady needs, and of the best. It is for you now to come down from the throne of heaven and make yourself look as the Queen **of** Heaven should look. Señora, will you snip? Señora, will you sew?"

He placed a prie-dieu for her and stood with bowed head waiting. A rustle of stiff old garments, and she was beside him, smiling. Then she gathered up the brocade, reached for the scissors that the brother had procured for her, snipped here, snipped there; took up her needle and went diligently to work. All that she said to Fray Benito was: "Molest yourself no further, my son. You might put your attention to the altar. It needs touching up. And there lies in the attic of the belltower, long forgotten, a chalice and cross which need burnishing."

When a second day broke over the old Dominican convent the Virgin was back on the High Altar. How splendid she looked—how magnificent—how precious and more beautiful than nothing!

Fray Benito ran to the street, distracted with joy. He found Concepción, the youngest child of the baker, playing already, and called to her in a kind of holy rapture. "Nena, go to the meadow outside the walls and gather flowers. This is our day of fiesta. We must make the altar of Our Lady as beautiful as the hills of heaven."

So Concepción ran, and returned soon with her arms full of lilies, branches of almond, jasmine, and spikenard. Together they achieved much loveliness. All those living close to the Roman walls heard of the miracle that had been performed in the old chapel. They came to see and stayed to worship at the feet of this Virgin who had been old and ugly for so many years and had now become young and beautiful.

Year followed year and Fray Benito served his Virgin well. Always he procured candles to burn on the High Altar; always Concepción kept flowers to grace it. The brother toiled in his small garden and grew the *frijoles,* cabbages, and herbs necessary to his simple fare. All Sevilla came to think of him as a very holy man; and the rich sent their sons to him for instruction. There was young Miguel—son of an *abogado*—a very prosperous lawyer. Every day he came; and as Concepción played about the cloisters the two were often together, listening to the gentle teachings of Fray Benito and to the marvelous tales of the *conquistadores,* those knights of Spain who had carried the Church and the worship of the Blessed Virgin into the New World.

As swallows who fly far together mate, so Miguel came to love Concepción and to desire her above all things. *"Chiquita mía,* I will wait for you to grow up," he would whisper to her. "When you are old enough we shall be married here, before the altar of Our Lady; and Fray Benito shall bless us; and we will live *muy contentos* all our days."

"But I am poor. My father is the poorest *panadero* in the city; he bakes fewer loaves than any. The poor do not marry with the rich."

"Love marries with love; you shall see. Ours will be the most glorious wedding since el Cid married Ximena."

How this other miracle was performed I do not know. Possibly Fray Benito loved them both so well that he made the lawyer see that the marriage was the will of God. Pos sibly the Virgin looked with pleasure on the *novios* and blessed their love. This I do know, that on the day before that one set for the marriage Concepción came running to the chapel and threw herself down weeping before the Virgin. Fray Benito found her prostrate there.

"*Qué tienes, niña mía!* What ails you?"

"How shall I marry tomorrow and bring anything but shame to Miguel, to his father and his mother? Nothing have I to wear but the black dress for mass, and that I split at the elbows last night. I tell you, Fray Benito, the bride of the son of a rich *abogado* should look almost as beautiful as the Bride of Heaven. Not quite, you understand, but almost."

"Such a little one—such a silly one! Weep no more." Fray Benito regarded her with gentle mockery. "Whatever happens we must not bring shame to Miguel, his father, and his mother. You shall look even like the Bride of Heaven."

He said it in a way to put peace into the heart of Concepción; but all that day he went about with a troubled mind, discoursing to himself on the vanities of women and the distractions of a worldly life. At nightfall he took the way again to the house of the rich *patrón* and asked to see the marquesa. "*Excelencia,* this time it concerns a wedding and the garments for a bride. Procure the materials for the making of those garments and I will never molest you again."

That night there were many candles lighted on the High Altar. Between the chalice and the cross was heaped the satin, shining like the breast of a white bird. Looking up at the Virgin, Fray Benito spoke his mind.

"You will understand better than I, Santa María, the meaning of all this trumpery. The ways of women are beyond the knowledge of men. Being a woman yourself, you will understand why Concepción must go to her Miguel looking more beautiful than nothing. Once again let me assist you down from the throne of heaven, *Madre Mía,* that you may take up the scissors and the needle and make as lovingly the garments for tomorrow as you would if sewing for your own daughter. Señora, will you snip? Señora, will you sew?"

Then he spread wide his arms and sang again that *saeta* that he had made for her years before:

De rosas, lirios y nardos,
Tengo que hacer una corona,
Para regarla a María,
Hermosísima Paloma,
Reina de Andalucia.

Laughter came from the High Altar. The Virgin was laughing at him as she stretched out her hand to his. "You take us too seriously, holy brother. Come, help me down to my good earth again, and be quick about it. If we are to have our little Concepción ready for her bridegroom there is no time to waste."

She gathered about her the lengths of white satin until they folded her in like the white clouds of heaven. Snip, snip, went the scissors; in and out flew the needle. Once only did she look up from her work, and then it was to cast about her a searching glance at those things Fray Benito had brought from the marquesa. "There is no white mantilla. I see you have forgotten that a rich bride must wear a white one. Go fetch the broom that lies back of the wicket. With it gather the cobwebs which the spiders have been spinning in the empty cells since the brotherhood left us behind. I must wind shuttles and make lace when the garments are finished."

All Sevilla came to that wedding. Never was there a bride more beautiful or a bridegroom less ashamed. More than once during the ceremony Fray Benito stole a look at the Virgin, so eternally still, so full of compassion. Once he nodded his head at her and there were unspoken words on his tongue: "A good thing we made of it last night, Santa María. Never before has there been a bride who has had her wedding garments made by the Queen of Heaven. For recompense, there should be many fine sons to sing *saetas* to you in the processions of the *semana santa*."

This all happened a century and more ago. That Virgin is among the best beloved of Sevilla. The young girls have a saying about her. When one of them is to be married and is too poor to buy a wedding dress they say: "Go to the Dominican Virgin and pray to her. She will see that you have a dress and a mantilla to wear with it. What is more, she will give you enough happiness to last through your life."

The Peddler of Ballaghadereen

Ballaghadereen lies in County Mayo, Ireland. There is an English version of "The Peddler," a fragment from a seventeenth-century diary written about the same time as Mr. Pepys's. In it it is Saint Swithin who appears to the peddler, instead of Saint Patrick.

I think the original source of the tale is a Hebrew legend from one of the lost books of the Apocrypha. Mr. M. R. James gives an excellent version of it in his *Old Testament Legends*.

I owe this tale to John Hegarty—to whom I owe much. He was the last of the long line of seanachies in Donegal. He could not read or write, but he could trace his lineage back to the chief bard of King Conal.

The Peddler of Ballaghadereen

MORE years ago than you can tell me and twice as
many as I can tell you, there lived a peddler in Ballaghadereen. He lived at the crossroads, by himself in a bit
of a cabin with one room to it, and that so small that a man
could stand in the middle of the floor and, without taking
a step, he could lift the latch on the front door, he could lift
the latch on the back door, and he could hang the kettle
over the turf. That is how small and snug it was.

Outside the cabin the peddler had a bit of a garden. In it
he planted carrots and cabbages, onions and potatoes. In
the center grew a cherry tree—as brave and fine a tree as you
would find anywhere in Ireland. Every spring it flowered,
the white blossoms covering it like a fresh falling of snow.
Every summer it bore cherries as read as heart's blood.

But every year, after the garden was planted the wee
brown hares would come from the copse near by and nibble-
nibble here, and nibble-nibble there, until there was not a
thing left, barely, to grow into a full-sized vegetable that a
man could harvest for his table. And every summer as the
cherries began to ripen the blackbirds came in whirling
flocks and ate the cherries as fast as they ripened.

The neighbors that lived thereabouts minded this and nodded their heads and said: "Master Peddler, you're a poor, simple man, entirely. You let the wild creatures thieve from you without lifting your hand to stop them."

And the peddler would always nod his head back at them and laugh and answer: "Nay, then, 'tis not thieving they are at all. They pay well for what they take. Look you—on yonder cherry tree the blackbirds sing sweeter nor they sing on any cherry tree in Ballaghadereen. And the brown hares make good company at dusk-hour for a lonely man."

In the country roundabout, every day when there was market, a wedding, or a fair, the peddler would be off at ring-o'-day, his pack strapped on his back, one foot ahead of the other, fetching him along the road. And when he reached the town diamond he would open his pack, spread it on the green turf, and, making a hollow of his two hands, he would call:

"Come buy a trinket—come buy a brooch—
Come buy a kerchief of scarlet or yellow!"

In no time at all there would be a great crowding of lads and lasses and children about him, searching his pack for what they might be wanting. And like as not, some bare-footed lad would hold up a jack-knife and ask: "How much for this, Master Peddler?"

And the peddler would answer: "Half a crown."

And the lad would put it back, shaking his head dolefully. "Faith, I haven't the half of that, nor likely ever to have it."

And the peddler would pull the lad over to him and whisper in his ear: "Take the knife—'twill rest a deal more easy in your pocket than in my pack."

Then, like as not, some lass would hold up a blue kerchief to her yellow curls and ask: "Master Peddler, what is the price of this?"

And the peddler would answer: "One shilling sixpence."

And the lass would put it back, the smile gone from her face, and she turning away.

And the peddler would catch up the kerchief again and tie it himself about her curls and laugh and say: "Faith, there it looks far prettier than ever it looks in my pack. Take it, with God's blessing."

So it would go—a brooch to this one and a top to that. There were days when the peddler took in little more than a few farthings. But after those days he would sing his way homeward; and the shrewd ones would watch him passing by and wag their fingers at him and say: "You're a poor, simple man, Master Peddler. You'll never be putting a penny by for your old age. You'll end your days like the blackbirds, whistling for crumbs at our back doors. Why, even the vagabond dogs know they can wheedle the half of the bread you are carrying in your pouch, you're that simple."

Which likewise was true. Every stray, hungry dog knew him the length and breadth of the county. Rarely did he follow a road without one tagging his heels, sure of a noonday sharing of bread and cheese.

There were days when he went abroad without his pack.

when there was no market-day, no wedding or fair. These he spent with the children, who would have followed him about like the dogs, had their mothers let them. On these days he would sit himself down on some doorstep and when a crowd of children had gathered he would tell them tales —old tales of Ireland—tales of the good folk, of the heroes, of the saints. He knew them all, and he knew how to tell them, the way the children would never be forgetting one of them, but carry them in their hearts until they were old.

And whenever he finished a tale he would say, like as not, laughing and pinching the cheek of some wee lass: "Mind well your manners, whether you are at home or abroad, for you can never be telling what good folk, or saint, or hero you may be fetching up with on the road—or who may come knocking at your doors. Aye, when Duirmuid, or Fionn or Oisin or Saint Patrick walked the earth they were poor and simple and plain men; it took death to put a grand memory on them. And the poor and the simple and the old today may be heroes tomorrow—you never can be telling. So keep a kind word for all, and a gentling hand."

Often an older would stop to listen to the scraps of words he was saying; and often as not he would go his way, wagging his finger and mumbling: "The poor, simple man. He's as foolish as the blackbirds."

Spring followed winter in Ireland, and summer followed close upon the heels of both. And winter came again and the peddler grew old. His pack grew lighter and lighter, until the neighbors could hear the trinkets jangling inside as he passed, so few things were left. They would nod their heads and say to one another: "Like as not his pockets are as empty as his pack. Time will come, with winter at hand, when he will be at our back doors begging crumbs, along with the blackbirds."

The time did come, as the neighbors had prophesied it would, smug and proper, when the peddler's pack was empty, when he had naught in his pockets and naught in his cupboard. That night he went hungry to bed.

Now it is more than likely that hungry men will dream; and the peddler of Ballaghadereen had a strange dream that night. He dreamed that there came a sound of knocking in the middle of the night. Then the latch on the front door lifted, the door opened without a creak or a cringe, and inside the cabin stepped Saint Patrick. Standing in the doorway the good man pointed a finger; and he spoke in a voice tuned as low as the wind over the bogs. "Peddler, peddler of Ballaghadereen, take the road to Dublin town. When you get to the bridge that spans the Liffey you will hear what you were meant to hear."

On the morrow the peddler awoke and remembered the dream. He rubbed his stomach and found it mortal empty; he stood on his legs and found them trembling in under him; and he said to himself: "Faith, an empty stomach and weak legs are the worst traveling companions a man can have, and Dublin is a long way. I'll bide where I am."

That night the peddler went hungrier to bed, and again came the dream. There came the knocking on the door, the lifting of the latch. The door opened and Saint Patrick stood there, pointing the road: "Peddler, peddler of Ballaghadereen, take the road that leads to Dublin Town. When you get to the bridge that spans the Liffey you will hear what you were meant to hear!"

The second day it was the same as the first. The peddler felt the hunger and the weakness stronger in him, and stayed where he was. But when he woke after the third night and the third coming of the dream, he rose and strapped his pack from long habit upon his back and took the road to Dublin. For three long weary days he traveled, barely staying his fast, and on the fourth day he came into the city.

Early in the day he found the bridge spanning the river and all the lee-long day he stood there, changing his weight from one foot to the other, shifting his pack to ease the drag of it, scanning the faces of all who passed by. But although a great tide of people swept this way, and a great tide swept that, no one stopped and spoke to him.

At the end of the day he said to himself: "I'll find me a blind alley, and like an old dog I'll lay me down in it and die." Slowly he moved off the bridge. As he passed by the Head Inn of Dublin, the door opened and out came the landlord.

To the peddler's astonishment he crossed the thoroughfare and hurried after him. He clapped a strong hand on his shoulder and cried: "Arra, man, hold a minute! All day I've been watching you. All day I have seen you standing on the bridge like an old rook with rent wings. And of all the people passing from the west to the east, and of all the people passing from the east to the west, not one crossing the bridge spoke aught with you. Now I am filled with a great curiosity entirely to know what fetched you here."

Seeing hunger and weariness on the peddler, he drew him toward the inn. "Come; in return for having my curiosity satisfied you shall have rest in the kitchen yonder, with bread and cheese and ale. Come."

So the peddler rested his bones by the kitchen hearth and he ate as he hadn't eaten in many days. He was satisfied at long last and the landlord repeated his question. "Peddler, what fetched you here?"

"For three nights running I had a dream—" began the peddler, but he got no further.

The landlord of the Head Inn threw back his head and laughed. How he laughed, rocking on his feet, shaking the whole length of him!

"A dream you had, by my soul, a dream!" He spoke when he could get his breath. "I could be telling you were the cut of a man to have dreams, and to listen to them, what's more. Rags on your back and hunger in your cheeks and age upon you, and I'll wager not a farthing in your pouch. Well, God's blessing on you and your dreams."

The peddler got to his feet, saddled his pack, and made for the door. He had one foot over the sill when the landlord hurried after him and again clapped a hand on his shoulder.

"Hold, Master Peddler," he said, "I too had a dream, three nights running." He burst into laughter again, remembering it. "I dreamed there came a knocking on this very door, and the latch lifted, and, standing in the doorway, as you are standing, I saw Saint Patrick. He pointed with one finger to the road running westward and he said: 'Landlord, Landlord of the Head Inn, take *that* road to Ballaghadereen. When you come to the crossroads you will find a wee cabin, and beside the cabin a wee garden, and in the center of the garden a cherry tree. Dig deep under the tree and you will find gold—much gold.' "

The landlord paused and drew his sleeve across his mouth to hush his laughter.

"Ballaghadereen! I never heard of the place. Gold under a cherry tree—whoever heard of gold under a cherry tree! There is only one dream that I hear, waking or sleeping, and it's the dream of gold, much gold, in my own pocket. Aye, listen, 'tis a good dream." And the landlord thrust a hand into his pouch and jangled the coins loudly in the peddler's ear.

Back to Ballaghadereen went the peddler, one foot ahead of the other. How he got there I cannot be telling you. He unslung his pack, took up a mattock lying near by, and dug under the cherry tree. He dug deep and felt at last the scraping of the mattock against something hard and smooth. It took him time to uncover it and he found it to be an old sea chest, of foreign pattern and workmanship, bound around with bands of brass. These he broke, and lifting the lid he found the chest full of gold, tarnished and clotted with mold; pieces-of-six and pieces-of-eight and Spanish doubloons.

I cannot begin to tell the half of the goodness that the peddler put into the spending of that gold. But this I know.

He built a chapel at the crossroads—a resting-place for all weary travelers, journeying thither.

And after he had gone the neighbors had a statue made of him and placed it facing the crossroads. And there he stands to this day, a pack on his back and a dog at his heels.

Where One Is Fed a Hundred Can Dine

I like to remember that two of the best tales I brought out of Spain were picked up in a third-class railway carriage. "The Flea," included in *The Picture Tales of Spain,* was one; this is the other.

Never again do I expect to smell goat's cheese, freshly cut, or thin, sour wine, being poured down the gullet of some traveler straight out of the wineskin; nor will I again taste Spanish peasant bread. But if I ever do I shall expect to hear again that exuberant laughter which accompanied the telling of this story. A young farmer told it; but he explained that it was a story for grandmothers to tell the *nietos* at bedtime. And at the Easter season. "It is then that we believe the Cristo comes back to walk the long road upon this earth; and with Him come the Twelve."

After the story was told, his little boy, taking his first ride on the train, pulled between the distraction of his father's storytelling and all that was passing outside the train window, explained with the care and seriousness of the Spanish child that the "One" in the story always meant the Cristo Himself.

Where One Is Fed a Hundred Can Dine

ONCE there was and was not a poor peasant. Always he had little to eat; today, yes; tomorrow, no. One night there came a great storm. The wind shook the trees like dusters. The rain covered the earth like a heavy mantilla. Out of the wind and the rain there came one knocking at the door of his hut.

It was late—late. As the peasant answered the knocking he said to his wife: "God forbid that these be hungry folk. This night there is nothing to eat."

One came in, covered with a great cape, and threw it down by the hearth to dry. He wore a beard. He was cold —cold. The peasant said: "Come, draw your stool close to the fire; it dries quickly here."

He drew his stool close—close. The peasant lifted a small table and put it beside him. Then in his grandest manner, as if he had good soup, tortillas, rice, sausage—everything to feed him—he asked, "Caballero, what can I bring you to eat?"

And the answer was: "Bring me whatever you have—it will be enough."

Now, the peasant thought he had nothing. But he looked

—looked—and found the quarter of a hard round loaf of bread. He put that on the table and filled a *copita* with water. "Let the food be blessed," he said sadly. And the answer was: "The food is blessed," and the one who had found refuge here from the storm broke the bread.

At that moment there came another knocking at the door. "Mary defend us!" exclaimed the peasant. "There is enough to stay your hunger until morning, perhaps. But what of these others?"

"Where one is fed a hundred can dine. Bid them enter."

There entered two, covered in long capes. They greeted the one at the fire as if they had known him long—long. "Sit you down," said the one who had come first and seemed to be master. And to the peasant: "Bring two more *copitas* of water. And have you not the smallest bit of fish?"

The peasant was now shaking all over with humiliation at his poverty. He could hardly speak. "Caballero, there is only the tail. It is not fit to eat."

"Bring it."

So the peasant brought the tail on a dish and the two *copitas* of water for the others, and said, with head sunk upon his breast: "Let the food be blessed."

"It is blessed."

As the one who seemed to be master answered, there came another knocking at the door. "Do not ask me to bid them enter," entreated the peasant. "It is right that one should keep one's poverty covered as with a great cloak."

"Where one is fed a hundred can dine," was the answer.

Two more entered, clothed as all had been, with capes. The peasant drew a bench to the table for them. He was too dumfounded to speak again, for when he had filled two more *copitas* with water and brought them to the table, he saw that the bread had been broken into a platterful of pieces and that the tail of the fish had become many fishes.

Seeing the peasant's amazement, the one who seemed to be master smiled. "Have you not one egg—or perhaps the shell of an egg?"

The peasant shook his head. He was about to answer when he remembered that the *golondrina* who had her nest under the eaves of the hut had hatched out her nestling that day; and the eggshells were scattered on the ground. So he went out into the wind and rain and gathered up small fragments of the eggshells and brought them in. He put them on a dish and set them upon the table, saying: "Let the food be blessed."

"It is blessed."

There came another knocking at the door. Two more entered. The floor around the hearth was spread with capes, drying; and on the table, on the dish where there had been the fragments of swallow's eggs, there was now a great pile of poultry eggs. "Take them," said the one who seemed to be master. "Make the good tortillas and let you and your wife eat abundantly."

When the tortillas were cooked, there had been more knocking, more to enter; until around the table sat thirteen —the one who had come first and seemed to be master, and twelve others. They ate as hungry men eat; and when they had had their fill, there was enough of bread, fish, and tor-tillas to feed the peasant and his wife well for days.

Each man slept, wrapped in his cape, about the fire. In the morning when they left, the first one said to the peasant: "Ask. Whatever you ask for shall be granted."

The peasant thought. "I ask that I shall win at whatever game I play."

The thirteen went their way. The peasant watched them from the door. It seemed as if they walked straight into the rising sun and were gone.

From that day forward, the peasant prospered at whatever he undertook. He lived kindly, sharing food with all, speak-ing well of his neighbors. So did he come to the end of a good life. On his way to heaven, he came upon the Devil, waiting for a rich and wicked man to die.

"What are you doing?" asked the peasant.

"Waiting to carry away this black soul with me."

"While you wait I will play a game with you. Whoever wins shall take with him this soul. Agreed?"

"Agreed."

They played. The peasant won. The rich man died and the peasant took his black soul upon his back and went on his journey to heaven. There stood Saint Peter. The peas-ant knew him at once. "Can I come in?" he asked.

"Enter—" and then Saint Peter stopped. "Wait! What do you carry, there?" The peasant showed him.

"You can't bring that heavy, black soul into heaven.

Throw it away. It will fall and land in the place meant for it."

Then the peasant reminded Saint Peter of the night of wind and rain, when he had taken refuge in the peasant's hut with the twelve others. He reminded him of the one who had seemed to be master and the words he had spoken: "Where one is fed a hundred can dine."

"So—you remember that?" said Saint Peter.

"I remember," said the peasant.

Saint Peter walked away from the gate of heaven, leaving it open. Then he turned his back that he might not see what the peasant did.

Through the gate the peasant hurried—hurried. He carried with him safely on his back the soul of the man who had been rich and wicked.

A Matter of Brogues

This story is a story of fairy music. It calls for little comment. But I give you the music Conal made to put enchantment on the brogues that you may sing it and so put enchantment on your listeners.

THE MUSIC OF ENCHANTMENT

Oh,—— hey—— there and hi—— there,——
Wee brogues, are ye hear-in' me? Tramp a-long to
Bal-ly-weel, For soon, I am fear-in' me, The
mas-ter'll have his po-teen drunk And be back a-ny
min-ute, And to-mor-row there's a
wed-din' And there'll be no Ka-tie in it.

A Matter of Brogues

HERE is a tale, how old I cannot be telling. It happened long back when fairies were plentiful over Ireland, before the great famine and the plague—which gives more than a hundred years to it, if it is time you care anything about.

It is told that much of the music in Ireland came at one time or another from the fairies. Many a soft lilting air we sing today was heard first by some lad who slept a night through by chance with his ear to a fairy rath and woke in the morning with the music ringing in his head. It is the way the song of the brogues came first to Conal of a Thousand Songs. And Conal lived back in that pleasant time before war, famine, or plague.

There are many tales told about this lad, how he could be getting music out of anything. He could cut a reed at the lough and make a pipe that would carry sweeter than the lark singing his matins. He could whittle a sally wand into a whistle with more notes to it than a blackbird. He could stretch dried sinews over a crack in the wall when the wind was blowing and make a caoining as wild and heart-breaking as the wail of the banshee. He could play the pipes and the harp and the fiddle; but of them all it was the fiddle he liked best. But that is not all about Conal. He slept not once but often and often with his ear to a fairy rath until he had his thousand songs by heart, and with those the music of enchantment.

He could pull his bow this way till he had laughter on every lip; he could draw it that way till he had tears instead of laughter. And he could put a charm on mute things that had no life of reason to them the way they would follow his fancy wherever it might lead.

Now there were, and are still, in an out-of-the-way corner of County Donegal two bits of places—like this and like that. They lie two sides of the Gap, with a town between. One place had the manor house, with the Marquis living there. The other place they called Ballyweel; and here the Marquis pastured his cattle with Thady as a cowherd, and his sheep with Manus as shepherd. And in cabins near to them lived Padraic, the weaver, with wee Katie, his one child; and old Shawn, who cut peat on the bogs; and Granny Dagh, who made creels to hold anything at all. These, with a twoscore more, made a contented place; for all they were so poor that, barring the shepherd, they owned not a pair of brogues, each to his name.

Now brogues are the queer things. If you think about them at all, you will know that there is more pride goes into the wearing of new brogues than of any other thing man or child can put on himself. At the time that Conal was still much of a lad a great happening took place, the like of which might not be happening again for a hundred years—

or ever. Love had come to Bridget, the shepherd's daughter, and Duirmuid, the Marquis's son; a love so wonderful that even the Marquis could not put a stop to it, although he had been thinking of ways for a year and a day. He had given in to it at the last; and the Bishop was coming from Dublin to marry the two in the chapel that stood half-way between the manor house and Ballyweel. It was the chapel, the store, the barracks, the tailor's, the public-house, and Tomais the cobbler's that, put together, made the town.

It was over this bit of road that Conal of the Thousand Songs liked best to be tramping. The lad had neither kin nor cabin of his own. Yet he claimed the whole of Donegal for his home; anyone was like to find him on that stretch of road lying between any two places that had a feis today and a wedding tomorrow. And there was never a cabin over all the countryside but had a welcome and more for him.

It was May Day that Bridget was to marry Duirmuid, but weeks ahead there was great fashing and talking of the Bishop's coming. For a bishop was a strange creature in those parts, and not a soul in Ballyweel had ever laid eyes on one, or was ever like to if aught happened to keep this one out of reach. It came to be a fortnight before the wedding, when Hughey O'Brian, the Marquis's agent, gave out the general invitations for the countryside: every man, woman, and child would be welcome; there would be room for all in the chapel who could come decent—with coats to their backs and brogues to their feet.

Brogues! I am wondering can you feel the heart-break in that one word for the people of Ballyweel. New coats for the men, made from Padraic's homespun, print dresses and aprons for the women and children; these could be managed. But who could be turning out brogues but Tomais the cobbler? And he was as tight-fisted and mean a dispositioned man as had ever been born into County Donegal— by the grace of God. Sour as a green gooseberry he was, with a mouth always full of whinings over poverty and a starving old age; while everyone was knowing there was more gold put by in his chimney corner than would keep food in a dozen mouths, and more. To get the gift or the loan of a pair of brogues out of Tomais, short of the five shillings sixpence ha'penny that he asked for the poorest of them, was as impossible a trick as to move the Causeway down to the bay of Cork. And who in Ballyweel had five shillings sixpence ha'penny!

"Faith, I'd like to be murtherin' that old spotted cow and sewing up every foot in the place with strips of her hide!" Thady shouted out his anger at last to the wife. "That cow's but an old bag of leather, anyways. Sure, death would bring her grand comfort."

The cowherd was all for taking an ax and clouting her. But the wife put sense into him, reminding him that, young or old, the cow belonged to the Marquis, and, if murder was done her, like as not Thady would be jailed. But staying Thady's hand was not staying his tongue; and he and the neighbors filled the days and nights with bitterness. The evening before the day of the wedding a fine wet rain began; and the children, urged on by wee Katie, took their last hope and tramped down the hill to the town to see

could they coax Tomais into some kind of good-heartedness.
With Katie as spokesman, they ventured as much as their
heads inside the door of his shop and cried out:

"Tomais, *agradh!* Ye are the grandest cobbler in Donegal.
Lend us the loan of your wee brogues till the Bishop has
gone the morrow, and like as not he'll pray ye a year out of
purgatory."

But before ever the last word was out, Tomais was after
them, a curse on his lips and a blackthorn in his fist. The
last they saw of him as they topped the hill he was still
shaking the stick at them; and his curses came up the wind,
daring them ever to show their faces inside his shop again.

With the coming of dusk a terrible gloom settled on every
cabin but the shepherd's. There Bridget was sprigging the
last bit of wedding finery. New brogues and coats and such-
like were spread everywhere for her family to go decent;
and, not knowing the trouble that had come to the neighbors, she was singing as gay as a throstle.

Tea had been drunk in Ballyweel and the turf stacked
fresh on the fires when over the crest of the highest hill
came Conal of the Thousand Songs, one foot before the
other. A set of pipes was slung over his shoulder and a
fiddle was under his arm, for he was to be making much
music for the wedding on the morrow. The first cabin he
came to was Thady's.

" 'Tis a fine soft evenin', glory be to God!" he called in
at the door.

"Aye, 'tis a grand bit of weather, glory be! Will ye come
in?" was the answer. But when Thady brought his face to

the door to follow his welcome Conal could see it was as black as a peat bog.

He shook his head by way of saying he would not be stopping the night. "What ails ye, man? 'Tis glower looks ye have. Has a murrain taken the cows?"

"It has not, worse luck. If it had taken one cow, just, maybe the black sorrow would not be so heavy this night on Ballyweel." And with that he went on to explain the matter of brogues and the morrow.

Aye, and it was the black sorrow Conal found in every cabin he passed. Outside the door of the weaver's he found wee Katie with her back to the rain and her face to the wall, making as much wetness as the weather. Conal laid a gentle hand on her curls. "And what is breaking your heart this night, *cailin astore?*"

"The same that is breaking them all—what but the matter of brogues?" The words came in a high, thin wail. "To be thinkin' of Bridget, a bride, in a dress fetched from Dublin by the Marquis, his own self, and a Bishop thrown in! All that to be missin'! Faith, I wish I was the whole sky to deluge the countryside proper!"

" 'Tis a terrible shame," Conal agreed. "But now ye hearken to me. If ye weep the night through 'tis a poor manner of wee lass ye'll be the morrow should a pair of wee brogues happen by. Are ye forgettin' entirely what night o' the year this might be? Sure, afore ye sleep this night mind ye put a bowl o' stir-about an' a sup o' fresh milk by the door for the Good People. Anything at all at all could be happenin' on May Eve."

Easing the weight of his pipes to his shoulder, Conal went on from cabin to cabin, leaving behind a trail of hope for the morrow. Then down the hill to the town he went, a queer bit of a smile on his lips. Straight as the crow flies he made for the window of the cobbler's shop, and there he stood looking in. On the shelf were neat rows of brogues— big brogues, soft brogues, stout brogues, wee brogues— stitched and pegged and ready for anyone who had five shillings sixpence ha'penny and upwards to pay for them.

"There's a fine lot of brogues, all waitin' for feet to put life in them," said Conal low, to himself. "But what's the good of empty brogues? Tell me that," and he broke into a laugh as he lifted the latch of the door and went in.

Old Tomais was pegging the last of a sole by the mean light of one tallow dip, and he grumbled Conal a welcome. "Ye can ease your bones on the pile of hides in the corner," says he. "I'll be through in a minute, an' ye can mind the shop whilst I go across yondther an' drink my mug," and he jerked his thumb towards the public-house.

Conal thanked him for his grand hospitality and gave a rascally wink at the brogues in the window. Then he sat down and laid his cheek to his fiddle, drawing his bow softly over the strings to sweeten them.

"Is that a new song ye are makin'?" mumbled the cobbler with a peg between his teeth.

"It might turn into one," agreed Conal.

"Maybe 'tis a new reel ye would be playin' at the weddin' the mornin'?" Tomais was as sharp-fingered for gossip as he was for gold.

' "Aye, an' it might be that, too."

"What name would ye be givin' it, then?" asked the cobbler.

Conal laughed. "Faith, I'm thinkin' of callin' it a tune for puttin' enchantment on brogues—any sort of brogues."

Tomais shot him an uneasy look from the tail of his eye. But the last peg was in and the thirst was on him; so, instead of getting at once to the bottom of such foolish talk, he set it back in his mind to see to as soon as he had finished his mug. Throwing his mallet and awl in the corner, he hurried away with a final word to Conal to mind the shop well.

"Aye, I'll mind it mortial well," the lad whispered after him. As the latch dropped back in its place he was on his feet, his bow beginning to sweep the strings in a mad, wild way. Slowly he moved over to the window, his head thrown back, his body keeping time to the music of his fiddle and a bewitched look coming into his eyes. From under his fingers sprang the music of enchantment like fairy primroses from under spring rains. Never was there a lilt with so much magic to it. By the time he was close to the window and the tidy rows of brogues he was humming the air and fitting words to it. Again he winked, this time at the weest pair, and he sang straight at them:

> Oh, hey there and hi there,
> Wee brogues, are ye hearin' me?
> Tramp along to Ballyweel,
> For soon, I am fearin' me,
> The master'll have his poteen drunk

And be back any minute,
And tomorrow there's a weddin'
And there'll be no Katie in it.

With the finishing of the song the wee brogues walked themselves off the shelf and made straight for the door! Conal lifted the latch to let them out, and waved them toward the hill road to Katie's cabin. If you had been there, you would have seen them splashing through the soft rain.

Fastening the latch after them, Conal came back to the window and winked at the biggest brogues, his fingers holding the music the while. This time he sang:

Oh, hey there and hi there,
Big brogues, are ye hearin' me?
Tramp along to Ballyweel,
For soon, I am fearin' me,
The master'll have his poteen drunk
And be back any minute,
And tomorrow there's a weddin'
And there'll be no Thady in it.

The big brogues walked off the shelf, same as the wee ones, taking the road close behind them; and Conal laughed long and hearty to see them go. And so it went. He sang the stoutest pair away to old Shawn and the easiest pair to Padraic the weaver, and the softest pair to Granny Dagh, till the shelf was as empty as a harvested field and Tomais the cobbler had not a pair of brogues left to his name. With the last gone, Conal blew out the candle and latched the door after him. He stopped but a moment before he passed

out into the darkness, and that was to look in at the window of the public-house. The cobbler was as drunk as a
lord. He was draining his fifth mug to the health of the
bride. And again Conal laughed. "Faith, by the time he is
back in his shop again he'll never be knowin' if he has
there a hundred brogues or none at all."

Maybe ye are thinking this is the end of the tale; but,
faith and all, 'twould make but a poor ending. With a man
as mean as the cobbler, you can guess he would never be
letting his shop empty itself of brogues without prying into
where they had gone. With the wedding day come and
Tomais sober and the people of Ballyweel tramping down
to the chapel—each one of them dandering out in a pair
of new brogues—it would have taken no time at all for the
cobbler to be swearing them his and running every man,
woman, and child off to the barracks and the constable,
to get them all jailed.

And maybe you are forgetting that this was May Eve, as
gentle a night as any in the whole year. No sooner had
Conal passed into the night than down from the fairy
rath above the town trooped hundreds and hundreds of
the Gentle People, in their little green caps and their little
green coats, and never a sound as they came. Straight to
the cobbler's shop they trooped, and, lifting the latch, they
crowded thick inside. There were wee men carrying rush
lights; there were others carrying bits of leather; and, last
of all, there were some with aprons tied over their coats
and mallets in their hands. These were the leprechauns,
the fairy cobblers. They pulled themselves up on Tomais's

bench, while all around them the others shouted to make haste.

If you had been listening then with your ear to a crack in the door, you would have heard the soft "tap-tap-tapping" of their wee hammers on the pegs, sounding like a flock of woodpeckers at a tree. And if you had had the courage to peek through that same crack, you would have seen the wee men handing the leprechauns the bits of leather to turn into brogues as fast as others could put them back on the shelves. So they worked with never a word between them; and in the whisk of an eye the window was full again, with a pair of brogues for every pair Conal had sent tramping up the hill that night.

With their work done, you would have heard the slow running of their laughter, like water running over moss-covered stones; and away they trooped to their rath again, to dance till the moon went down behind the rain.

But here is the strangest part of the tale. Tomais the cobbler never found out the difference between the fairy brogues and his own; for a brogue was naught but a brogue to him—something made of leather to be sold for five shillings sixpence ha'penny and upward. Not so was it for those who came to buy. For as soon as ever they tried on a pair their toes were pinched so hard they cried out sharp with pain, and lost no time kicking them off and leaving them behind in the shop while they went searching another cobbler in another town. So, for all the brogues on his window shelf, Tomais never sold another pair till the day he died.

And what of the wedding? Why, Thady and wee Katie and all of them came down to the chapel, made decent enough, in their new brogues and all. They looked as hard at the Bishop as they liked, until their eyes were full of him and they could tell their children and their grand-children what manner of creature a bishop was. And Conal played the merriest reels for them all to dance. Never was there a gayer wedding or a grander feast; and at the last Conal made a song for Bridget, the shepherd's daughter, and Duirmuid, the Marquis's son. It was a song to lay en-chantment on their hearts so that love should last between them till life's end, and afterward.

The Juggler of Notre Dame

This is an old French legend about the Virgin in the Abbey of Cluny. Anatole France has written a version of it. Massenet has made it into an opera. Those who have ever seen a production of the *Jongleur of Notre Dame* will never forget it. I have tried to put something of the loveliness of the opera into this arrangement for storytelling.

The Juggler of Notre Dame

HERE is an old story, told by French mothers to their children for many centuries. It is as old as the marketplace at Cluny, old as the Abbey and the figure of Our Lady over the doorway. She has been listening to the feet of all who pass these hundreds of years.

It is the month of Marie—May, you call it. It is market-day. Look—you can see the square before the Abbey filled with children, with lads and maidens sweethearting, with farmers selling their wares. You can hear them calling from here, from there:

"Leeks, turnips, good white cabbages!"

"Prunes from Tours!"

"Good cheese—cream cheese!"

"New beets. Strawberries, strawberries, fine early strawberries!"

"Who will buy . . . who will buy?"

One of the monks of the Abbey passes, chanting his call to all sinners: "Come . . . come. Pardons for all at the central altar."

Suddenly the children begin to shout and to point: "Look who is coming! A juggler . . . a juggler. . . ."

Everybody takes up the shouting. A fat farmer shouts: *"Mon dieu,* may he be a good juggler!" For everybody knows no market-day is properly gay without a juggler—his tricks, his songs.

Look with the children and you will see him coming down the road. He is a little one, a boy still; he has twelve years, perhaps. His stockings are in shreds, his doublet in tatters. Famine shows in his cheeks; his body looks as if the wind could blow straight through it as it blows through a young pear tree in wintertime. For many nights now he has had nowhere to sleep but under the hedge, along the road. He has walked far and eaten nothing. He holds fast to his bag of tricks. It takes all his courage to laugh boldly at the crowd and shout: *"Holà!* Behold you see me—Jean, king of the jugglers!"

How the crowd laughs—how it mocks! "Ho-ho! A pretty king! A king of tatters and starvation. Well, what can you do, Jean, king of the jugglers?"

Look again, and you will see how carefully he has to balance himself against the stone bench facing the Abbey. It is the only way he can persuade his legs to hold him up. Mark how he pretends not to hear their mocking. He has learned a great deal in his few years: always to be gay, always to have a laugh waiting, always to treat a crowd as if it were his own good brother.

"What can I not do! Tricks—marvelous! Ballads—five new ones! And for dancing . . . But first, good my friends, a penny for my bowl. It brings luck to all who give

Jean a penny. And you will see. I will make music with them . . . if there are enough."

The people hold back. Two children toss their pennies into the bowl. But the fat farmer cries: "First let us see what he can do. He may not be worth a penny."

A face he makes at those two pennies, that juggler; then carefully he takes from his bag the golden balls. That is a trick all jugglers know—to keep six balls in the air. He tosses them: one . . . two . . . three. . . . He never gets beyond the fourth before he spills them. The crowd laughs. The fat farmer jeers: "I could toss cabbages better than that."

He tries the hoops, tossing them, twirling them, catching them on the stick. But his arms, they ache, they are as weak as his legs; and for the moment he allows himself to be very solemn. "Your pardons. I am clumsy today. It is the empty stomach which travels always with me. Look, good sirs! Watch but a moment. I will take a fresh brown egg out of anyone's hat."

But this is an old trick. Not funny. The crowd starts to break, each to go about his own business. *"Holà—holà!"* the king of the jugglers shouts. "I will sing for you. Name any song, I will sing it."

The fat farmer calls: "Sing us a drinking song—something gay and very wicked."

Jean looks across the square to the doorway of the Abbey, where stands the figure of Our Lady. The crowd is shouting again and no one hears him address her: "Holy Mother, forgive me; and I beg You to close Your ears, for I am about to sing a song that is not proper for You to hear. Today the stomach is master, it will not go another day without being filled." He makes a slight reverence and bursts into the maddest, the lustiest drinking song sung in all of France three hundred years ago.

And who is coming now? Look down the road and you will see the Prior of the Abbey coming back from visiting the sick. He arrives at the square to hear Jean singing his song; and, *mon dieu,* he is a very pious prior. He scatters the crowd and lays a tight hand over Jean's mouth. "Sacrileges . . . blasphemies! You dare profane our Abbey and Our Lady! Apprentice of the Devil, begone!"

These are terrible words; at them the very small juggler's knees begin to knock together, to bend. And he thinks: it would be well to smile. But what a smile!—one to tear the heart out of a stone. "I asked pardons of the Holy Mother before I began. As for the Devil, tell me, holy father, how can I be his apprentice when I have never seen him?"

Look again, down the road. You will see the good Brother Boniface riding in on his small gray donkey. He is the cook of all the brothers. He has been out in the countryside gathering food for the feast-day of Sainte Marie. The baskets on his donkey are filled with fruit, with vegetables. He speaks to the Prior:

"Father, here are lilacs, lilies, sweet violets for the altar of Our Lady. Here are onions, white as pearls, leeks and basil for savory, cheeses, cabbages. And, look you, two fine fat capons! The better the brothers feast the better they can pray, eh, Father?"

As he holds up one good thing after another, it is too much for Jean, that starved king of the jugglers. His knees drop wholly from under him and he pitches forward, fainting, almost beneath the doorway of the Abbey. The Prior's tongue clicks to his cheek in sounds of compassion. He kneels beside the ragged little one, then, bewildered for a prior, he looks up into the gentle face of Brother Boniface. "I think I was mistaken. There is here less of the Devil and more of starvation. Come, Brother, let us take him in. We have found before that one of the pathways to the soul leads through the stomach." And as Jean opens his eyes: "Come, child—come to table."

"To table!" Jean repeats it in a kind of holy ecstasy. He is lifted to the donkey's back in place of Brother Boniface; and together the three enter the courtyard of the Abbey, the king of the jugglers sobbing against the white cassock of the cook-brother.

So, that is the way a juggler came to the Abbey of Cluny three hundred years ago. Jean hid his tattered clothes and the bag of tricks in the hollow of the old tree in the square. He put on the brown robe of the novitiate and became helper in the kitchen to Brother Boniface. That poor, travel-worn, starved little body and that ignorant, vagrant soul together found sanctuary in the old monastery. All about him was beauty and consecration. All day there was beauty to touch, to see, to hear: the monks chanting the

Magnificat . . . the musician-brother playing through his new mass on the organ . . . candles, tall candles, always burning in the chapel before the Virgin, who looked across the light to the kneeling brothers, Her sad, lovely face so filled with compassion.

Soon, very soon, Jean forgot the world outside with its noisy, jeering crowds, the long, lonely roads, the barking, snapping dogs at his heels, the cold dark of the nights, hidden under a hedge or some cock of hay. He became happy; such a bounding joy filled his small body as nearly to split it asunder, so tremendous was it. He had only one disturbing thought and this he shared with Brother Boniface one day as they were preparing dinner.

"All day I watch the brotherhood, busy, doing things for the glorification of Our Lady. The painter-brother is making a new Holy Family. Very beautiful. The carving-brother is making a new font for the holy water. The singing-brother is composing a new Gloria for Our Lady's Day. But me—what can I do for the glorication of Our Lady? Nothing!"

The cook laughed and held up the big cabbage he was slicing. "Look, my little one, what do I do for the glorification of Our Lady. I make fine this cabbage. I pare these carrots, so. I take these pearls of onions and quarter them. All to put in the pot of broth to fill the stomachs of the brothers. We cannot all serve in ways of beauty; but we can serve humbly and lovingly, with our hands and our hearts. And I think that in the eyes of Our Lady all service is acceptable—the painting of the Holy Family by Brother

Joseph . . . the making of the pot of broth by Brother Boniface."

He threw his head far back and laughed, filling the kitchen with merriment. Then he laid down knife and cabbage and put his hands on the small, narrow shoulders of the juggler-novitiate. *"Mon dieu,* what is the use of my making good broth if it puts no flesh on your bones? You are nothing but a fledgling, skin and eyes. Some day you will blow away like a feather. Pouf! You will be gone. Then who will help me glorify Our Lady in the kitchen with the beautiful vegetables?"

But the disturbing thought grew apace, until it cloaked heavily the happiness. Jean took the disturbance to the Holy Mother Herself. Kneeling before Her in the chapel he spoke slowly, that no word might be lost. "How sad You always look, Holy Mother. . . . Is it because of what You are always thinking? . . . You never forget Your Son who died upon the cross? . . . I have a great wish to make You smile. . . . That would be something—to have Jean make You smile."

This thought, with the disturbing one, dwelt with him many days. He took it to bed with him, after complin; he awoke with it in the morning and carried it along with his beads to matins. It was at daybreak that the inspiration came to him—that way in which he could truly serve Our Lady. He waited until mass had been said and each brother gone to his appointed task, the chapel deserted. Hurrying secretly to the old tree in the square he pulled out his bag of tricks, his juggler's clothes. In a dim corner of the chapel he changed. Capping his head with the conical cap and long feather he skipped down the nave and stood making deep reverences before Our Lady. "Holy Mother . . . Adored Virgin . . . here I stand, Jean, a poor juggler. He has made other mothers, sadder mothers than You, to smile. . . . See, he falls at Your feet and begs the honor of doing for You his tricks. He will do all things for You, of the best. *Voilà!*"

First the golden balls. Jean takes them out and keeps the six in the air, each one aloft catching the light of all the candles. "Look, they are magnificent. Now for the hoops."

He does them all, every trick he has ever learned; and how gloriously he performs! Now the drum. He is marching with it, beating time, singing an old French marching song: "Tra-la-la-la-la-la . . . tra-la-la-la-la-la!" That is what he is singing when the musician-brother returns to the chapel to play over a part of his mass.

For a moment he stands transfixed beside the organ. A novice! Doing desecration in front of the altar! It is unthinkable—it is horrible! He finds movement at last and hurries out to summon the Prior, the whole brotherhood. Like white wraiths they come into the chapel, without sound. And there is Jean, once a juggler, still marching, still beating his drum, still singing bravely his "Tra-la-la-la-la-la."

Mutterings grow. It is like the gathering of a black, angry storm. Words are spoken under bitter breath: "Sacrilege!" . . . "A limb of Satan!" . . . "Cast him forth!". . . "Let him die in the streets!"

The Prior raises his hand to curse, to fling the anathema upon the boy. It is Brother Boniface who catches the Prior's sleeve and points. "Be not rash, Father; look! It is the Virgin Herself who gives sanctuary."

The drum beats: Boom-boom-boom! Jean sings; "Tra-la-la-la-la-la!" And Our Lady? Watch Her, even as the brotherhood is watching Her. Slowly, very slowly, She is beginning to smile. Jean is looking up at Her face. He laughs aloud with his great happiness. He casts away his drum and kneels before the altar, crying out: "See—see—She smiles at last! I have brought happiness this day to Our Lady."

It is no longer a figure there who smiles—it is the living Mother of Jesus. She leans far down and gathers that small king of the jugglers into Her arms and cradles him. He who has never known cradling knows a mother's arms at last, the close, everlasting blessing they give.

A great light fills the chapel. A chorus, unseen, of heavenly music fills the spaces. The monks kneel in awe and silence. Only Brother Boniface speaks: "It is a miracle. Our eyes have looked upon it."

From that day on—so the old story runs—Our Lady of Cluny has always smiled.

The Deserted Mine

This has been taken from *Peasant Tales of Russia* by Nemirovitch-Dantchenko. The original story runs the length of a short novel. In cutting for storytelling I have kept as close to the original as it has been possible, not wishing to lose any of that sense of cumulative drama with its undercurrent of simple faith. It is to me as strong and beautiful as Tolstoy's "Where Love Is There God Is Also," and goes beyond it in dramatic force.

The Deserted Mine

AT THE entrance of the new mine stood a group of miners. They wore leather jerkins and small lamps that flickered at their belts. The young overseer was talking to the oldest miner, whose gray beard fell untidily over his hollow chest. The old man's breath came in thin, whistling sounds; his black eyes burned like black holes shot through with strange, fantastic light; his feeble arms hung at his sides, his legs tottered under him. They called him Ivan the Silent.

"Listen, old man," said the overseer. "You can never manage the ladders. We'll put you in the bucket and lower you in."

The other miners laughed good-humoredly. "Think of old Father Ivan thinking he could go down the ladders with the best of us. Ho-ho!"

Ivan looked at the bucket they were making ready. He hadn't been lowered in a bucket since he was a baby, eighty years ago. He had been born in the old mine—the deserted one. His father had been killed in it; his mother had gone on working in his place so there might be food enough for two when he was born. He had been born down there in the eternal darkness. The first noises he remembered were sounds of picks and blasting rocks. He lay all through his babyhood on an old blanket in a hole, sucking away at his milk rag. His eyes followed the flickerings of his mother's lamp. He learned to walk in the mine, his hand on the ledges of rock; and as he grew he came to know new sounds —rushing water, sudden crashing, swishing, hollow echoes. Sometimes a miner sang; sometimes he swore or groaned. Sometimes there was silence. The silences were terrible.

"Get in, old man," said the overseer.

He pushed him in and Ivan squatted down at the bottom.

"Now in the name of God you'll turn round a bit," said one.

"Look you, we'll get him down in the wink of an eye," said another.

Nevertheless, there was time for many memories as old Ivan swung and creaked down on the rusty chain. He watched the square of daylight over his head dim out until it was only a speck of gray. The lamp at his belt threw timid shadows on the damp trickling walls of the shaft. At last the daylight above him closed its gray eye and he was in the dark.

"Already the shaft is old. Old and rotten. Some day it will come crashing in with all the earth on top of it. Then those who are inside will stay in, and those that are out will stay out."

He said all this to himself. He never spoke aloud. No one had heard him speak in ten years. He stirred his memories about and pulled out one that he liked. He was still very little—talking some—walking as one does in such darkness —listening to everything. He had a friend, an old miner. old as he was himself now. Down there in what he called the comfortable darkness, he had told him about the Lord Jesus Christ.

"I tell you, Ivanovitch," he would say, "He has His Kingdom here, under the earth, the same as above. He is here, moving about us, often. Listen some day and you will see it is the truth. You will hear the rustle of His garments as He passes through the long galleries. If you are lucky you will see Him; if not today, why, then tomorrow."

"And do you see Him?"

At the question his friend had laughed in his throat. "Now why should I see Him! I am old—everything has grown too thick about me. But when I was little like you, Ivanovitch, I heard Him often—and saw Him. If I had not, how could I be telling you about Him now?"

One day his friend was telling him again about Jesus when there came a long sighing. And the sighing changed to a rumble and grumble, and there was a sense of tossing as if Mother Earth was shaking herself. "Pray, Ivanovitch," said the old man and he thrust him down on his knees.

So, for the first time in his life he had prayed. He did not know what this praying was supposed to be like, so all he said was: "Good Jesus, good old Jesus."

He said it over a great many times and after that he put his hands in his friend's and together they felt their way down to the other end of the pit where his mother had been working. All they found was a mountain of fresh earth and underneath her boots sticking out. He had tried to get those boots. He had tugged and tugged but the mine held them fast.

He had a playmate, a little boy like himself. One day they were playing at being miners, each with a pick of his own. Some way a stone became dislodged in the vault over them. It came crashing down, straight on top of the playmate, and that was the end of him. When Ivan was half grown he lost his old friend, too. He tripped on one of the ladders and came tumbling down the shaft. They buried him above ground in the churchyard. He was the only one of all Ivan knew who had been buried above ground.

Ivan grew up and became a miner. His eyes were all now for his pick and the bright masses of ore he struck. He saw Jesus no longer and forgot how His garments sounded rustling through the long galleries. Long ago they had left the old mine, deserted it. The new mine held no memories.

Down went the bucket—down went Ivan. All around him now sounded rushing water. "There is too much water," he said to himself. "If Jesus comes into the new mine He will see it is not safe, that shaft. If He pays no attention to it, it will go quickly one day."

The bucket scraped on the bottom. The old miner got out and shouldered his pickax. He tottered forward, mumbling: "Earth—water—darkness—they are all in God's hands."

He passed other miners who spoke to him kindly but with humor: "See who comes here!". . . "Good day, Father.", . . "Here's better walking." He answered them all alike—with a doffing of his old cap. He never spoke.

The gallery where he worked was high. He felt at home here. Sometimes when a terrible feeling of loneliness came over him he would sleep here all night. The comfortable security of the dark—that was the way he felt about it. The sun frightened him: it was too big and blazing. The stars he liked: they were small and friendly. He liked flowers. Sometimes he brought down clumps of sod with daisies growing in them. The water kept them alive for days; they gleamed like stars in the flicker of his lamp.

He began to work. Then he rested—he was tired. He looked out for rock that was not so hard to break. When he had a pile he broke the metal out and put it on the wheelbarrow, to wheel into the main gallery. This was hard work. He stumbled and fell many times. It was exhaustion that felled him. When he passed his fellow-workers, one stopped him. "Here, wait a minute, I'll help you."

But another laughed. "What, do you think now that anyone is allowed to help old Father Ivan? He is the proud, ancient one."

Ivan brushed away angrily the one who had come to help. He lifted his shoulders, he straightened his tottering legs, he pushed on with his barrow.

The others watched him go, wagging their heads with approval. "He is as proud as Croesus," laughed one. "He is the ancient child," said another and tapped his forehead meaningly.

And then someone cried out: "God! What was that!"

A few paces ahead Ivan dropped his barrow and stood huddled over it. No one stirred. It began with a sound of deep breathing, not human but the earth's. It was as if the mountain over them was taking great gusts of air into its lungs. Far off at first, then closer and closer. A rush of wind came upon them and blew out all their lights; water started gushing down on them from everywhere. Miners came running from other galleries like sheep in a pen. Only Ivan stood quite still.

The overseer came hurrying up—he had a lighted torch. They stumbled after him toward the shaft. There they came upon nothing but a mountain of fresh damp earth, and half of the bucket that had lowered Ivan into the mine. Under the earth one could see a face with eyelids set, and far from that a hand still clutching a slice of bread with salt on it. At the bottom of the pile the earth was changing fast to mud. At that rate, Ivan said to himself, it wouldn't take long to flood the mine.

"We are lost!" shouted one miner.

"Caught like rats in a trap!" screamed another.

Panic took them. They dug their nails into the rock that penned them in. They trod on each other; they clawed each other's faces. They cursed like madmen.

"Stop!" The overseer kept shouting at them. "It will not save your skins to kill your neighbors. Come! On to the long gallery—there may be a way out!"

The overseer led. They followed, quieted a little. But in the long gallery it was no better. Air was growing thin;

water rushed at their heels. "Half an hour and we'll all be choking," groaned one. "If we knew the way into the old mine," said another. And another answered, crying out with hope: "Always as a boy I was told there was a way from the new into the old mine."

Hope was killed the next moment. "What of it? No one knows the way. Better die here where we know where we are than go wandering, lost into strange parts."

Behind them came another sound of shifting earth, soft, caressing. Then a crash: earth, rocks, driving water. Then a tumbling at their very backs. "We can't go back.". . . "We're shut off.". . . "God have mercy on our souls!"

A worse panic took them. They dug like beasts at the mass that shut them in until their nails hung torn and bleeding. They beat at one another with fists as hard as rock. They would have gone quite mad if something had not happened. Ivan took the torch from the overseer and spoke. It was the first time in ten years he had spoken, and the men in their amazement forgot their terror and stopped to listen.

"Hush," he was saying, "keep quiet, you men." His voice was strong, his eyes blazed. "How will we hear the rustle of His garments if you make such noise?"

"Look at him—he has gone mad," whispered one. But they kept listening to him just the same.

He was cocking his ear now, his eyes were searching the dark, narrow passage ahead. He kept sucking his lips in and out in a hushing sound. At last a look of foolish delight swept his face. "Ah, what did I tell you? Look! There

He goes, the light about His head, just as I remember seeing it as a child. It is seventy years since I have seen Him."

He swung the torch above his head, beckoning. Then he
stepped his way into the passage, crying: "I come, Lord, I
come!"

"Stop!" cried the overseer. "What in the name of saints
and devils do you see?"

Ivan turned. "See? What you yourself see. Come. It is
Jesus. He will lead us safely out." He turned away and
started along the passage again, repeating his cry: "I come,
Lord, I come!"

Holding their breath, not daring to speak, they followed,
to a man. At the end of the passage they came upon a blank
wall. Noway dismayed, Ivan pointed to the loose earth at
the bottom and bade the men dig. "See"—he pointed—
"His shining footsteps. He marches through the darkness
like the sun."

Amazed, doubting, the men plied their picks. The rock
crumbled. In no time there was an aperture. Gusts of fresh
air rushed through. The men crowded about the diggers,
pulling bits of rock away with their bare hands. Ivan
slipped through the opening; the others followed. He led
them along winding galleries; he led them through fissures
and around yawning chasms where they could hear water
rushing forty feet below; along narrow ledges with sheer
walls on one side and horrible precipices on the other,
where they had to crawl on hands and knees; and always
Ivan leading with his cry: "I come, Lord, I come!"

He was sobbing with eagerness now, like a child. In and

out, through this gallery and that, he wound. The floor of rock under them now was dry. Water no longer dripped from roof and walls. Suddenly he stopped, stock-still, and looked above his head. The men crowded and looked. They saw a small gray eye. They had reached the shaft of the deserted mine.

A hoarse shout went up, but it died as quickly as it had been born.

"The ladders are rotten as dead fish."

"A man might as well try to climb to heaven on cobwebs."

"What good is it to us to see daylight if we cannot reach it!"

"Let one of us try the ladders," said the overseer. "If one can get to the top, he can fetch ropes for the rest."

They turned, one to another, appraising, comparing. Who was the lightest, the most agile? Who had courage to try? No one noticed Ivan. He was following the rise of the ladders, as if watching for a signal. Suddenly he placed his old tottering legs on the first rung. He was thirty feet up the shaft before the others saw him.

"Merciful God."

"He will fall in a second and come down like a bag of stones."

"Look you," said the overseer, "Ivan is climbing on faith. While his faith lasts, the ladders may hold."

They climbed after him. Quickly, breathlessly; so close they went it was as if each man mounted on the next man's shoulders. Up and up—they could hear Ivan's panting breath. At last they were above ground; strong Mother Earth was under their feet. Ivan scanned the blazing blue sky over him for an instant. He looked frightened, bewildered. Then he smiled suddenly, his face alight with the radiance of his Lord whom he had followed. Down he went like a tottering old tree. Only the overseer caught his last cry: "I come, Lord, I come!"

The Bird Who Spoke Three Times

This is a Spanish tale within a tale. It is not an easy one to tell, bringing in as it does a confusion of names and incidents. It calls for a quick, staccato timing when the bird is talking, for a changing of voice quality and a careful marking of pauses. It is a rollicking tale to tell, full of humor, life. The Spanish storyteller gives it many gestures, laughs, nods his head, and wags a fore-finger as the action proceeds. He is always as surprised as his listeners when the bird begins to talk. He has such a good time telling it that it adds much to the flavor.

This is a very typical story of old Spain—Spain in the fourteenth and fifteenth centuries, when the Moors swarmed over it. The woman with the sad face, bearing a child, who helps Mariana, is the Spanish way of bringing the Virgin into a folk-tale. The good, the kind, she always helps; the sly, the false, the cruel, she passes by or sends misfortune to overtake them. Often I have seen a storyteller cross himself when he speaks of "the woman with a sad face, carrying a small child."

The Bird Who Spoke Three Times

LONG ago and far away there lived a soldier. He was handsome, brave, and not afraid to fight for his king and his country. One day he was at home; the next he was ordered off to defend Spain against the Moors.

Before leaving he went to the market and bought a bird. I cannot tell you what kind it was. He brought it home in a cage, gave it to his wife Rosita, and said: "You are too young and too lovely to be left alone without a companion. Here is one for you. Promise me you will not leave the house until I return. There are Moors and brigands in the streets everywhere."

Rosita promised. Away went the soldier, content; march, march, one foot forward and the other following.

Every day the old woman who served Rosita went into the streets and bought what was needed. Rosita stayed at home, with her fan and her rockingchair and her bird. Through the heat of the mornings she sat in the shaded patio; through the cool of the afternoons she sat on her balcony. One day a Moor passed below. He was handsome, wicked. He fell in love at once with her and swore to himself that he would steal her and carry her off to Africa with him.

He watched—watched. He saw the old woman going out every day. He painted his face lighter; he dressed himself like a grandee of Spain. He stopped the old woman one day and said: "I am Don Eulalio, a rich oil merchant. I admire your mistress. Arrange a meeting with her and here is a purse of gold. It is yours for a few little minutes with your mistress."

The purse of gold looked enormous, magnificent, to the old woman. She began to think of ways of getting Rosita out of the house. One day she said to her: "Doña Rosita, my daughter's youngest child will be christened tonight. We beg you to stand godmother to the baby."

But Rosita would not listen. Had she not promised her husband never to leave the house? Did not danger lurk in the streets? She would remain at home.

But the old woman was very clever. She knew how to make words have a coaxing sound; she knew how to make a promise seem smaller than nothing. Was it not a kind act for a rich woman to stand godmother to a poor baby? And was not her husband, the soldier, glad for her to do kindly acts? In the end Rosita consented.

That night the old woman dressed Rosita in a lovely dress of yellow satin, with many ruffles. In her hair she put the high comb and covered it with the finest mantilla. All was ready. She turned the great key in the door to let out her mistress and herself. The door creaked on its hinges for the first time; and for the first time the bird spoke:

"Doña Rosita—Doña Rosita! Come back. I am going to tell you a story."

Rosita was charmed. She would not go with the old woman. She returned to the patio, drew her rockingchair close to the cage, and tne bird began:

"Know then, Señora, that once there lived a fisherman with one daughter—good, clever, and lovely to look upon. One day the fisherman caught in his nets a cuidado. (That is a kind of fish, but what kind I cannot tell you.) He brought the cuidado home to his daughter; and Mariana put it in a little dish filled with water.

"So happy was the cuidado that it began to sing. All day it sang a little song like this:

> Over valley, over hill,
> bom—bom!
> Over river, over rill,
> bom—bom!
> Love travels far—
> Love travels far.

"It made Mariana so happy that she put the cuidado outside the door of the hut, so that all who passed by might hear. A red bull came charging down the street. It knocked over the dish, broke it. It caught up the cuidado in its mouth and vanished.

"All day Mariana cried. The next day, early, she put on her shawl and started forth to find the cuidado. She traveled over valley and hill; she crossed over river and rill. After many days she reached the country around about the king's palace."

Here the bird came to a sharp stop. "Go on, go on!" begged Rosita.

"You want to know what is now going to happen?" asked the bird.

"Yes, oh, yes!"

"Then it is time to stop." The bird closed its beak and would not utter another word.

Many days went by. Many times the Moor, dressed as a grandee of Spain, met the old woman on the street and shook the purse of gold in her face. "For just a few little moments," he would say.

So again she said to her mistress: "Doña Rosita, my daughter could not bear to have the christening without you for godmother. She has set the time again—it will be tonight." Again she made words that had a coaxing sound; and at last Rosita consented.

This time Rosita was dressed in a lovely dress of blue satin, with many ruffles. Into her hair the old woman put the high comb, and covered it with the finest mantilla. All was again ready. She turned the great key in the lock. The door creaked on its hinges; and again the bird called:

"Doña Rosita, Doña Rosita! Come back. I am going to tell you the rest of the story."

Rosita was charmed. She would not go with the old woman. She returned to the patio, drew her rockingchair close to the cage, and the bird began:

"As you remember, the red bull ran off with the cuidado and Mariana followed as far as the king's court. There she heard everybody talking about the infante. He had gone quite mad. Nobody knew why; and nobody could bring him back to his right mind.

"Mariana sat down under a cork tree and kept thinking: Maybe I could—maybe I could. A woman with a sad face, carrying a small child, stopped beside her. She said. 'Mariana, maybe you could. Listen. Do as I tell you. Dress yourself like a gypsy. Go to the palace. Say that you have herbs and a charm to cure madness. When they take you into the infante's room ask for a great kettleful of oil to be put over the fire on the hearth. In that kettle you must throw three sprigs of yerbabuena, and whatever you find hidden under the infante's pillow. Now go!'

"Mariana went to the palace and asked for the king. She told him what she could do. 'Do it,' said the king, 'and I will grant any wish. But if the infante clings to his madness you lose you life.'

"The fire was built on the hearth; the kettle, full of oil, was hung. It grew hot—hot. Into it Mariana threw the three sprigs of yerbabuena. Then she went to find what lay hidden under the infante's pillow."

Here the bird came to a sharp stop. "Go on, go on!" begged Rosita.

"You want to know what she found under the pillow, yes?"

"Yes, oh, yes!"

"Then it is time to stop," and the bird closed its beak and would not utter another word.

Many more days went by; weeks, months. Again the old woman came to Rosita. "If my daughter's baby is not soon

christened we will be getting her ready for her wedding.
Do not refuse this time. Remember the old saying: A good
act lays a paving-stone on the road to heaven."

At last Rosita consented. This time she was dressed in
white, with ruffles that came to her waist, a red carnation
in her hair, the high comb, and the finest mantilla. All was
ready. The old woman was thinking as she turned the great
key in the lock: This time I shall have that purse of gold.

But the door creaked again on its hinges; and the bird
called:

"Doña Rosita—Doña Rosita! Come back. I am going to
finish the story for you."

Rosita was charmed. She would not go with the old
woman. She returned to the patio, drew her rockingchair
close to the cage, and the bird began:

"Know then that what Mariana found under the infante's pillow was the skin of the cuidado, shriveled, dead.
The infante was raving like a *tonto*. Into the kettle Mariana threw the skin, dropping on her knees to cry hard—
hard. Never again would she hear her own little fish sing
so prettily about love.

"Smoke rose from the kettle. It took form. It became
a great Moor—black—terrible. What shall I do now?
thought Mariana. The Moor will kill me, if the king does
not. And he may kill the infante afterward.

"She heard the voice of the sad-faced woman saying:
'Push him back into the kettle. Push him back three times
and you will be safe.'

"So Mariana put her hands on the hot smoking shoulders of the Moor and pushed him back into the boiling oil. He rose again, blacker, more terrible. She pushed again. He rose a third time. His eyes were like burning coal, his face was like a fiend's. Mariana was frightened—frightened. But she shut her eyes and pushed with all her might.

"What was that she heard, singing back of her? The song of the cuidado:

> Over valley, over hill,
>   bom—bom!
> Over river, over rill,
>   bom—bom!
> Love travels far—
> Love travels far.

"She looked over her shoulder. The infante was raving no more. He was looking at her with light, shining eyes He was singing the cuidado's song. The Moor had enchanted him into a fish; as a red bull he had come to devour him. The Moor had perished in the boiling oil. So may all wicked, black magicians perish! Mariana married the infante."

The bird fluttered its wings and turned around on its perch.

"Is that all?" asked Rosita.

The bird did not answer. But there came a great knocking at the door. The key was turned. The door was flung wide. There stood the soldier, home from the war. He was safe. Rosita was safe. The Moor went back to his city of Tetuán. The old woman never got her purse of gold. The baby was never christened, because there had been no baby. And the bird never spoke again. Never!

The Legend of Saint Elizabeth

This is typical of medieval stories. It has an ornateness and a certain grandiloquent consciousness of words that were characteristic of all storytellers of that time, whether minnesinger, troubadour, monk, or tirewoman. It has as well a quaint charm that is combined of romance and religious fervor, equally characteristic. I have drawn on Baring-Gould, records of minnesingers, and the cantata by Franz Liszt for the story. The prayer of Elizabeth at the end is a literal translation from the Latin, supposed to have been taken down by one of the sisterhood as she was dying. Against the simplicity and directness of the other stories included in this book "The Legend of Saint Elizabeth" stands out in marked and perhaps needed contrast.

The Legend of Saint Elizabeth

HERE is a tale that is old and very beautiful. It has been sung and told throughout Europe for a thousand years and more, at the courts of Provence, Navarre, Spain, and in every little duchy and principality. Mothers of Hesse and Thuringia have been telling it to their children since the time of the Crusades; and the poor in Hungary still say: "For each prayer offered to Elizabeth there is one less suffering soul on earth."

Like a troubadour of olden time let me tell the story; and you shall listen as if you were sitting in kings' houses.

Here followeth the legend of our good Saint Elizabeth. . . . Born in the year of Our Lord 1207, received into blessed martyrdom in the year 1231. May the Lord have a like mercy on our souls.

Hermann, landgrave of Thuringia and Hesse, sat at meat in his castle at Wartburg. About him were his knights, squires, men-at-arms, the ladies of the court, and certain minnesingers who had come to try for that yearly prize of gold given by the landgrave. Among these was one Klingsor of Hungary, greatly renowned for his songs and his prophecies. Coming before Hermann he spoke in this wise: "Knowest thou, my lord, that unto Gertrude, consort of Andrew of Hungary, there will be born this night a daughter to be named Elizabeth and destined to be the bride of thy eldest son, Ludwig?"

Straightway the landgrave dispatched unto the court of Hungary a trusty knight, one Walter of Vargila, to make certain of the truth of the prophecy, and to ask the hand of the infant Elizabeth for his son. Further did he beseech the lord of Hungary, should he deem it prudent, to entrust to the messenger no lesser thing than the child herself, that both infants might be reared together at Wartburg and so grow strong in love, honor, and courtesy, each for the other.

Thus it did come to pass that the young Elizabeth was brought to Wartburg in a silver cradle. Feasting was held; vassals, serfs, even children came to pay homage to the little princess. The young Ludwig was placed beside her in the cradle as sign and symbol of their betrothal. They were gently rocked to sleep while garlands were strewn and children sang them sweet lullabies:

> Lightly we'll dance to thee,
> Sweet songs we'll sing to thee,
> Fair little bridal pair,
> Much joy we'll bring to thee.

But out of all the court who attended on that day there was one who paid no homage—Sophie, landgravine and mother of Ludwig. She looked down upon the sleeping infant in the cradle and felt a burning jealousy which turned straightway to hatred. And the ladies of the court, perceiving this, murmured among themselves: "Our landgravine loveth not the child. It would be well that we treat her with coldness and displeasure lest we bring Sophie's anger upon our own heads."

Thus the young Elizabeth grew into maidenhood with little showing of kindness from the ladies of the court. Only the landgrave and young Ludwig showed tenderness and adoration. The harsh ways of Sophie and her women for the princess carried much wounding of heart; which was the more strange because of her loveliness. She was a child of grace, perfect in body, kindly in speech, modest in all ways, and full of a godly love toward all creatures.

Once, at the Feast of the Assumption, she threw herself weeping before the altar of Our Blessed Lord, and laid her crown of gold and precious gems at His feet. Full of rage at this display of sorrow, Sophie rebuked her in the church, saying: "Stand up, thou silly child. Art mad to prostrate thyself like any common peasant and throw away thy coronet? Stand up, I say."

Whereupon Elizabeth answered: "From whom shall I find comfort if not from my dear Lord? And how may I pass Him by, proudly, with my crown of gold, when He wears so humbly His crown of thorns!"

Finding no refuge in the castle for her sore heart, Elizabeth went abroad among the serfs and peasants, ministering to all who were afflicted in body or soul. Early she learned the art of nursing, often sitting the day through beside some pallet praying. And when the day ended, often it would come to pass that fever and pain would depart, and the sick one would be made whole.

Word of this was spread throughout the land, until there came to the castle gates many who were maimed, diseased, or blind. In the courtyard they would be packed like dogs, waiting to touch the hem of her little garment as she passed, or to beg her to lay hands upon them. And Sophie, angered the more at this, would look down from the castle turret and say scoffingly to her women: "Look at yonder fools— carrion! And she among them!"

Ten years passed away. The landgrave died; and now was Ludwig left alone to care for Elizabeth, alone to stand between her and Sophie's hatred. But Ludwig loved Elizabeth with a love that knew neither faltering nor blindness. It stood as shield and bulwark against the treacheries of the landgravine. So wondrous was that love that when within the compass of it Elizabeth forgot all cruelties. Then did her heart grow light as any singing bird's.

But ever Sophie waited for a time to break that love; ever jealousy cried that she must part these two.

A spring came, covering the land with fair lilies, filling the valleys with a gentle fragrance and the sound of the cuckoo calling to his mate. Ludwig departed to the far end of his lands on business that was urgent and troublesome and that held him from Elizabeth for a goodly time. Then did Sophie have rumors spread abroad concerning Ludwig—black, ugly tales of his loving a peasant wench. When the tales reached Elizabeth's ears she did straightway dispatch Walter of Vargila—the same knight that did bring her to Wartburg in her silver cradle—to beg Ludwig to send her some token of his love. And when Ludwig received the messenger and heard the tales at court he was filled with a great anger. Putting in the hands of the knight a mirror, wondrously wrought with a crucifix, he bade Walter of Vargila give it to Elizabeth with these words: "I would as soon betray my Savior as to suffer unfaithfulness toward my dear love."

When she received the token, Elizabeth's heart bounded with joy; and she hurried abroad to her sick and poor, that she might praise God with acts of service.

Upon Ludwig's return he dispatched heralds throughout the land proclaiming his marriage to Elizabeth. The good bishop married them; and there were set aside three days of feasting and splendor for all. This came to pass in Elizabeth's fifteenth year.

There followed then endless deeds of compassion—far too many to recount. I might tell of how Elizabeth opened the great dungeons under the castle and made those cells of torture and imprisonment into a place of harborage for the sick and homeless, and of how, with the dungeons overflowed, she did open a hospital near to the city and gave it into the care of holy women.

I might tell further of how upon a certain day when there came to Wartburg envoys from emperors and kings to make alliance with Ludwig that Elizabeth was abroad among her sick. So great was her diligence for them that the hour for meat had drawn near before she remembered the need of her presence at the castle. Then, lest she put shame upon Ludwig by keeping his guests waiting, she entered the hall as she was, clothed in her gray gown of service. But as she crossed the threshold angels descended from heaven bearing fitting raiment for her; one, a coronet for her head, one a dress of golden tissue, and one a mantle. So that when Elizabeth took her seat beside her consort she appeared in the sight of all who beheld her as fair as the Lady of Heaven herself.

And greater than these is that tale of the leper that came, crawling to the castle, seeking help from Elizabeth. Ludwig was far distant; and the leper being far gone in his foul disease and all other places filled, Elizabeth carried him in her arms and laid him in Ludwig's own bed. When Sophie discovered this she was greatly enraged and dispatched a messenger for Ludwig; and upon his arrival at the castle at midnight, she conveyed him to his bedroom, saying as they went: "A pretty wife thou hast. So little doth she care for thee or thy love that she has placed in thy very bed a dying leper. This, that thou mayest take the scourge thyself."

But at the door they both stood confounded. For on the bed there lay none other than Christ the Savior. Seeing Ludwig and Sophie, He smiled right pityingly upon them and said: "Behold, the Son of Man had not where to lay His head. I pray you let me bide here until morning cometh."

And when morning came, Ludwig, kneeling in adoration, saw the Christ had gone and in His place lay the leper, cleansed and whole.

But of all wondrous miracles wrought by God's hand for Elizabeth the greatest came to pass when the land was stricken with famine. Crops failed, grain blighted, cattle sickened and died. The granaries of the castle dwindled until there was little wheat left. All about the land could be heard the rap-rap of the joiners' hammers, making coffins. Then did the landgravine come to Ludwig with terror, saying: "Thy wife gives and gives to the poor and soon we will have no bread. A fortnight ago the cooks baked a thousand loaves for thy knights and those in the castle; today they bake a scant fifty. Another fortnight and there will be no flour left. I beseech thee curb this madwoman of yours lest we all die."

Fearing more that Elizabeth might come to a grievous want, and fearful always that she might take upon herself some dread disease with all her nursing of the sick, Ludwig sternly bade her feed the poor no more, nor tend the sick.

"But, my lord, what will they do if they have not anyone to care for them?"

"Leave them in God's hands. And go thou not again until the famine be spent, the grain stand ripened in the fields, and pestilence no longer walk the earth."

But in the dark of the night Elizabeth heard the cries of hungry and the dying, nor could she sleep for the sound. There came a time when she could bear it no longer. Leaving her bed, she stole forth into the night, her arms laden with bread that she had pillaged from the larder. Hardly had she compassed the garden when Ludwig came upon her, unawares; and seeing her, his face hardened for the first time with anger.

"Why dost thou steal abroad like a thief, under cover of the night? What hidest thou under thy mantle?"

With an angry hand he flung aside her garment, and, lo, where there had been bread there were now roses—pale, ghostly roses, and out of their hearts dripped red, red blood like sacramental wine. The face of Elizabeth confounded him with its compassion and he knelt at the miracle, praying God for His merciful forgiveness. From that night famine departed from the land, the grain shot from the dry earth and ripened within a handful of days; and plenty dwelt again in their midst.

There is little more of the tale to be told. The land being at peace, Ludwig gathered his knights and marched forth to the Holy Wars. For a breath as they passed there was a great flying of colors, the neighing of gallant horses, the shining of splendid armor in the sun, the marking of brave singing to the tramp of surging feet. Amid the shouting and singing Ludwig bent at the last to take his sorrowful farewell of Elizabeth. A twelvemonth later, runners from the south brought her word of his death.

Then did Sophie, the landgravine, seize the tenury of Thuringia and Hesse. Elizabeth and her young children she drove forth into the night, while a terrible storm raged. The castle gates were barred fast against them; the serfs and vassals were forbidden to give them harborage under pain of death. Weak with much wandering, Elizabeth took sanctuary at last in that same hospital she had had built, near the city gates. Here she ended her life in days of service and prayer.

At the moment of her dying, there gathered many holy ones in the cloisters below, to chant the requiem for the repose of her soul. Above their chanting Elizabeth prayed her last prayer on earth in this wise:

"Now cometh the hour when Mother Maid Mary brought the Child Jesus into the world, and the star appeared in the east to guide the Wise Men to His cradle. He came to redeem the world—and He will redeem me. Now is the time when He arose from the dead and broke the prison doors of hell to release all imprisoned souls—and now will He release me."

The Princess and the Vagabone

So often it happens in Ireland that if you would hear a tale you must first tell one. So it was that I came by this north of Ireland version of *The Taming of the Shrew* in exchange for our best-known legend of the Catskills.

Before I had finished, the oldest seanachie was knocking the ashes from his pipe, ready to begin. "That's grand," he said. "I have a tale. . . . Do you know Willie Shakespeare?" I nodded. "Well, ye may not be knowin' this; he was afther writin' a play a few hundthred years ago which he took straight out of a Connaught tale. Like as not he had it from an Irish nurse or a rovin' tinker. He has it changed a bit, turned and patched and made up in a strange fashion, but 'tis the same tale for all of that." "Tell it," said I. "Aye, tell it," said the wife. "I wish ye had the Gaelic so I could tell it right; I'm never so good at giving a tale in English." Thus did the oldest seanachie begin "The Princess and the Vagabone."

I wish I might make you see the cabin as it was that night: overflowing with neighbors, the men smoking, the women knitting, the boys and girls stretched tired-limbed beside the hearth; the children peering out, sleepy-eyed, from the outshot bed; the old gray piper in the chimney corner, his pipes laid lovingly across his knees; the kettle hung fresh over the turf, the empty griddle near by, ready for a late baking of currant bread; the singing kettle and the clicking needles making a low running accompaniment for the story.

The Princess and the Vagabone

ONCE, in the golden time, when an Irish king sat in every province and plenty covered the land, there lived in Connaught a grand old king with one daughter. She was as tall and slender as the reeds that grow by Lough Erne, and her face was the fairest in seven counties. This was more the pity, for the temper she had did not match it at all, at all; it was the blackest and ugliest that ever fell to the birthlot of a princess. She was proud, she was haughty; her tongue had the length and the sharpness of the thorns on a *sidheog* bush; and from the day she was born till long after she was a woman grown she was never heard to say a kind word or known to do a kind deed to a living creature.

As each year passed, the King would think to himself: "'Tis the New Year will see her better." But it was worse instead of better she grew, until one day the King found himself at the end of his patience, and he groaned aloud as he sat alone, drinking his poteen.

"Faith, another man shall have her for the next eighteen years, for, by my soul, I've had my fill of her!"

So it came about, as I am telling ye, that the King sent word to the nobles of the neighboring provinces that whosoever would win the consent of his daughter in marriage should have half of his kingdom and the whole of his blessing. On the day that she was eighteen they came: a wonderful procession of earls, dukes, princes, and kings, riding up to the castle gate, a-courting. The air was filled with the ring of the silver trappings on their horses, and the courtyard was gay with the colors of their bratas and the long cloaks they wore, riding. The King made each welcome according to his rank; and then he sent a serving-man to his daughter, bidding her come and choose her suitor, the time being ripe for her to marry. It was a courteous message that the King sent, but the Princess heard little of it. She flew into the hall on the heels of the serving-man, like a fowl-hawk after a bantam cock. Her eyes burned with the anger that was hot in her heart, while she stamped her foot in the King's face until the rafters rang with the noise of it.

"So, ye will be giving me away for the asking—to any one of these blithering fools who has a rag to his back or a castle to his name?"

The King grew crimson at her words. He was ashamed that they should all hear how sharp was her tongue; moreover, he was fearsome lest they should take to their heels and leave him with a shrew on his hands for another eighteen years. He was hard at work piecing together a speech when the Princess strode past him on to the first suitor in the line.

"At any rate, I'll not be choosing ye, ye long-legged corn-crake," and she gave him a sound kick as she went on to the next. He was a large man with a shaggy beard; and, see-

ing how the first suitor had fared, he tried a wee bit of a
smile on her while his hand went out coaxingly. She saw,
and the anger in her grew threefold. She sprang at him, digging the two of her hands deep in his beard, and then she
wagged his foolish head back and forth, screaming: "Take
that, and that, and that, ye old whiskered rascal!"

It was a miracle that any beard was left on his face the
way that she pulled it. But she let him go free at last, and
turned to a thin, sharp-faced prince with a monstrous long
nose. The nose took her fancy, and she gave it a tweak, telling the prince to take himself home before he did any dam-
age with it. The next one she called "pudding-face" and
slapped his fat cheeks until they were purple, and the poor
lad groaned with the sting of it.

"Go back to your trough, for I'll not marry a grunter, i'
faith," said she.

She moved swiftly down the line in less time than it takes
for the telling. It came to the mind of many of the suitors
that they would be doing a wise thing if they betook themselves off before their turn came; as many of them as were
not fastened to the floor with fear started away. There happened to be a fat, crooked-legged prince from Leinster just
making for the door when the Princess looked around. In a
trice she reached out for the tongs that stood on the hearth
near by, and she laid it across his shoulders, sending him
spinning into the yard.

"Take that, ye old gander, and good riddance to ye!" she
cried after him.

It was then that she saw looking at her a great towering

giant of a man; and his eyes burned through hers, deep down into her soul. So great was he that he could have picked her up with a single hand and thrown her after the gander: and she knew it and yet she felt no fear. He was as handsome as Nuada of the Silver Hand; and not a mortal fault could she have found with him, not if she had tried for a hundred years. The two of them stood facing each other, glaring, as if each would spring at the other's throat the next moment; but all the while the Princess was thinking, and thinking how wonderful he was, from the top of his curling black hair, down the seven feet of him, to the golden clasps on his shoes.

What the man was thinking I cannot be telling. Like a breath of wind on smoldering turf, her liking for him set her anger fierce-burning again. She gave him a sound cuff on the ear, then turned, and with a sob in her throat she went flying from the room, the serving-men scattering before her as if she had been a hundred million robbers on a raid.

And the King? Faith, he was dumb with rage. But when he saw the blow that his daughter had given to the finest gentleman in all of Ireland, he went after her as if he had been two hundred million constables on the trail of robbers.

"Ye are a disgrace and a shame to me," said he, catching up with her and holding firmly to her two hands; "and, what's more, ye are a disgrace and a blemish to my castle and my kingdom; I'll not keep ye in it a day longer. The first traveling vagabone who comes begging at the door shall have ye for his wife."

"Will he?" and the Princess tossed her head in the King's face and went to her chamber.

The next morning a poor singing *sthronshuch* came to the castle to sell a song for a penny or a morsel of bread. The song was sweet that he sang, and the Princess listened as Oona, the tirewoman, was winding strands of her long black hair with golden thread.

> "The gay young wren sang over the moor.
>   'I'll build me a nest,' sang he.
> ' 'Twill have a thatch and a wee latched door,
>   For the wind blows cold from the sea.
> And I'll let no one but my true love in,
>   For she is the mate for me.'
>   Sang the gay young wren.

> The wee brown wren by the hedgerow cried,
>   'I'll wait for him here,' cried she.
> 'For the way is far and the world is wide,
>   And he might miss the way to me.
> Long is the time when the heart is shut,
>   But I'll open to none save he,'
>   Sang the wee brown wren."

A strange throb came to the heart of the Princess when the song was done. She pulled her hair free from the hands of the tirewoman.

"Get silver," she said; "I would throw it to him." And when she saw the wonderment grow in Oona's face, she added: "The song pleased me. Can I not pay for what I like without having ye look at me as if ye feared my wits had flown? Go, get the silver!"

the sky. The Princess sat there until hunger drove her to her feet. She rose wearily and stumbled to the road. It might have been the sound of wheels that had started her, I cannot be telling; but as she reached the road a great coach drawn by six black horses came galloping up. The Princess made a sign for it to stop; though she was in rags, yet she was still so beautiful that the coachman drew in the horses and asked her what she was wanting.

"I am near to starving," and as she spoke the tears started to her eyes, while a new soft note crept into her voice. "Do ye think your master could spare me a bit of food—or a shilling?" and the hand that had been used to strike went out for the first time to beg.

It was a prince who rode inside the coach that day, and he heard her. Reaching out a fine, big hamper through the window, he told her she was hearty welcome to whatever she found in it, along with his blessing. But as she put up her arms for it, just, she looked—and saw that the prince was none other than the fat suitor whose face she had slapped on the day before. Then anger came back to her again, for the shame of begging from him. She emptied the hamper—chicken pasty, jam, currant bread, and all—on top of his head, peering through the window, and threw the empty basket at the coachman. Away drove the coach; away ran the Princess, and threw herself, sobbing, on the ground, near the vagabone.

" 'Twas a good dinner that ye lost," said the vagabone; and that was all.

That night they reached a wee scrap of a cabin on the

side of a hill. The vagabone climbed the steps and opened the door. "Here we are at home, my dear," said he.

"What kind of a home do ye call this?" and the Princess stamped her foot. "Faith, I'll not live in it."

"Then ye can live outside; it's all the same to me." The vagabone went in and closed the door after him; and in a moment he was whistling merrily the song of the wee brown wren.

The Princess sat down on the ground and nursed her poor tired knees. She had walked many a mile that day, with a heavy heart and an empty stomach—two of the worst traveling companions ye can find. The night came down, black as a raven's wing; the dew fell, heavy as rain, wetting the rags and chilling the Princess to the marrow. The wind blew fresh from the sea, and the wolves began their howling in the woods near by; and at last, what with the cold and the fear and the loneliness of it, she could bear it no longer, and she crept softly up to the cabin and went in.

"There's the creepy-stool by the fire, waiting for ye," said the vagabone; and that was all. But late in the night he lifted her from the chimney corner where she had dropped asleep and laid her gently on the bed, which was freshly made and clean. And he sat by the hearth till dawn, keeping the turf piled high on the fire, so that cold would not waken her. Once he left the hearth; coming to the bedside, he stood a moment to watch her while she slept, and he stooped and kissed the wee pink palm of her hand that lay there like a half-closed lough lily.

Next morning the first thing the Princess asked was where

was the breakfast, and where were the servants to wait on her, and where were some decent clothes.

"Your servants are your own two hands, and they will serve ye well when ye teach them how," was the answer she got.

"I'll have neither breakfast nor clothes if I have to be getting them myself. And shame on ye for treating a wife so," and the Princess caught up a piggin and threw it at the vagabone.

He jumped clear of it, and it struck the wall behind him. "Have your own way, my dear," and he left her, to go out on the bogs and cut turf.

That night the Princess hung the kettle and made stirabout and griddle bread for the two of them.

" 'Tis the best I have tasted since I was a lad and my mother made the baking," said the vagabone, and that was all. But often and often his lips touched the braids of her hair as she passed him in the dark; and again he sat through the night, keeping the fire and mending her wee leather brogues, that they might be whole against the morrow.

Next day he brought some sally twigs and showed her how to weave them into creels to sell on coming market-day. But the twigs cut her fingers until they bled, and the Princess cried, making the vagabone white with rage. Never had she seen such a rage in another creature. He threw the sally twigs about the cabin, making them whirl and eddy like leaves before an autumn wind; he stamped upon the half-made creel, crushing it to pulp under his feet; and catching up the table, he tore it to splinters, throwing the fragments into the fire, where they blazed.

"By Saint Patrick, 'tis a bad bargain that ye are! I will take ye this day to the castle in the next county, where I hear they are needing a scullery-maid; and there I'll apprentice ye to the King's cook."

"I will not go," said the Princess; but even as she spoke fear showed in her eyes and her knees began shaking in under her.

"Aye, but ye will, my dear," and the vagabone took up the tongs quietly from the hearth.

For a month the Princess worked in the castle of the King, and all that time she never saw the vagabone. Often and often she said to herself, fiercely, that she was well rid of him; but often, as she sat alone after her work in the cool of the night, she would wish for the song of the wee brown wren, while a new loneliness crept deeper and deeper into her heart.

She worked hard about the kitchen, and as she scrubbed the pots and turned the spit and cleaned the floor with fresh white sand she listened to the wonderful tales the other servants had to tell of the King. They had it that he was the handsomest, aye, and the strongest, king in all of Ireland; and every man and child and little creature in his kingdom worshiped him. And after the tales were told the Princess would say to herself: "If I had not been so proud and free with my tongue, I might have married such a king, and ruled his kingdom with him, learning kindness."

Now it happened one day that the Princess was told to be unusually spry and careful about her work; and there was a monstrous deal of it to be done: cakes to be iced and puddings to be boiled, fat ducks to be roasted, and a whole sucking pig put on the spit to turn.

"What's the meaning of all this?" asked the Princess.

"Ochone, ye poor feeble-minded girl!" and the cook looked at her pityingly. "Haven't ye heard the King is to be married this day to the fairest princess in seven counties?"

"Once that was I," thought the Princess, and she sighed.

"What makes ye sigh?" asked the cook.

"I was wishing, just, that I could be having a peep at her and the King."

"Faith, that's possible. Do your work well, and maybe I can put ye where ye can see without being seen."

So it came about, as I am telling ye, at the end of the day, when the feast was ready and the guests come, that the Princess was hidden behind the broidered curtains in the great hall. There, where no one could see her, she watched the hundreds upon hundreds of fair ladies and fine noblemen in their silken dresses and shining coats, all silver and gold, march back and forth across the hall, laughing and talking and making merry among themselves. Then the pipers began to play, and everybody was still. From the farthest end of the hall came two and twenty lads in white and gold; and these were followed by two and twenty pipers in green and gold and two and twenty bowmen in saffron and gold, and, last of all, the King.

A scream, a wee wisp of a cry, broke from the Princess, and she would have fallen had she not caught one of the curtains. For the King was as tall and strong and beautiful as Nuada of the Silver Hand; and from the top of his curling black hair down the seven feet of him to the golden clasps of his shoes he was every whit as handsome as he had been that day when she had cuffed him in her father's castle.

The King heard the cry and stopped the pipers. "I think," said he, "there's a scullery-maid behind the curtains. Some-one fetch her to me."

A hundred hands pulled the Princess out; a hundred more pushed her across the hall to the feet of the King, and held her there, fearing lest she escape. "What were ye do-ing there?" the King asked.

"Looking at ye, and wishing I had the undoing of things I have done," and the Princess hung her head and sobbed piteously.

"Nay, sweetheart, things are best as they are," and there came a look into the King's eyes that blinded those watch-ing, so that they turned away and left the two alone.

"Heart of mine," he went on, softly, "are ye not know-ing me?"

"Ye are putting more shame on me because of my evil tongue and the blow my hand gave ye that day."

"I' faith, it is not so. Look at me."

Slowly the eyes of the Princess looked into the eyes of the King. For a moment she could not be reading them; she was as a child who pores over a strange tale after the light fades and it has grown too dark to see. But bit by bit the meaning of it came to her, and her heart grew glad with the wonder of it. Out went her arms to him with the cry of loneliness that had been hers so long.

"I never dreamed that it was ye, never once."

"Can ye ever love and forgive?" asked the King.

"Hush ye!" and the Princess laid her finger on his lips.

The tirewomen were called and she was led away. Her rags were changed for a dress that was spun from gold and woven with pearls, and her beauty shone about her like a great light. They were married again that night, for none of the guests were knowing of that first wedding long ago.

Late o' that night a singing *sthronshuch* came under the Princess's window, and very softly the words of his song came to her:

> "The gay young wren sang over the moor.
>   'I'll build me a nest,' sang he.
> ' 'Twill have a thatch and a wee latched door,
>   For the wind blows cold from the sea.
> And I'll let no one but my true love in,
>   For she is the mate for me,'
>   Sang the gay young wren.
>
> The wee brown wren by the hedgerow cried.
>   'I'll wait for him here,' cried she.
> 'For the way is far and the world is wide,
>   And he might miss the way to me.
> Long is the time when the heart is shut,
>   But I'll open to none save he,'
>   Sang the wee brown wren."

The grating opened slowly; the Princess leaned far out, her eyes like stars in the night, and when she spoke there was naught but gentleness and love in her voice.

"Here is the silver I would have thrown ye on a day long gone by. Shall I throw it now, or will ye come for it?"

And that was how a princess of Connaught was won by a king who was a vagabone.

A Reading List

One of the instincts most deeply embedded in the human race is the instinct to dig—to dig for water that the thirst may be quenched; to dig into the ground that something may be planted and grow; to dig for treasure, to dig for records; to dig and to find.

It is to the diggers among storytellers that this list is dedicated. Within it lies much treasure for those who have the patience and the enthusiasm to dig. And I promise this—that instinct grows with effort; and each one will discover more books for himself to add to the list.

For the Building of Folk Background

Anderson, R. B. *Norse Mythology.* Chicago, Scott, Foresman.
Arabian Nights Entertainment, ed. E. W. Lane. London, Routledge.
Baring-Gould, S. *Curious Myths of the Middle Ages.* London, Rivingtons.
———. *The Lives of the Saints.* London, Hodges.
Beckwith, Benjamin A. *Treasury of American Folklore.* New York, Crown.
Bulfinch, Thomas. *Age of Fable.* New York, Dutton.
Campbell, J. F. *Popular Tales of the West Highlands.* London, Gardner.

Childs, F. J. *English and Scottish Ballads*. Boston, Houghton.

Clough, Ben C., ed. *American Imagination at Work*. New York, Knopf.

Clouston, W. A. *Popular Tales and Fictions*. Edinburgh, Blackwood.

Crane, T. F. *Italian Popular Tales*. Boston, Houghton.

Curtin, Jeremiah. *Myths and Folklore of Ireland*. Boston, Little, Brown.

Cushing, F. H. *Zuni Folk Tales*. New York, Knopf.

Dasent, G. W. *Popular Tales from the Norse*. London, Blackie.

———. *Dialogues of Saint Gregory, Surnamed the Great*, trans. P. W., ed. E. G. Gardner. London, Warner.

Emerson, P. H. *Tales from Welsh Wales*. London, Nutt.

Fiske, John. *Myths and Myth-Makers*. Boston, Houghton.

Frazer, J. G. *Folk-Lore in the Old Testament*. New York, Macmillan.

———. *The Golden Bough*. New York, Macmillan.

Freeman, Margaret B. *The Story of the Three Kings*. New York, Metropolitan Museum of Art. Retelling of a 14th-century version.

Gregory, Lady. *Cuchulain of Muirthemne*. New York, Scribner.

———. *Gods and Fighting Men*. London, Murray.

Grimm, Jakob. *Teutonic Mythology*. London, Bell.

Grimm, J. L. K. and W. K. *Household Stories*. New York, Macmillan.

Grinnell, G. B. *Blackfoot Lodge Tales*. New York, Scribner.

———. *Pawnee Hero Stories and Folk Tales*. New York, Scribner.

Guerber, Helene A. *Legends of the Middle Ages*. New York, American Book.

Halliday, W. R. *Indo-European Folk-Tales and Greek Legends*. Cambridge, England, Cambridge University Press.

Hazlitt, W. Carewe. *Tales and Legends*. London, Sonnenschein.

Hyde, Douglas. *Legends of Saints and Sinners*. London, Unwin.

Jones, W. H. R., and Kropf, L. L. *The Folk-Tales of the Magyars.* London, Folk Lore Society Publications, v. 13.

Kennedy, Patrick. *Legendary Fictions of the Irish Celts.* London, Macmillan.

Lang, Andrew. *Custom and Myth.* London, Longmans.

Macculloch, J. A. *The Childhood of Fiction.* London, Murray.

Macdougall, James. *Folktales and Fairy Lore,* ed. G. Calder. Edinburgh, Grant.

Malory, Sir Thomas. *Le Mort d'Arthur.* New York, Dutton.

Parker of Ceylon, H. *Village Folk-Tales of Ceylon.* London, Luzac.

Parry, Jones, D., ed. *Welsh Legends and Fairy Lore.* London, Batsford.

———. *Popular Tales and Romances of the Northern Nations.* London, Simpkin.

Pulszky, Ferencz and Terez. *Tales and Traditions of Hungary.* London, Colburn.

Rhys, Ernest. *Fairy Gold.* New York, Dutton.

Skinner, C. M. *Myths and Legends of Our Own Country.* Philadelphia, Lippincott.

Somadeva Bhatta. *The Ocean of Story,* trans. C. H. Tawney. (Privately printed.) London, Sawyer.

Swynnerton, Rev. Charles. *Romantic Tales from the Punjab, with Indian Nights Entertainment.* London, Stock.

Tylor, Sir Edward Burnett. *Primitive Culture.* New York, Holt.

Werner, E. T. C. *Myths and Legends of China.* London, Harrap.

Yeats, W. B. *The Celtic Twilight.* London Bullen.

Records, Journals, and Periodicals

American Folk Lore
Ballad Society of London
Bibliography of Folklore. W. W. Thompson

Finding List of Fairy Tales and Folk Tales. Boston Public
Library
The Folklore Foundation of Vassar College
The Gypsy Lore Society
Revue de Folklore Français
South African Folk Lore Society

For the Building of Literary Values

Chadwick, H. M. *The Growth of Literature.* Cambridge, England, Cambridge University Press. Background reading, covering a wide area.

Drinkwater, John. *The Outline of Literature.* New York, Putnam. Long, comprehensive. Take leisure to it.

Ford, Ford Madox. *The March of Literature.* London, Unwin. Written with charm and authority. Recommended for Book I.

Horn Book, The. An invaluable guide. The only magazine devoted exclusively to children's literature, authors, and illustrators. Published bi-monthly. Boston, 585 Boylston Street.

Jackson, Holbrook. *The Reading of Books.* New York, Scribners.

Macy, John. *Story of the World's Literature.* New York, Liveright. Good, on the whole.

Pater, Walter. *The Renaissance.* London, Macmillan. For flavor, delight, and good reading. In paperback, New American Library.

Pound, Ezra. *A.B.C. of Reading.* New Haven, Yale University Press. A zestful, provocative book. In paperback, New Directions.

Quiller-Couch, Sir Arthur. *On the Art of Reading.* Cambridge, England, Cambridge University Press. Read the chapters on children's reading.

Woolf, Virginia. *The Common Reader*. New York, Harcourt. A fine appetizer, brilliant commentaries. In paperback, Harvest Books.

Of Children's Books and Stories

Duff, Annis. *"Bequest of Wings." "Longer Flight."* New York, Viking. Invaluable guides to what parents may do with their children.

Eaton, Anne T. *Reading with Children. Treasure for the Taking*. New York, Viking. Two books of appreciation and wisdom.

Meigs, Cornelia, and others, eds. *Critical History of Children's Literature*. New York, Macmillan.

Miller, Bertha Mahony, and Whitney, Elinor. *Realms of Gold in Children's Books*. New York, Doubleday. Three centuries of children's books delightfully reviewed: good bibliography.

Moore, Anne Carroll. *My Roads to Childhood*. New York, Doubleday. In paperback, Boston, Horn Book. *Three Owls*. New York, Macmillan. Invaluable. Here is literature about children's literature.

Richards, Laura E. *What Shall the Children Read?* New York, Appleton. Good commentaries on the long-ago books.

Shedlock, Marie L. *The Art of the Story-Teller*. Introduction by Anne Carroll Moore; list of stories compiled by Eulalie Steinmetz Ross. New York, Dover.

On a Variety of Interests

Barber, Sara M. *Speech Education*. Boston, Little, Brown. The best and most complete.

Barrows, Sarah T., and Pierce, Anne E. *The Voice: How to Use It*. Boston, Expression Co. A concise, thorough book.

Bauer, Marion, and Peyser, Ethel. *How Music Grew*. New York, Putnam. A good folk feeling.

Everts, Katherine J. *The Speaking Voice*. New York, Harpers. An untechnical, simple approach.

Finck, Henry T. *Success in Music*. New York, Scribner.

Manchester, Arthur L. *Twelve Lessons in the Fundamentals of Voice Production*. Boston, Oliver Ditson. Condensed and thorough. For anyone who wants to go conscientiously about training.

Saint-Saëns, Camille. *Outspoken Essays on Music*. New York, Dutton. For enjoyment and feeling.

Scholes, P. A. *The Listener's History of Music*. London, Oxford University Press. A fine commentary, not too technical.

Taylor, Deems. *The Well-Tempered Listener*. New York, Simon & Schuster.

———. *Of Men and Music*. New York, Simon & Schuster.

Van Loon, Hendrik. *The Arts*. New York, Simon & Schuster. For general appreciation and a tangy flavor.

$\mathcal{A}$ Story List

Such a list must inevitably be very personal, and therefore somewhat limited. But it gives stories to tell on the *short breath*, and more to tell on the *long breath*. It gives books, a few, from which stories spring naturally to be told; it gives other books where there is good material for condensing or adapting, books that cannot be left out of the storyteller's collection.

And there are suggestions for poetry and ballad. These make good grist for the mill out of which may truly come fairy bread.

OLD AND NEW STORIES FOR TELLING

Picture Books

Artzybasheff, Boris. *The Fairy Shoemaker and Other Fairy Poems.* New York, Macmillan.
——. *Aesop's Fables.* New York, Viking.
Aulaire, Ingri and Edgar Parin d'. *Children of the Northlights.* New York, Viking.
——. *Leif the Lucky.* New York, Doubleday.
——. *Abraham Lincoln.* New York, Doubleday.
Bannerman, Helen. *The Story of Little Black Sambo.* New York, Stokes.
Belpré, Pura. *Perez and Martina.* New York, Warne.
Bemelmans, Ludwig. *Hansi.* New York, Viking.

Beskow, Elsa. *Peter's Voyage*, New York, Knopf.

Bishop, Claire H. *The Five Chinese Brothers*. New York, Coward.

———. *The Ferryman*. New York, Coward.

Brock, Emma. *The Runaway Sardine*. New York, Knopf.

Brooke, Leslie. *Johnny Crow's Garden*. New York, Warne.

———. *Johnny Crow's New Garden*. New York, Warne.

———. *The Golden Goose Book*. New York, Warne.

Brown, Palmer. *Cheerful*. New York, Harpers.

Carrick, Valer. *Picture Tales from the Russian*. New York, Stokes.

———. *More Russian Picture Tales*. New York, Stokes.

Dickens, Charles. *The Magic Fishbone*. New York, Warne.

Ets, Marie. *Mister Penny*. New York, Viking.

———. *Play With Me*. New York, Viking.

———. *Mister Penny's Circus*. New York, Viking.

Fatio, Louise. *The Happy Lion*. New York, Whittlesey.

Flack, Marjorie. *Ask Mr. Bear*. New York, Macmillan.

———. *The Story about Ping*. New York, Viking.

Gág, Wanda. *The A.B.C. Bunny*. New York, Coward.

———. *Millions of Cats*. New York, Coward.

———. *Gone Is Gone*. New York, Coward.

———. *Nothing at All*. New York, Coward.

Gibson, Katherine. *Cinders*. New York, Longmans.

Gramatky, Hardie. *Little Toot*. New York, Putnam.

Hill, Mabel B. *Down along Apple Street*. New York, Stokes.

Jones, Elizabeth Orton. *Maminka's Children*. New York, Macmillan.

Leaf, Munro, and Lawson, Robert. *The Story of Ferdinand*. New York, Viking.

McCloskey, Robert. *Lentil*. New York, Viking.

———. *Make Way for Ducklings*. New York, Viking.

———. *Blueberries for Sal*. New York, Viking.

Nicholson, William. *Clever Bill*. New York, Doubleday.

Potter, Beatrix. *The Tailor of Gloucester*. New York, Warne.

———. *The Tale of Benjamin Bunny*. New York, Warne.

———. *The Tale of Peter Rabbit*. New York, Warne.

———. *The Tale of Squirrel Nutkin*. New York, Warne.

Prokofieff, Serge, and Chappell, Warren. *Peter and the Wolf*. New York, Knopf.

Rey, H. A. *Curious George*. Boston, Houghton.

Sawyer, Ruth. *Journey Cake, Ho!* New York, Viking.

Seuss, Dr. *The 500 Hats of Bartholomew Cubbins*. New York, Vanguard. All his better books are loved.

Stong, Phil. *Honk, the Moose*. New York, Dodd, Mead.

Van Stockum, Hilda. *A Day on Skates*. New York, Harper.

Ward, Lynd. *The Biggest Bear*. Boston, Houghton.

Stories for All of Story-Hour Age

Boggs, R. S., and Davis, M. G. "The Goatherd Who Won a Princess" in *Three Golden Oranges*. New York, Longmans.

Browne, Frances. "The Christmas Cuckoo," and "The Greedy Shepherd" in *Granny's Wonderful Chair*. New York, Macmillan.

Colum, Padraic. "Thor and Loki in the Giant's City," "How Thor and Loki Befooled Thrym the Giant," and "Aegir's Feast: How Thor Triumphed" in *Children of Odin*. New York, Macmillan.

Dane, B. J., and G. E. "The Well of the Moon," and "The Castle of Thou Shalt Go and Not Return" in *Once There Was and Was Not*. New York, Doubleday.

Dasent, G. W. "East o' the Sun and West o' the Moon," "The Giant Who Had No Heart in His Body," and "The Three Billy-Goats Gruff" in *East o' the Sun and West o' the Moon*. New York, Putnam.

Davis, Mary Gould. "The Truce of the Wolf" in *The Truce of the Wolf*. New York, Harcourt.

Eels, Elsie Spicer. "How the Brazilian Beetles Got Their Gorgeous Coats" in *Fairytales from Brazil*. New York, Dodd.

Farjeon, Eleanor. "Tom Cobble and Coney," and "Elsie Piddock Skips in Her Sleep" in *Martin Pippin in the Daisy-field*. New York, Stokes.

Fillmore, Parker. "The Twelve Months," and "The Shoemaker's Apron" in *The Shoemaker's Apron*. New York, Harcourt.

————. "Mighty Mikko," and "The Terrible Olli" in *Mighty Mikko*. New York, Harcourt.

Finger, Charles. "The Hero Twins," "The Four Hundred," and "The Killing of Cabrakan" in *Tales from Silver Lands*. New York, Doubleday.

Grimm, J. L. K., and W. K. "The Golden Bird," "The Bremen Town Musicians," "The Frog Prince," "The Elves," and "Snow White" in *Household Stories*. New York, Macmillan.

Hawthorne, Nathaniel. "The Gorgon's Head," "The Golden Touch," and "The Three Golden Apples" in *A Wonder Book*. New York, Doubleday. "The Chimera" in *Tangle-wood Tales*. New York, Doubleday.

Housman, Laurence. "The Cloak of Friendship" in *All-Fellows and the Cloak of Friendship*. New York, Harcourt.

————. "Rocking-Horse Land," "A Capful of Moonshine," and "A Chinese Fairytale" in *Moonshine and Clover*. New York, Harcourt.

Jacobs, Joseph. "Tom Tit Tot," "Master of All Masters," "The Laidly Worm of Spindleston Heugh," and "Teeny-Tiny" in *English Fairy Tales*. New York, Putnam.

Jewett, Eleanore M. "When Isis Sought Her Lord," and "King Setnau and the Assyrians" in *Egyptian Tales of Magic*. Boston, Little, Brown.

Kipling, Rudyard. "The Elephant's Child," and "How the Rhinoceros Got His Skin" in *Just So Stories*. New York, Doubleday.

Leamy, Edmund. "The Little White Cat," and "The Fairy Tree of Dooros" in *The Golden Spears*. New York, Longmans.

Macmanus, Seumas. "Rory the Robber," "Jack and the King

Who Was a Gentleman," and "Billy Beg and the Bull"
in *In Chimney Corners*. New York, Doubleday.

Malcolmson, Anne. "John Henry," "Mike Fink," and "Davy
Crockett" in *Yankee Doodle's Cousins*. Boston, Houghton.

Pyle, Howard. "The Stool of Fortune," and "Much Shall Have
More and Little Shall Have Less" in *Twilight Land*.
New York, Harper.

———. "Peterkin and the Little Grey Hare," "How the Good
Gifts Were Used by Two," and "How Boots Befooled
the King" in *The Wonder Clock*. New York, Harper.

Sawyer, Ruth. "The Flea," "The Frog," and "The Little Cock
Who Sang *Coplas*" in *Picture Tales from Spain*. New
York, Stokes.

Smedley, Constance. "The Stone Lion" in *Tales from Timbuktu*. New York, Harcourt.

Steel, Flora A. "The Rat's Wedding," "The Lambikin," and
"The Grain of Corn" in *Tales of the Punjab*. New York,
Macmillan.

Tregarthen, Enys. "The Boy Who Played with the Piskeys,"
and "The Nurse Who Broke Her Promise" in *Piskey
Folk*. New York, Day.

Wheeler, Post. "The Little Humpbacked Horse" in *Russian
Wonder Tales*. New York, Appleton.

Wilde, Oscar. "The Selfish Giant" in *The Happy Prince and
Other Fairy Tales*. New York, Putnam.

Zeitlin, Ida. "Kirilo, the Tanner," and "The Golden Cock"
in *Skazki, Tales and Legends of Old Russia*. New York,
Farrar & Rinehart.

Collections from Which It Is Difficult to Select Just One or Two Good Stories

Adams, Julia. *The Swords of the Vikings*. New York, Dutton

Andersen, Hans Christian. *Fairy Tales*, trans. Mrs. Edgar
Lucas. New York, Dutton.

Bay, J. C. (comp.). *Danish Fairy and Folk Tales,* from S. Grundtvig, E. T. Kristensen, I. Bondeson, and L. Budde. New York, Harper.

Berry, Erick. *Black Folk Tales.* New York, Harper.

Bosschère, Jean de. *Folk Tales of Flanders.* New York, Doubleday.

Brown, Abbie F. *In the Days of the Giants.* Boston, Houghton.

Bryson, Bernada. *The Twenty Miracles of Saint Nicholas.* Boston, Little, Brown.

Buckley, Elsie Finnimore. *Children of the Dawn.* New York, Stokes.

Carpenter, Frances. *Tales of a Russian Grandmother.* New York, Doubleday.

Chrisman, A. B. *Shen of the Sea.* New York, Dutton.

Coatsworth, Elizabeth. *The Cat Who Went to Heaven.* New York, Macmillan.

Colum, Padraic. *The Boy Who Knew What the Birds Said.* New York, Macmillan.

————. *The Big Tree of Bunlahy.* New York, Macmillan.

————. *The Forge in the Forest.* New York, Macmillan.

Credle, Ellis. *Tall Tales from the Far Hills.* New York, Nelson.

De La Mare, Walter. *Told Again.* New York, Knopf.

Dunbar, Aldis. *Sons o' Cormac.* New York, Dutton.

Estabrook, Helen S. *Seventy Stories of the Old Testament.* Massachusetts, The Bradford Press.

Field, Rachel, ed. *American Folk and Fairy Tales.* New York, Scribner.

Harris, Joel Chandler. *Uncle Remus, His Songs and His Sayings.* New York, Appleton.

————. *Nights with Uncle Remus.* Boston, Houghton.

Haviland, Virginia. *Favorite Fairy Tales* (retold). *Told in England. Told in France. Told in Germany. Told in Ireland. Told in Norway. Told in Russia.* Boston, Little, Brown. All excellent.

Hosford, Dorothy G. *Sons of the Volsungs,* adapted from *The*

Story of Sigurd the Volsung, by William Morris. New York, Macmillan.

Hull, Eleanor. *The Boys' Cuchulain*. New York, Crowell.

Irving, Washington. *The Bold Dragoon and Other Ghostly Tales*, sel. and ed. by Anne Carroll Moore. New York, Knopf.

———. *Tales from the Alhambra*. Sel. and re-arr. by Mabel Williams. New York, Macmillan.

James, Grace. *Green Willow*. New York, Macmillan.

Jewett, Eleanore M. *Told on the King's Highway*. New York, Viking. Best collection of medieval tales.

Kipling, Rudyard. *Puck of Pook's Hill*. New York, Doubleday.

———. *Rewards and Fairies*. New York, Doubleday.

———. *Two Jungle Books*. New York, Doubleday.

Lagerlöf, Selma. *Christ Legends*, trans. V. C. Howard. New York, Holt.

Macmanus, Seumas. *The Donegal Wonder Book*. New York, Stokes.

Meigs, Cornelia. *Master Simon's Garden*. New York, Macmillan.

Pyle, Howard. *The Merry Adventures of Robin Hood*. New York, Scribner.

———. *The Story of King Arthur and His Knights*. New York, Scribner.

Ransome, Arthur. *Old Peter's Russian Tales*. New York, Nelson.

Rasmussen, Knud. *The Eagle's Gift*, trans. Isobel Hutchinson. New York, Doubleday.

Shedlock, Marie L. *Eastern Stories and Legends*. New York, Dutton.

Sherwood, Merriam. *The Tale of the Warrior Lord*. New York, Longmans.

Stephens, James. *Irish Fairy Tales*. New York, Macmillan.

Tyler, Anna Cogswell. *Twenty-Four Unusual Stories*. New York, Harcourt.

Wiggin, Kate Douglas, and Smith, Nora Archibald, eds. *Tales of Laughter*. New York, Doubleday.

Young, Ella. *Celtic Wonder Tales*. New York, Dutton.

————. *The Tangle-Coated Horse*. New York, Longmans.

The collections of colored fairy tales: *The Green Fairy Book, The Violet Fairy Book,* etc., by Andrew Lang (Longmans) cannot be slighted. There are some excellent stories nowhere else to be found at easy hand.

Poetry and Ballad

Allingham, William. *Robin Redbreast and Other Verses*. New York, Macmillan.

Behn, Harry. *The House Beyond the Meadow*. New York, Pantheon.

————. *The Little Hill. Wizard in the Well*. New York, Harcourt.

Carroll, Lewis. *The Hunting of the Snark*. New York, Macmillan.

de la Mare, Walter. *Down-Adown-Derry*. New York, Holt.

————. *Peacock Pie*. New York, Holt.

————. *A Child's Day*. New York, Holt.

————. *Bells and Grass*. New York, Viking.

————. *Come Hither*, Anthology. New York, Knopf.

Fyleman, Rose. *Fairies and Chimneys*. New York, Doubleday.

Grahame, Kenneth. *Cambridge Book of Verse*. New York, Putnam. Anthology.

Greenaway, Kate. *Mother Goose*. New York, Warne.

Lear, Edward. *Nonsense Books*. Boston, Little Brown.

Lindsay, Vachel. *Collected Poems*. New York, Macmillan.

Masefield, John. *Salt Water Poems and Ballads*. New York, Macmillan.

McCord, David. *Far and Few*. Boston, Little, Brown.

Millay, Edna St. Vincent. *Poems Selected for Young People*. New York, Harpers.

Milne, A. A. *When We Were Very Young. Now We Are Six*. New York, Dutton.

Quiller-Couch, Sir Arthur. *The Oxford Book of Ballads*. Anthology. London, Oxford University Press.
Roberts, Elizabeth M. *Under the Tree*. New York, Viking.
Rossetti, Christina. *Sing-Song*. New York, Macmillan.
Stevenson, Robert Louis. *A Child's Garden of Verses*. New York, Scribner.
Teasdale, Sara. *Rainbow Gold*. Anthology. New York, Macmillan.
Untermeyer, Louis. *This Singing World*. New York, Harcourt.
———. *Rainbow in the Sky*. New York, Harcourt.

Books Which Lend Themselves to the Storyteller's Art

The Bible. King James Version.
Carroll, Lewis. *Alice's Adventures in Wonderland*. New York, Macmillan.
———. *Through the Looking-Glass*. New York, Macmillan
French, H. W. *The Lance of Kanana*. Boston, Lothrop, Lee.
Grahame, Kenneth. *The Wind in the Willows*. New York, Scribner.
Kipling, Rudyard. *Kim*. New York, Doubleday.
Lagerlöf, Selma. *The Girl from the Marshcroft*, trans. V. S. Howard. New York, Doubleday.
Macdonald, George. *The Princess and the Goblin*. Philadelphia, McKay.
Milne, A. A. *Winnie-the-Pooh*. New York, Dutton.
———. *The House at Pooh Corner*. New York, Dutton.
Ruskin, John. *The King of the Golden River*. Philadelphia, McKay.
Stephens, James. *The Crock of Gold*. New York, Macmillan.
———. *In the Land of Youth*. New York, Macmillan.
White, T. H. *The Sword in the Stone*. New York, Putnam.
Yates, Elizabeth. *Amos Fortune*. New York, Aladdin.

Index

VERTICAL COMICS

MYSTERIOUS GIRLFRIEND X

RIICHI UESHIBA

MYSTERIOUS GIRLFRIEND X

Ayuko Oka (17)

At 4'8", she's very small, but her figure is well-developed and quite gorgeous. She is Ueno's girlfriend. She often toys with Urabe through her impish personality. Like Tsubaki, she is responsive to Urabe's drool.

Kouhei Ueno (17)

Tsubaki's best friend. He's been going out with their classmate, Oka, since they were sophomores. Ueno's fond way of talking about Oka frequently influences Tsubaki's ideas about relationships.

Ryouko Suwano (17)

Tsubaki's classmate who shares his class duties. Her drooping eyes are her most charming feature. She knows Tsubaki has a girlfriend, though she doesn't know that it's Urabe.

Characters

Mikoto Urabe (17)

A transfer student who joined Tsubaki's class. She can convey her own feelings through her drool, as well as pick up on Tsubaki's feelings through his. She's anti-social and everything she says and does is mysterious, but her ideas about love are very pure. Her hobby is using scissors, which she can use to cut up anything.

Akira Tsubaki (17)

The protagonist of the story. His bizarre relationship with Urabe began after he licked her drool one day. He is as interested in girls as any boy his age, but Urabe takes the lead in their relationship and Tsubaki can't seem to initiate any progress between them.

CHAPTER 61: MYSTERIOUS BODY DOUBLE

YOU SHOULD HAVE SOMETHING IN YOUR STOMACH.

THAT'S GOOD!

I GUESS I'LL HAVE SOME.

OKAY...

DO YOU WANT TO TRY?

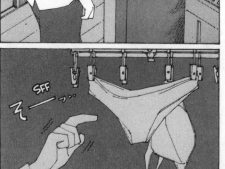

SFF

DO YOU HAVE A GRATER?

IT'S IN THE DRAWER BY THE SINK.

TSUBAKI...

MM...

HUH...?

AH...

DIDN'T YOU GO HOME...?

IT FEELS NICE...

IT'S COOL...

TSUBAKI'S HAND...

I CAN FEEL...

MM...

HM?

JUST QUICKLY BEFORE I GO TO SCHOOL.

WOULD THAT BE OKAY?

OKAY!

I THOUGHT I'D STOP BY TO SEE YOU

I PLAN TO.

I'LL BE A BIT LATE, BUT SOMETIME BEFORE NOON...

ARE YOU COMING TO SCHOOL TODAY?

GACHAK

MORN-ING,

OH,

URA—

DING DONG

SURE...

THAT SHIRT...

TH...

HUH ...?!

IT'S THE SHIRT YOU LEFT HERE.

YES.

SO I PUT THIS ON.

THE SWEATS I WAS WEARING YESTERDAY GOT ALL SWEATY OVERNIGHT

THAT MEANS... SHE'S WEARING IT OVER HER BARE SKIN, RIGHT...?

OH,

RIGHT...

BECAUSE OF THE SHIRT YOU LEFT HERE AS YOUR DOUBLE.

MIGHT ALSO BE

MY FEVER GOING DOWN OVERNIGHT

IS KINDA...

THAT I USUALLY WEAR...

TO SEE URABE WEARING A SHIRT

SINCE WE DIDN'T DO OUR ROUTINE YESTERDAY...

WHAT?

WHY?

SO IF I GIVE YOU MINE

MY FEVER ONLY JUST BROKE,

YOUR DROOL TODAY?

CAN I TASTE

INSTEAD,

YOU MIGHT GET SICK.

SO IF I TASTE YOURS...

B...

BE-CAUSE...

NO WAY!!

GRIP

IN MY SHIRT.

REALLY EXCITED SEEING YOU

I FEEL

IF YOU TASTE MY DROOL NOW,

YOUR FEVER

MIGHT COME BACK...

SWAP

YOU FEEL HOT...

AH...

D...

DUMMY!

BATAM

I WISH I COULD BE MY SHIRT'S DOUBLE.

BUT RIGHT NOW,

I LEFT MY SHIRT WITH HER TO ACT AS MY OWN DOUBLE...

TSUBAKI,

LET ME KEEP THIS SHIRT.

I'M SO JEALOUS

OF THAT SHIRT...

BATAM

CLINGING TO URABE'S BARE SKIN LIKE THAT...

I WANT

TO USE IT AS A PAJAMA TOP FROM NOW ON.

CHAK

END OF CHAPTER 61

CHAPTER 62: MYSTERIOUS MOVIE PRODUCTION (1)

THE 45TH KAZAMIDAI HIGH
CULTURE FESTIVAL
11/5 (SAT)・11/6 (SUN)

AH,

IT'S THAT TIME OF YEAR ALREADY?

THE CULTURE FESTIVAL, HUH?

I WOULDN'T MIND HELPING WITH SHOPPING FOR MATERIALS.

WELL,

PSHTS

SAME HERE.

I'M NOT IN ANY CLUBS, SO I HAVE NOTHING ELSE TO DO AFTER SCHOOL...

GULP

GULP

WHAT IS OUR CLASS

DOING THERE AGAIN?

SONTORY

CAFÉ.

KAZUUNK!

AMIN

TSUBAKI?

THE FILM STUDIES CLUB! OR DID YOU FORGET,

YOU ARE IN A CLUB.

SO,

OUR CLUB IS GETTING READY TO MAKE A SELF-PRODUCED MOVIE TO SHOW AT THE CULTURE FEST...

AS A CLUB MEMBER!

I'M HERE TO ASK YOU A FAVOR

OH!

YEAH!

HUH?

YOU'RE IN THE FILM CLUB?

I NEVER KNEW THAT.

I AM, ACTUALLY.

I'M KIND OF A GHOST MEMBER, THOUGH...

I'M YAMA-ZAKI.

PREZ OF THE FILM CLUB.

YOU'RE
...
UHM
...
UHH
...

AH, SUWANO, HUH?

R...

RYOUKO SUWANO.

I TOLD HER WE SHOULD TRY TO CAST PEOPLE IN THE CLUB, TOO...

THERE ARE GIRLS IN THE CLUB!

WHY SUWANO?

SINCE YOU'RE IN HER CLASS,

SO, TSU-BAKI!

I WANT YOU TO TALK HER INTO TAKING THE ROLE.

SHE SAYS THE GIRL FROM CLASS 2-A WITH THE LONG HAIR

FITS HER IMAGE PERFECTLY, AND SHE WON'T TAKE NO FOR AN ANSWER.

BUT

THE DIRECTOR REMEMBERS THE SUMMER SWIM MEET.

KLATTER

HM?

SUWANO!

BAKERY

AND WE'RE GOING TO MAKE A MOVIE FOR THE CULTURE FEST.

THE FILM STUDIES CLUB,

I AM IN

THERE'S SOMETHING I WANTED TO TALK TO YOU ABOUT.

LISTEN,

WHAT?

KLATTER

OHH...?

THEY REALLY WANT YOU TO PLAY THE LEAD IN THE MOVIE.

AND APPARENTLY,

BUT IF YOU DON'T WANT TO,

IT'D BE GREAT IF YOU WANTED TO DO IT,

YOU DON'T HAVE TO!

HONESTLY,

I DON'T HAVE ANY INTENTION TO FORCE YOU INTO IT.

BUT ONLY YOU CAN DECIDE WHETHER

TO BE IN THE MOVIE OR NOT.

THEY ASKED ME TO TRY TO TALK YOU INTO IT.

SINCE WE'RE IN THE SAME CLASS,

HUH?

WHAT KIND OF MOVIE IS IT?

AND I'LL RELAY YOUR ANSWER TO THE CLUB!

SO JUST GIVE ME A YES OR A NO,

I'M ASKING,

WHAT IS THE MOVIE ABOUT?

I DON'T HAVE ANY WAY TO DECIDE

WHETHER I WANT TO BE IN IT OR NOT!

WELL, THEN,

THEY DIDN'T REALLY TELL ME ABOUT THAT...

UH...

I THINK THEY'LL ALL BE THERE.

...THAT'S FAIR.

WANT TO GO TO THE CLUB ROOM AFTER LUNCH, THEN?

WHO KNOWS WHAT IT'S ABOUT AND CAN TELL ME

I'D RATHER MEET WITH SOMEONE

BEFORE I MAKE A DECISION.

ESPECIALLY LOOKING FOR FEMALE MEMBERS ♡

RECRUITING NEW MEMBERS! I ♡ CINEMA!

2011

A SPACE ODYSSEY

TABE ♡

BIG NATION

FILM STUDIES CLUB

OPEN

No MOVIE! No LIFE!

WHY ARE YOU TAGGING ALONG?

OH,

IT JUST SOUNDED INTERESTING.

OF COURSE, I DON'T KNOW...

SKRITCH SKRITCH

BECAUSE I ALMOST NEVER COME TO THE CLUB...

I'D LIKE TO KNOW, TOO.

OF THIS MOVIE YOU GUYS ARE MAKING,

SO I'LL DECIDE AFTER I HEAR MORE ABOUT IT.

I DON'T KNOW ANYTHING ABOUT THE PLOT

YAMADA! I'M HUNGRY!

GO

CLOSE THIRD

WHAT?

THIS IS

THE PROPOSAL FOR OUR MOVIE.

HERE.

SWIP

FILMS

YES, YOU'RE RIGHT!

TAKE A SEAT, THEN?

WOULD YOU ALL

I'LL EXPLAIN!

KLATTER

"MYSTERIOUS GIRLFRIEND... Y"?

...

BUT SINCE IT HAS "GIRL-FRIEND" IN IT,

IS IT A ROMANCE?

THAT'S AN ODD TITLE...

A Film Studies Club Production

"MYSTERIOUS GIRLFRIEND Y"

Director, Screenplay: Minori Matsuzawa
Producer: Kenji Yamazaki

CAST

BUT THIS BOY...

IT'S ABOUT A BOY WHO FALLS IN LOVE WITH THE HEROINE,

IT IS A ROMANCE,

BUT IT'S A DIFFERENT SORT OF LOVE STORY.

IF TSUBAKI WILL PLAY THIS PART,

I'LL DO IT.

IT'S WISE TO TRUST YOUR STAR'S TASTE!

AT TIMES LIKE THESE,

THE ROLE OF THE HEROINE'S ROMANTIC RIVAL...

-HE[...]

-BOY WHO FALL FOR HEROINE

-HEROINE'S ROMANTIC RIVA[...]

-BOY'S [...]IEND [...]

I HAVE ANOTHER CONDITION!

I ACCEPT!

SO FAST...

WHIP

HEY...

ACCEPTED!

SO FAST AGAIN!

WHIP

WAIT A MINUTE!!

I'LL DO MY BEST!

TSU-BAKI!

IT SOUNDS LIKE FUN!

WHY NOT?

BESIDES...

B...

I HAVEN'T AGREED TO BE IN IT YET!!

WHETHER I'LL

GIVE ME ANOTHER DAY TO CONSIDER

PLAY THE PART OR NOT.

URABE, DOESN'T KNOW ANYTHING ABOUT THIS, EITHER...

U...

THE GIRL FROM OUR CLASS,

ARE YOU WHY

ASKING ME?

I HAVE NO INTENTION OF BEING IN IT...

I'M NOT INTERESTED IN MOVIES.

YOU'LL APPEAR WITH SUWANO IN THE MOVIE.

IT'S UP TO YOU TO DECIDE WHETHER OR NOT

...WELL, SURE...

WELL, TSUBAKI...

BUT HER EMOTIONS TEND TO RAGE LIKE A STORM ON THE INSIDE...

SHE SAID WITH NO EXPRESSION THAT

IT'S UP TO ME TO DECIDE...

SO WHY ASK ME?

OUR USUAL ROUTINE.

HERE.

SHLP

BADUM BADUM BADUM...

SEEEEE? I KNEW IT! IT FEELS LIKE THERE'S A BOULDER ON MY SHOULDERS!

THAT PROVES URABE'S MAD!!

OWW...

ZWOOOM

POK

WE EVEN KNOW IF THIS MOVIE WILL COME TOGETHER YET.

WHAT?

BUT WAIT,

HEY, YOU THINK THEY CAN WRITE A ROLE FOR ME NOW?

IF URABE WILL AGREE TO IT...

AND WE STILL DON'T KNOW

REALLY?

HUH?

I CAN'T BLAME HIM FOR BEING HUNG UP ON THAT,

BUT A MOVIE IS PURE FICTION.

BESIDES...

AH...

IS TSUBAKI HUNG UP ON THE IDEA OF SUWANO PLAYING HIS LOVER?

WELL, URABE IS DATING TSUBAKI IN REAL LIFE...

TSUBAKI SAID HE'LL DECIDE WHETHER HE'LL BE IN IT OR NOT BY TOMORROW.

AND SUWANO SAYS SHE WON'T DO IT

IF TSUBAKI ISN'T IN IT.

ABOVE ALL, A CULTURE FESTIVAL'S GOTTA BE FUN!

Welcome Home! My Master ♡

Moe

UENO!

LET'S MAKE SURE

THIS MOVIE GETS FILMED!

BUT

TSUBAKI AND URABE...

WE'LL CONVINCE THEM!

AS THEIR BEST FRIENDS,

LISTEN...

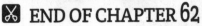

CHAPTER 63: MYSTERIOUS MOVIE PRODUCTION (2)

AH, I GET IT.

YOU'RE AFRAID.

EVEN THOUGH A MOVIE IS JUST FICTIONAL...

I GUESS A BOND THROUGH DROOL IS STILL FRAGILE.

TO THINK YOU HAVE SUCH LITTLE FAITH IN HIM,

WHAT?

ARE N'T YOU?

SUWANO IS PLAYING TSUBAKI'S GIRLFRIEND,

SO YOU'RE AFRAID

HE'LL FALL IN LOVE WITH HER FOR REAL WHILE THEY'RE FILMING,

MUNCH MUNCH MUNCH

THUNK

TSUBAKI WOULDN'T TAKE THE ROLE,

SO I ENDED UP WITH THE PART OF SUWANO'S BOYFRIEND...

SLIDE

TAKE THE PART IN TSUBAKI'S PLACE.

I KNEW THAT YOU'D

IT'S OKAY.

REALLY?

HUH?

NOT ONE BIT.

I MEAN, IT'S ONLY FOR A MOVIE!

IT SOUNDS REALLY INTERESTING, AND IT'S FOR THE CULTURE FESTIVAL,

SO WE SHOULD ALL TRY TO HAVE FUN!

OH...

AND SHE SAID SHE MIGHT ASK YOU TO TAKE THE PART IF TSUBAKI REFUSED.

I TALKED TO SUWANO ABOUT THE MOVIE THIS MORNING,

BUT YOU DON'T MIND ME

PLAYING ANOTHER GIRL'S BOYFRIEND?

WILL YOU FALL FOR SUWANO INSTEAD OF ME?

IF YOU PLAY SUWANO'S BOYFRIEND IN THE MOVIE,

OR...

WELL, UENO,

I TRUST YOU...

OF—

OF COURSE NOT!

I SEE...

THAT GIRL, OKA FROM CLASS 2-A, CALLED US ALL TOGETHER THIS MORNING,

AND SAID IF TSUBAKI REFUSED THE ROLE,

WE SHOULD MAKE UENO HIS REPLACEMENT,

AND ASK HIM AGAIN TOMORROW...

WAS THAT THE RIGHT THING TO DO?

STILL...

FILM STUDIES CLUB

OPEN

TSUBAKI WOULD AGREE TO IT THEN.

SHE WAS SURE

LET'S

GO ALONG WITH OKA'S PLAN.

SHE SAID IT WITH SUCH CONFIDENCE, AFTER ALL.

I THINK IT'LL BE FINE.

WILL IT REALLY TURN OUT THAT WAY?

AT LEAST, THAT'S WHAT SHE SAID...

I

TURNED THEM DOWN TODAY.

ABOUT THE MOVIE...

URABE...

SAID TO GIVE HER MY FINAL ANSWER TOMORROW, THOUGH...

THE DIRECTOR, MATSU-ZAWA,

UENO SAID

HE'LL PLAY MY PART INSTEAD.

THAT'S WHAT YOU WANT, RIGHT?

OF COURSE, I INTEND TO DECLINE.

I KNOW FULL WELL THAT URABE HATES THE IDEA OF THIS MOVIE.

IT PROBABLY WASN'T NECESSARY TO ASK HER THAT...

WAIT...

SHLP

OUR DAILY ROUTINE...

WELL, TSUBAKI,

AH...

OKAY!

MAKE HER ANGRY AGAIN?

DID I

TSUBAKI?

HUH?

WHAT?

BUT MY SHOUL-DERS...

NO, MY WHOLE BODY FEELS LIGHT!

DOES THIS MEAN URABE... ISN'T MAD ANYMORE ?!!

I THOUGHT I'D GET THAT HEAVY FEELING AGAIN, LIKE YESTERDAY...

HUH ...?

WHAAAT?!!

THE FILM STUDIES CLUB'S MOVIE.

I DON'T MIND IF YOU ACT IN

I REALIZED SOME-THING.

B...

BUT,

I'D BE PLAYING SUWANO'S BOYFRIEND...

WAS THE SAME AS NOT TRUSTING YOU...

MY NOT WANTING YOU TO APPEAR IN THE MOVIE

DOUBTING THE BOND I HAVE WITH YOU.

IT WAS THE SAME AS

GRIP

...

ARE YOU SURE YOU DON'T MIND?

NOD

SO, TSUBAKI,

YOU CAN TELL THE CLUB TOMOR-ROW

THAT YOU'LL BE IN THE MOVIE.

BECAUSE I

TRUST YOU, TSUBAKI...

HUH?

WH... WHAT?

WHAT?

"NEVER MIND" WHAT?!

HUH?

HUH?

...

ACTUALLY, NEVER MIND...

SHFF

WHAT THE HECK HAPPENED TO URABE TODAY?!

WH...

WHAT'S WITH THE SUDDEN 180?!

I'LL BE IN THE MOVIE, TOO!

ANYWAY, I'LL GO TO THE CLUB ROOM WITH YOU TOMOR-ROW.

DID THAT HAVE ANYTHING TO DO WITH TSUBAKI AND URABE SUDDENLY CHANGING THEIR MINDS?

YOU DID KISS ME AFTER SAYING THAT...

WHAAAT?!

AFTER YOU TELL ME,

I'LL

GIVE YOU A KISS!

WELL,

WHAT DOES IT MATTER?

AFTER ALL!

IS BACK TO ITS ORIGINAL CASTING,

NOW THE MOVIE

I'M SO HAPPY!

TSUBAKI!

TRANSFER STUDENT FROM HELL

URABE IS SUCH A STRAIGHT-FORWARD GIRL ♥

IT LOOKS LIKE WHAT WE DID IN THE CLASSROOM WORKED JUST LIKE I PLANNED!

?

WILL BE AKIRA TSUBAKI.

THE BOY WHO FALLS FOR THE HEROINE

WILL BE PLAYED BY RYOUKO SUWANO.

THE HEROINE, THE MYSTERIOUS GIRLFRIEND

WILL BE KOUHEI UENO.

AND THE BOY'S FRIEND

WILL BE MIKOTO URABE.

THE HEROINE'S ROMANTIC RIVAL

KLAK
KLAK

WHUMP

END OF CHAPTER 63

CHAPTER 64: ✂ MYSTERIOUS MOVIE
PRODUCTION (3)

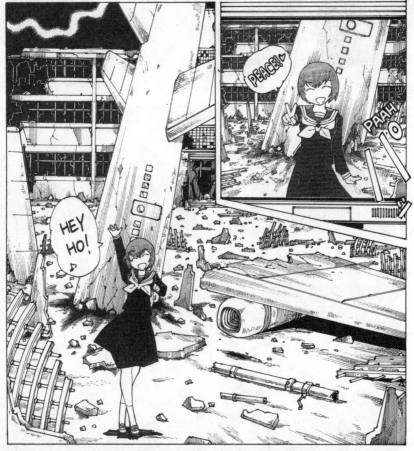

IS THE ENDING OF THE STORY!

AND THAT

THE SCRIPT TELLS IT IN MORE DETAIL,

SO EVERYONE READ THIS AND...

WAIT!

I THOUGHT IT WAS A LOVE STORY, BUT IT'S ACTUALLY SCI-FI?

OH.

YOU COULD SAY THAT.

BUT IT'S STILL A LOVE STORY UP TO THE VERY END.

STILL,

THE MOVIE

SEEMS INTERESTING SOMEHOW...

AFTER WHAT MATSUZAWA TOLD US TODAY...

BUT

LIKE MAKING MOVIES AT ALL,

I WASN'T INTERESTED IN THINGS

AT FIRST,

NOW I THINK...

I SEE...

I...

I WOULDN'T MIND

PLAYING A ROLE IN THIS MOVIE.

WOW...

SHE WAS SO AGAINST IT, AND NOW SHE'S ALL FOR IT...

I'M SURPRISED...!

IT WOULD FEEL WEIRD CALLING HIM A DIFFERENT NAME FOR THE MOVIE,

TO ME, TSUBAKI IS TSUBAKI.

SHOULD I HAVE GIVEN YOU DIFFERENT NAMES?

AND IT

FEELS MORE NATURAL TO ME IF HE CALLS ME "SUWANO."

IF THEY'RE THE SAME.

I THINK IT'S FINE

IT'S TIME TO GO HOME!

SUWANO!

SHE'S HOPELESS...

ACTION!

WAKE UP!

WELL,

EITHER IS FINE WITH ME...

ROLLING!

YOU WAKE UP SUWANO WITH THOSE LINES!

OKAY, IN THIS SCENE,

AND CUT!

WHERE SUWANO IS DROOLING

AS SHE LIFTS HER HEAD FROM THE DESK.

NOW, NEXT IS...

THE BIG SCENE ...

TWIST キュポ。

PRESI- DENT!

THE SPORTS DRINK!

YEP!

WE'LL USE THIS FOR THE DROOL.

AND LET JUST A BIT DRIBBLE OUT WHEN YOU LIFT YOUR HEAD.

HOLD SOME SPORTS DRINK IN YOUR MOUTH

SU- WANO,

THIS IS JUST LIKE...

AH...

CUT!

AND

FALL FOR URABE...

THE SITUATION THAT MADE ME

OKAY, NEXT SCENE!

THIS IS WHERE!

TSUBAKI LICKS THE DROOL ON THE DESK!

I KNEW MY CASTING CHOICE WASN'T WRONG!

WE GOT A GREAT TAKE, SUWANO!

YOU'RE DEFINITELY THE RIGHT GIRL TO PLAY THE HEROINE!

OH?

OF COURSE, WE CAN'T HAVE YOU

LICK SUWANO'S DROOL FOR REAL, SO...

AND PUT SOME ON YOUR FINGER AND TASTE IT.

THINK OF THIS SPORTS DRINK

TSU-BAKI!

ON THE DESK AS HER DROOL,

DRIBBLE

YOUR EXPRESSION WAS PERFECT!

TSU-BAKI!

SHLP

AND

CUT!

YES, I DID.

DID YOU REALLY

HEY,

MATSU-ZAWA...

COME UP WITH THIS STORY YOUR-SELF?

END OF CHAPTER 64

CHAPTER 65: ✂ MYSTERIOUS MOVIE PRODUCTION (4)

AND

CUT!

GLANCE

FILMING FOR THE FILM STUDIES CLUB'S CULTURE FESTIVAL MOVIE, "MYSTERIOUS GIRLFRIEND Y,"

IS GOING SMOOTHLY SO FAR, BUT...

WE'RE FINISHED WITH

THE PARK SCENE!

AS YOU WATCH SUWANO AND I ACT AS LOVERS... AND PLAYING CHARACTERS BONDED THROUGH DROOL, NO LESS...

URABE ...?

WHAT ARE YOU FEELING AS YOU WATCH THIS,

WE'RE ONLY DOING SCENES WITH TSUBAKI AND SUWANO FOR A WHILE...

AH...

I FEEL LIKE I'M MISSING OUT IF I'M JUST WATCHING!

ARE YOU SURE YOU CAN'T MAKE A PART FOR ME?

OH, THANKS!

THIS ACTUALLY LOOKS LIKE

A REAL FILM SET!

MATSU-ZAWA!

LET'S GO BACK TO THE SCHOOL!

OKAY, WE'RE SHOOTING A SCENE IN THE CLASSROOM NEXT!

AND AS SOON AS HE OPENS THE DOOR...

TSUBAKI COMES BACK TO THE CLASSROOM AFTER SCHOOL,

NOW, IN THE NEXT SCENE,

AH...

CUT!

BUT IN THIS MOVIE,

YOU'RE PLAYING THE LEAD

AND I'M PLAYING YOUR GIRLFRIEND, RIGHT?

I DON'T MIND A LITTLE FAN SERVICE IN THAT CASE.

EASILY SAYING STUFF THAT WOULD MAKE ANYONE'S HEART FLIP...

SHE'S MAKING ME BLUSH...

YES!

SU- WANO!

GEEZ...

OKAY, IN THE NEXT SCENE,

TSUBAKI TASTES SUWANO'S DROOL

AFTER SEEING HER CHANGING,

AND IT TASTES REALLY SWEET.

THAT'S THE SCENE!

WE CAN'T HAVE TSUBAKI TASTE SUWANO'S DROOL FOR REAL,

SO WE USE THIS SPORTS DRINK

IN PLACE OF REAL DROOL.

NOW,

WE'LL CUT THE FILMING THERE...

SO,

WE'LL START WITH THE SHOT OF SUWANO PUTTING DROOL ON HER FINGER.

SHLP

PUT SOME ON HER FINGER...

TWIST

THIS REACTION...

IS JUST LIKE

WHAT HAPPENS WHEN I TASTE URABE'S DROOL...

BUT THAT MIGHT HAVE POISONED IT A LITTLE...

THE MOST IMPORTANT THING WAS TO LIVEN UP THE CULTURE FESTIVAL...

ALL THIS TIME, I THOUGHT

THIS CAN'T

BE GOOD...

THIS

CAN'T BE GOOD...

IF I WAS IN YOUR PLACE, I COULD NEVER SAY THAT SO EASILY!

YOU SAID THAT WITH CONFIDENCE!

SLAP

'ATTA GIRL,

URABE!

I'M SO MOVED!

YOU EVEN

YOU'RE THE ONE WHO TOLD ME TO TRUST TSUBAKI.

WHY ARE YOU MOVED?

MADE ME WATCH YOU KISS UENO.

OF COURSE I DID!

YOU KNEW I DID THAT ON PURPOSE?

AH,

AND CUT!

OKAY.

TODAY'S DOSE.

SHLP

TSUBAKI. HERE,

OKAY, SUWANO,

PUT THIS SPORTS DRINK ON YOUR FINGER...

TWIST

THIS WILL BE THE DROOL

THAT TSUBAKI LICKS OFF YOUR FINGER.

YOU'RE ALWAYS

TASTING SOMEONE ELSE'S DROOL

DOING "THAT" WITH SUWANO.

IS DISGUSTING!

BUT IN REALITY, URABE IS MY GIRLFRIEND...

AND URABE PLAYS THE GIRL WHO BASHES US...

SO SUWANO AND I PLAY A COUPLE,

SERIOUSLY,

...

URABE! YOUR SHARP EXPRESSION WAS PERFECT FOR A RIVAL CHARACTER!

WHERE IS THIS MOVIE GOING?

✂ **END OF CHAPTER 65**

THUP

AH...

U—

URABE!

CUT!

ALL IS VANITY

CHAPTER 66: ✂ MYSTERIOUS MOVIE PRODUCTION (5)

YOUR DROOL... JUST... OH,

WHAT'S WRONG, TSU-BAKI?

ALWAYS TASTES SO SWEET...

THAT'S ALL...

ZHFF

HUH...?

REALLY ALL? ...IS THAT

EVERYONE, GATHER!!

ALL RIGHT!

WHERE SUWANO AND TSUBAKI ARE WALKING HOME FROM SCHOOL

NEXT IS SCENE 90,

BUT THAT...

IF YOU'RE BOTH OKAY WITH IT, I WOULDN'T MIND IF YOU KISSED FOR REAL,

WOULD BE A BAD IDEA, HUH?

KLAP

BUT I PLAN TO JUST HAVE YOU BRING YOUR FACES AS CLOSE TOGETHER AS POSSIBLE SO IT LOOKS LIKE YOU'RE KISSING...

AND THEY SHARE THEIR FIRST KISS.

BESIDES, EVEN IF IT'S ONLY A MOVIE,

A KISS... I HAVEN'T EVEN KISSED MY REAL GIRLFRIEND, URABE, YET...

I WANT IT TO LOOK REALISTIC!

EVEN IF YOU DON'T REALLY KISS,

REALLY GET AS CLOSE AS HUMANLY POSSIBLE!

OH, SHUT UP ALREADY...

ROLLING!

HAVING TO DO THIS SCENE IN FRONT OF URABE...

ACTION!

STEP

WHAP

WHOA ....!

SFF

THIS CLOSE UP...

SEEING A GIRL'S FACE

CUT!

WHAP

SHE SMELLS NICE...

WOW...

THIS LOOKS EVEN BETTER THAN I THOUGHT!

WOW,

TSUBAKI. HERE,

OKAY...

SHLP

URABE!

SORRY TO KEEP YOU WAITING!

THIS WILL BE OUR LAST SCENE FOR THE DAY!

OKAY!

IT'S YOUR TURN!

Urabe is watching from the top of the steps.

THESE ARE TSUBAKI'S LINES.

Tsubaki: "...Urabe, why are you following me around?"

Urabe runs off without a word.

Tsubaki: "Uh, hey... Wait!"

...watches Urabe

THAT'S OUR SCENE.

AND YOU'RE WATCHING HIM FROM THE TOP OF THOSE STEPS.

AFTER KISSING SUWANO,

TSUBAKI IS ON HIS WAY HOME,

OKAY, URABE, WHENEVER YOU'RE READY!

URABE IS HIDING A SECRET.

ACTUALLY,

HEH HEH,

WHY DOES URABE SHOW UP LIKE THIS EVERY TIME I'M WITH SUWANO?

IS THAT WHAT URABE'S CHARACTER IS LIKE?

LET'S BEGIN!

AH, LOOKS LIKE THE CAMERA IS READY.

A SECRET...?

URABE...

WHY ARE YOU FOLLOWING ME AROUND?!

KI— WELL... HUH?

KISS SCENE WITH SUWANO TODAY...

I HAD THAT...

I THOUGHT IT MIGHT BOTHER YOU...

FOR WHAT?

AFTER ALL, IT'S ONLY

IT DOESN'T BOTHER ME.

FOR THE MOVIE.

URABE... WAIT,

IT REALLY DOESN'T BOTHER YOU?

BUT MY FACE WAS SO CLOSE TO ANOTHER GIRL'S...

AND WE DIDN'T ACTUALLY KISS...

YEAH...

W... WELL,

I SEE... I...

IT DOESN'T BOTHER ME.

MAKES HER SOUND LIKE A ROBOT...

...I MEAN, IT'S JUST A MOVIE, SO I WOULDN'T WANT HER TO GET REALLY JEALOUS...

BUT HEARING HER SAY SO PLAINLY THAT IT DOESN'T BOTHER HER KIND OF...

OKAY.

TSUBAKI,

TODAY'S ROUTINE.

SHLP

!

WHAT'S WRONG,

TSUBAKI?

HUH?

WHAT THE HECK IS HAPPENING

BETWEEN URABE AND ME?!

IT'S USUALLY REALLY SWEET...

IT HAD NO FLAVOR AT ALL...

THIS HAS NEVER HAPPENED BEFORE...

URABE...!!

✂ END OF CHAPTER 66

CHAPTER 67: MYSTERIOUS MOVIE PRODUCTION (6)

DAAAAAZE...

WH-WHAT IS IT?!
WHAT'S GOING ON?!

THAT WAS THE FIRST
TIME URABE'S DROOL
DIDN'T TASTE SWEET...

WHY DID THIS HAPPEN ...?!

TSUBAKI!

DAAAAAZE...

TSUBAKI.

WAH ...!!

EARTH TO TSUBAKI!!

IS SOMETHING ON YOUR MIND?

S... SUWANO ...!

WHAT IS IT?

I'VE BEEN CALLING TO YOU, AND YOU'RE JUST SPACING OUT...

WELL, W...

KIND OF...

YESTER-DAY ?

WERE YOU REMEM-BERING

WHAT HAPPENED YESTERDAY ?

WE FILMED YOU TASTING MY DROOL AFTER THAT SCENE, RIGHT?

BUT, HOW WAS IT FOR YOU?

OUR KISSING SCENE.

THAT'S NOT IT!!

IT WASN'T.

I GUESS THEY MAKE SPORTS DRINKS WITH MORE SUGAR THESE DAYS.

IT WAS PRETTY SWEET.

W... WELL...

HUH?

WAS IT SWEET?

WHEN YOU TASTED IT,

URABE...!!

EVERY-ONE,

OKAY!

THE NEXT CUT WILL BE THE LAST OF THE DAY.

TSUBAKI AND

URABE,

THIS SCENE IS FOR YOU TWO!

AFTER PARTING WAYS WITH SUWANO,

TSUBAKI IS ON HIS WAY HOME WHEN THE WAITING URABE APPROACHES.

AND SAYS,

"IF YOU TASTE

MY DROOL JUST ONCE,

WILL DO WHAT

SUWANO ALWAYS DOES,

AND THEN

URABE,

AND THEN...

STOP FOLLOWING YOU AROUND,"

I WILL

SUWANO'S DROOL TASTES, URABE'S DROOL

HE REPLIES THAT, COMPARED TO HOW SWEET

BUT WHEN HE DOES,

TSUBAKI TASTES HER DROOL.

UPON HEAR-ING THIS,

HAS NO FLAVOR AT ALL.

AH...

TSUBAKI! WHAT ARE YOU DOING?!

HEY!

...

TUG

TUG

TUG

THEN,

HEARING HIS RESPONSE,

THAT'S YOUR SCENE.

URABE RUNS AWAY WITHOUT A WORD.

URABE'S CHARACTER

A POINT...?

IS IN FACT

I ALREADY TOLD YOU!

HIDING A SECRET!

COMPARED TO SUWANO'S DROOL

AND WHAT DO YOU MEAN,

HER DROOL HAS NO FLAVOR...?

IS THERE ANY POINT IN DOING THAT?!

IS THIS SCENE REALLY NECESSARY?

WHAT?!

YOU GUYS WERE THE ONES WHO ASKED ME NOT TO GIVE YOU THE ENTIRE STORY YET!

IS AN IMPORTANT PIECE OF FORESHADOWING FOR THE ENDING!

THE FACT THAT URABE'S DROOL HAS NO FLAVOR

JUST PLAY YOUR PART EXACTLY AS I SAY!

UNTIL WE GET TO THAT POINT,

ACTION!

AND BACK TO THE SCENE!

I'LL POUR THE SPORTS DRINK ON YOUR FINGER...

OKAY, NOW

AND

CUT!

TSUBAKI, TASTE THIS...

URABE...

NO FLAVOR AT ALL...

YOUR DROOL HAS

Y...

TASTES REALLY SWEET, BUT...

SU-WANO'S DROOL

DASH

WHIRL

AND CUT!

THAT'S IT FOR TODAY!

SEE YOU ALL TOMORROW

IN THE CLUB ROOM AFTER SCHOOL!

OF DROPPING OUT OF THE MOVIE...

URABE, I...

I'M THINKING

BUT TASTING MY GIRLFRIEND'S DROOL ON THE WAY HOME...

THE WHOLE STORY

SEEMS SO CLOSE TO WHAT YOU AND I DO IN REALITY...

YEAH, BUT...

I DON'T KNOW IF IT'S A COINCI-DENCE,

BUT THE FILMING

HAS COME

SO FAR ...

NOW?

IT'S FICTIONAL, RIGHT?

THAT WAS JUST A LINE IN THE MOVIE.

BUT,

WHEN I THINK OF YOUR DROOL HAVING NO FLAVOR...

I DON'T KNOW...

I JUST DON'T LIKE IT.

AND ALSO,

FOR THE LEADING ACTOR TO QUIT NOW.

I DON'T THINK IT WOULD BE RIGHT

ANYWAY, WE'VE ALREADY COME THIS FAR.

W...

WELL,

YEAH, BUT...

TSUBAKI,

TODAY'S DOSE...

SHLP

AH...

YEAH...

SEE YOU TOMOR-ROW!

SEE YOU TOMOR-ROW!

WELL,

TSUBAKI,

IT STILL...

THIS IS JUST LIKE IN THE MOVIE.

IF THIS GOES ON UNTIL THE FILMING IS OVER,

WOULDN'T THAT MEAN...

HAS NO FLAVOR.

TASTE SWEET TO ME AGAIN?!

URABE'S DROOL MIGHT NEVER

DING

コンカン

キンコン

DING

DONG

DONG

はぁ

SIGH...

ESPECIALLY LOOKING FOR FEMALE MEMBERS ♥

2011

SPACE ODYSSEY

RECRUITING NEW MEMBERS!

FILM STUDIES CLUB

JOKER

PHANTOM CITY WAR

SWORD ASH

MAGIC

LOVE ♥

ガチャ

KA-CHAK

VIOLENT NEET

THAT'S WHERE TODAY'S FILMING WILL BE.

YOU KNOW THAT UNUSED CLASSROOM

UH,

AT THE FAR END OF THE 3RD FLOOR OF BUILDING 2?

EVERYONE ELSE IS ALREADY THERE,

SO YOU CAN HEAD ON OVER.

AH, TSUBAKI!

CLASS-ROOM IN BUILDING 2?

AN UN-USED ...

SLIDE

IN FACT,

I EXPLAINED IT TO URABE JUST NOW...

I SAID

THAT HER CHARACTER IS HIDING A SECRET, RIGHT?

THIS MACHINE

HAS SOMETHING TO DO WITH THAT.

URABE IS ACTUALLY...

AH!

IT LOOKS JUST RIGHT!

DURING THE FILMING,

WE'LL ATTACH MORE CABLES TO YOU, SO IT MIGHT BE HEAVY.

I DON'T MIND.

H...

HANG ON!

WHAT THE HECK IS THIS?

AH...

✄ END OF CHAPTER 67

CHAPTER 68: MYSTERIOUS MOVIE
PRODUCTION (7)

IN FACT, URABE IS ACTUALLY...
AN A.I.
THAT'S HER SECRET.
AN...
A.I. ?
TO PUT IT SIMPLY,
SHE'S A ROBOT.

IS THE FINAL SCENE OF THE MOVIE.

AND THAT

HERE ARE THE LINES FOR BOTH OF YOU!

I NEED TO HOOK UP THE ILLUMINATION TO YOU NOW.

OKAY, URABE,

IS THAT OKAY?

THAT'S FINE.

THEN LET'S START GETTING READY!

TSUBAKI...

URABE...

ARE YOU...

NOT HUMAN?

YES,

THERE IS NO ONE BUT YOU.

URABE...

I'M REALLY

THE ONLY HUMAN LEFT IN THE WORLD?

WAS NOTHING MORE THAN A DREAM.

EVERYTHING THAT YOU EXPERIENCED WITH SUWANO

THE LAST HUMAN ON EARTH.

I AM AN A.I., HERE TO MONITOR YOU,

I AM NOT.

I'M A MACHINE, NOT A HUMAN...

IT HAD NO FLAVOR BECAUSE...

WHEN I INTERVENED IN YOUR DREAM TO FEED YOU MY DROOL,

AND CUT!

TASTE THIS...

TSUBAKI,

IS THE SCENE WHERE

SHE FEEDS TSUBAKI HER DROOL.

AND NEXT...

NOW, WE'LL PUT THE SPORTS DRINK ON YOUR FINGER...

AFTER TSUBAKI TASTES HER DROOL,

HE SHEDS A TEAR AND WHISPERS, "IT HAS NO FLAVOR."

IN THE SCRIPT,

OKAY, LET'S RESUME FILMING!

ROLLING!

BUT WE'LL CUT WHILE HER FINGER IS IN YOUR MOUTH

AND USE EYE DROPS FOR THE TEARS,

SO DON'T WORRY ABOUT CRYING!

TSUBAKI,

TASTE THIS...

ACTION!

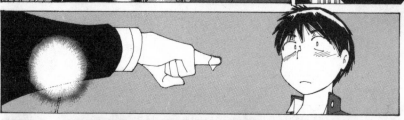

AND URABE TURNED OUT TO BE A ROBOT...

AT THE END OF THE WORLD...

URABE AND I WERE THE ONLY ONES LEFT ALIVE

IF...

I WOULD NEVER TASTE THE SWEET FLAVOR OF URABE'S DROOL AGAIN...

CU—

AND ...

WAIT!

KLAP

WHAT DO YOU THINK, PRESIDENT?

WH...

HRMM...

BUT I THINK THIS ENDING WORKS JUST AS WELL.

IT'S NOT WHAT WAS IN THE SCRIPT,

THE DROOL OF A ROBOT THAT SHOULD HAVE NO FLAVOR,

HIS OWN TEARS SPILL IN HIS MOUTH AND MIX WITH

CAUSING HIM TO ACTUALLY TASTE SOMETHING...

ACTUALLY, I AGREE WITH YOU.

WHAT DO YOU THINK, DIRECTOR?

SHLP

TSUBAKI,

TODAY'S DOSE.

HERE,

UH...
NOTH-ING...

WHAT IS IT, TSUBAKI?

HEY... TSUBAKI.

WHEN WE WERE FILMING THE FINAL SCENE...

IT TASTES LIKE URABE'S DROOL AGAIN...

IT'S SWEET...!

URABE...

TASTE IT.

IT'S SWEET !

...

!

CAN TASTE SWEET, TOO,

EVEN TEARS

SOMETIMES.

IF YOUR DROOL DIDN'T TASTE SWEET,

THAT, TO ME...

W... WELL,

ANYWAY...

ANYWAY, THE FILMING

IS FINALLY OVER.

NOW ALL THAT'S LEFT IS

THE CULTURE FESTIVAL IN A WEEK!

LET'S HAVE A GOOD TIME THERE!

✂ END OF CHAPTER 68

LEMON

CHOMP

THAT'S SOUR!

FROM THE AUTHOR'S VIEWPOINT

THE "MYSTERIOUS GIRLFRIEND X" ANIME CHRONICLES

I LIKE "X," BUT I LIKE "DISCOM-MUNICATION" TOO!

...IS WHAT HE TOLD ME.

I... I SEE...

UE

DIRECTOR AYUMU WATANABE (MY IMAGE)

TO THINK MATSUBUE AND TOGAWA FROM "DISCOMMUNICATION" WOULD BE IN THE LIMITED EDITION OAD...

I USED A CUT LIKE THIS, BUT I'VE MET MANY PEOPLE WHO LEARNED OF THE STORY FROM THE ANIME BROADCAST.

IT'S SPINNING MORE THAN USUAL!

ANIME VERSION

THE NEW VOLUME WAS BEHIND SCHEDULE...

I WANTED TO GO AND WATCH BUT I WAS TOO BUSY WORKING.

THE DRAMA CD WAS BASED ON JAPAN'S VOLUME 8, SO IT ACTUALLY WENT BEYOND THE END OF THE ANIME. LISTENING TO IT AFTER THE ANIME ENDED WAS STRANGE, SINCE TSUBAKI AND URABE'S RELATIONSHIP HAD PROGRESSED FURTHER BUT STILL SOUNDED SO NEW. THE BONUS FREE TALK WAS ALSO VERY INTERESTING.

JUN. 2010 RECEIVED PROPOSAL FROM KING RECORDS TO PRODUCE A "MYSTERIOUS GIRLFRIEND X" ANIME.

FEB. 2011 FIRST MEETING WITH THE ANIME STAFF IN A CONFERENCE ROOM AT KODANSHA.

EARLY SUMMER, 2011 • RECEIVED EPISODE 1 SCRIPT FROM SCRIPT WRITER AKAO. READ WITH DEEP INTEREST AND FOUND THAT IT COVERED CHAPTER 0 WELL.
• RECEIVED STORYBOARDS FROM DIRECTOR WATANABE. IT WAS DONE IN COLORED PENCILS AND VERY COLORFUL.

AUG. 2011 DINNER AT A NEARBY PUB AFTER A STAFF MEETING. DIRECTOR WATANABE SIGNED MY "DORAEMON THE MOVIE: NOBITA'S DINOSAUR (2006)" DVD (WHICH HE DIRECTED).

DEC. 2011 • ANNOUNCEMENT OF THE "MYSTERIOUS GIRLFRIEND X" ANIME IN AFTERNOON MONTHLY.
• ALL VOICE ACTORS EXCEPT URABE CHOSEN.

JAN. 15, 2012 MEETING TO SELECT URABE'S VOICE ACTRESS. AYAKO YOSHITANI WAS CHOSEN.

JAN. 20, 2012 RECORDED THE DRAMA CD INCLUDED WITH THE MANGA VOLUME TO BE RELEASED IN FEBRUARY.

FEB. 23, 2012 MANGA VOLUME 8 LIMITED EDITION WITH DRAMA CD RELEASED.

MAR. 1, 2012 RECORDING OF "MYSTERIOUS GIRLFRIEND X" ANIME EPISODE 1.

I LIKED THE SCENE WHERE URABE SAID, "TSUBAKI! STARTING TODAY, I'M YOUR GIRLFRIEND!" AND THEN ALL THE LIGHTS IN THE TOWN FLICKERED ON.

MIYU IRINO PLAYS TSUBAKI. I'M INCREDIBLY IMPRESSED THAT JINTAN FROM "ANO HANA" WILL BE PLAYING TSUBAKI.

UNDER-GROUND MAN

YOSHITANI'S DELIVERY OF THE LINE, "THE SICKNESS YOU CAME DOWN WITH WAS JUST LOVESICKNESS," WAS THE STRAIGHTEST AND MOST POWERFUL OF EVERYONE WHO AUDITIONED. I WAS SURPRISED THAT THE ACTRESS HERSELF WAS SO CHEERFUL, THE EXACT OPPOSITE OF THE ANTISOCIAL URABE.

I WANTED TO GO AND WATCH, BUT I WAS TOO BUSY WORKING.

NOT SO MUCH BUSY AS JUST WRITING TOO SLOWLY...

WATCHING THE RECORDING, I THOUGHT, NOT ONLY IS THE ACTING DURING THE REGULAR SCENES GOOD, BUT EVEN THE BACKGROUND LINES ARE FUN! THE VOICE ACTORS AD-LIB THEM ALL, SO THEIR PERSONALITIES REALLY COME THROUGH. IT MADE ME REALIZE THAT LISTENING TO THE BACKGROUND LINES BEING RECORDED IS A PRIVILEGE OF THOSE WHO GET TO OBSERVE A RECORDING STUDIO!

THAT'S ALL I EVER SAY...

I WANTED TO SNEAK IN AND WATCH, BUT I WAS TOO BUSY WORKING.

HIRO YUUKI AND MEGUMI HAYASHIBARA, WHO PLAYED MATSUBUE AND TOGAWA IN "DISCOMMUNICATION" 16 YEARS AGO, REPRISED THEIR ROLES ON THIS OAD AS WELL. I MET HAYASHIBARA IN THE STUDIO (YUUKI WAS RECORDING SEPARATELY).

I TALKED OUT LOUD WITHOUT THINKING...

I WANTED TO GO, BUT I WAS TOO BUSY WITH WORK AND COULDN'T MAKE IT. FROM THE CAST, RYOU HIROHASHI ATTENDED. I'VE BEEN WATCHING THE "WORKING!!" ANIME RECENTLY AND I REALLY LIKE YAMADA, SO I WISH I COULD'VE GONE...

THE AUDIO COMMENTARY WAS REALLY INTERESTING!

I FORGOT TO RECORD IT! (CRY) O KING RECORDS, IF YOU CAN... ONLY IF IT'S OKAY WITH YOU, COULD YOU PLEASE SEND ME THE RECORDED DATA?

MAR. 15, 2012 RECORDING OF "MYSTERIOUS GIRLFRIEND X" ANIME EPISODE 3. WENT TO WATCH FOR THE FIRST TIME.

APR. 7, 2012 "MYSTERIOUS GIRLFRIEND X" ANIME BEGINS AIRING ON TOKYO MX.

APR. 21, 2012 EPISODE 3 OF "MYSTERIOUS GIRLFRIEND X" AIRS ON TOKYO MX. FIRST TIME USING THE COMPLETE OPENING ANIMATION.

MAY 19, 2012 EVENT AT TOKYO UNIVERSITY'S MAY FESTIVAL. DIRECTOR WATANABE, YOSHITANI, HIROHASHI, IKEDA FROM KING RECORDS, AND MY EDITOR MR. N FROM AFTERNOON MONTHLY STOOD ONSTAGE.

MAY 24, 2012 RECORDING OF "MYSTERIOUS GIRLFRIEND X" FINAL EPISODE. MANAGED TO FINISH WORK SO I COULD WATCH.

JUN. 21, 2012 RECORDED THE DRAMA CD INCLUDED WITH MANGA VOLUME 9 LIMITED EDITION TO BE RELEASED AUGUST 23. MANAGED TO FINISH WORK SO I COULD WATCH. TALKED WITH DIRECTOR WATANABE, WHO WAS IN THE SAME STUDIO.

JUN. 30, 2012 FINAL EPISODE OF "MYSTERIOUS GIRLFRIEND X" ON THE AIR. THERE WAS AN EVENT AT SHINJUKU LOFT PLUS ONE WHERE FANS COULD WATCH THE FINAL EPISODE TOGETHER.

JUL. 4, 2012 "MYSTERIOUS GIRLFRIEND X" ANIME VOL. 1 RELEASED ON BLU-RAY AND DVD.

JUL. 23, 2012 AYAKO YOSHITANI APPEARED ON MEGUMI HAYASHIBARA'S RADIO SHOW. THE DISCUSSION BETWEEN TOGAWA FROM "DISCOMMUNICATION" AND URABE FROM "X" REALLY MOVED ME, AS THE AUTHOR OF BOTH.

AUG. 23, 2012 MANGA VOLUME 9 LIMITED EDITION WITH OAD RELEASED.

HONESTLY, IT WAS VERY ENGAGING. AT SOME POINT I FORGOT I WAS THE AUTHOR AND JUST GOT ABSORBED IN IT. I WAS IMPRESSED WITH THE DREAM TOWN.

WAS THE BOY WITH THE FOX MASK ON THE TRAIN MATSUBUE?

THE SHOT FROM THE OPENING OF URABE TROTTING UP THE STEPS WITH HER HANDS RAISED A LITTLE IS CUTE.

AFTER THE RECORDING, I GAVE EACH CAST MEMBER AN ILLUSTRATION OF THEIR OWN CHARACTER, AND THEY WERE SO HAPPY! I WAS REALLY MOVED!

WHILE WE WERE TALKING, DIRECTOR WATANABE SAID, "IT'S ALWAYS GIRLS WHO GUIDE BOYS THROUGH GROWING UP AND BECOMING ADULTS. THAT'S WHY, IN THE DREAM TOWN SCENE IN EPISODE 1, IT'S URABE, A GIRL, PULLING TSUBAKI'S HAND AS THEY RUN." THAT IMPRESSED ME.

I THINK HE'S GIVEN IT MORE THOUGHT THAN I HAVE...

ON THE COVER OF THE LIMITED EDITION, I DREW MATSUBUE AND TOGAWA FROM "DISCOMMUNICATION" FOR THE FIRST TIME IN 12 YEARS. DRAWING TOGAWA'S ROUND GLASSES IS A CHALLENGE.

AS YOU CAN SEE, IT WAS A VERY EXCITING EXPERIENCE. EVERYONE WHO WAS INVOLVED IN MAKING THE ANIME, AND EVERYONE WHO WATCHED IT,

SO GRATEFUL!

THANK YOU VERY MUCH!!

MYSTERIOUS GIRLFRIEND **X**

MYSTERIOUS GIRLFRIEND X

RIICHI UESHIBA

Ayuko Oka (17)

At 4'8", she's very small, but her figure is well-developed and quite gorgeous. She is Ueno's girlfriend. She often toys with Urabe through her impish personality. Like Tsubaki, she is responsive to Urabe's drool.

Kouhei Ueno (17)

Tsubaki's best friend. He's been going out with their classmate, Oka, since they were sophomores. Ueno's fond way of talking about Oka frequently influences Tsubaki's ideas about relationships.

Ryouko Suwano (17)

Tsubaki's classmate who shares his class duties. Her drooping eyes are her most charming feature. She knows Tsubaki has a girlfriend, though she doesn't know that it's Urabe.

Minori Matsuzawa (16)

Tsubaki's junior and a member of the film studies club. She is the director and script writer for the club's self-produced movie. She has rather eccentric taste in movies.

Youko Tsubaki (24)

Akira's sister, seven years his senior. She handles all the housework in place of their mother, who died when they were young. Akira is highly indebted to her.

MYSTERIOUS GIRLFRIEND X

Characters

Mikoto Urabe (17)

A transfer student who joined Tsubaki's class. She can convey her own feelings through her drool, as well as pick up on Tsubaki's feelings through his. She's antisocial and everything she says and does is mysterious, but her ideas about love are very pure. Her hobby is using scissors, which she can use to cut up anything.

Akira Tsubaki (17)

The protagonist of the story. His bizarre relationship with Urabe began after he licked her drool one day. He is as interested in girls as any boy his age, but Urabe takes the lead in their relationship and Tsubaki can't seem to initiate any progress between them.

AN UNIDENTIFIABLE ROMANCE MOVIE

KAZA01

MYSTERIOUS GIRLFRIEND Y

THE FILM STUDIES CLUB'S SELF-PRODUCED MOVIE?

YES.

IT'S SCREENING IN THE A.V. ROOM AT 3 O'CLOCK,

SO PLEASE COME AND WATCH.

DIRECTOR/SCREENPLAY: MINORI MATSUZAWA
PRODUCER: KENJI YAMAZAKI

RYOUKO SUWANO
AKIRA TSUBAKI
MIKOTO URABE

SHOWING AT 3:00 IN THE AV ROOM!

PRODUCED BY THE KAZAMIDAI
HIGH SCHOOL FILM STUDIES CLUB

IS IT A GOOD MOVIE?

YEAH?

OF COURSE!

OH, COME HERE!

AFTER ALL...

SQUEEZE

AN UNIDENTIFIABLE ROMANCE

MYSTERIOUS GIRLFRIEND Y

PRODUCED BY THE KAZAMIDAI HIGH SCHOOL FILM STUDY CLUB

MYSTERIOUS GIRLFRIEND Y | MYSTERIOUS GIRLFRIEND Y | MYSTERIOUS GIRLFRIEND Y | MYSTERIOUS GIRLFRIEND Y | MYSTERIOUS GIRLFRIEND Y

THERE! PERFECT!

THAT'S IT.

AH, IT'S TILTED.

RAISE THE LEFT END HIGHER.

WE'VE ALREADY HANDED OUT FLYERS

THE MOVIE'S NOT EVEN DONE YET, IS IT?

BUT

SAYING IT STARTS AT 3:00.

PRODUCED BY THE KAZAMIDAI FILM

WHAT DO YOU WANNA DO?

YOU GUYS SHOULD EAT NOW,

WHILE THERE'S STILL TIME.

HEY.

ARE STILL IN THE CLUB ROOM WORKING ON THE EDITING...

THE PRESIDENT AND MATSU-ZAWA

GRAB SOMETHING FROM A STALL SOME-WHERE?

OH, SURE.

THEY HAVE LESS THAN TWO HOURS!

YEAH, THAT'S FINE.

I'LL DO AS YOU ASKED...

IF YOU DO IT,

NEVER HAPPENED.

AND PRETEND "THAT"

I USED MY FAMILY'S SECRET SEASONING TECHNIQUES.

RIGHT?!

IT'S GOOD!

OH...

KAZAMIDAI LOVE ATTACK!! I-C

SWING GIRL

AH...

I'LL SLIP OUT TO COME WATCH!

OH!

YOU GUYS ARE GOING TO GREET THE AUDIENCE BEFORE THE SCREENING, RIGHT?

I GOTTA GO TO THE A.V. ROOM AFTER THIS, TOO...

WHERE'S TSUBAKI?

BY THE WAY,

I HAVEN'T SEEN HIM SINCE THIS MORNING.

WHAT ARE YOU GOING TO WEAR FOR THE GREETING?

ME?

MY SCHOOL UNIFORM.

HE'S HELPING WITH PREPARATIONS FOR THE MOVIE SCREENING.

HE IS TECHNICALLY A CLUB MEMBER, AFTER ALL.

URABE...

WAIT A MINUTE!

THE PERSON WITH THE HIGHEST SCORE IS SUPPOSED TO DO AN ENCORE AT THE END...

HEY! WAIT!

JUMP

DRAMA CLUB

ROBOT CONTEST ♥

100 POETS CARD TOURNEY

KAZA MIDAI FEST

KAZA MIDAI FES

TSUBAKI...

AH...

WAKE UP!

MATSU-ZAWA!

HEY!

mm...

FILM STUDIES CLUB

NO MOVIE! NO LIFE!

OPEN

WHOA!

AH!

BUMP!!

TSUBAKI
...

SUWANO
...

URABE'S ALREADY ON THE STAGE!

LET'S HURRY!

IT'S FOR THE STAGE GREETING EVENT, RIGHT?

IT...

AH...

UHM...

THIS DRESS...

HUH...?

LOOKS GREAT ON YOU, TOO...

YOUR DRESS

HM?

SUWANO...

REALLY GUILTY, FOR SOME REASON...

I FEEL...

URABE IS THE GIRL I LOVE MOST,

SO THE FACT THAT I TASTED YOUR DROOL

IS MY LIFE'S BIGGEST SECRET.

PFFT....

HEH HEH HEH...

I WASN'T ACTUALLY DATING.

I WOULD NEVER DO THAT WITH ANYONE

SOMETHING LIKE

TASTING SOMEONE'S DROOL...

THAT SPORTS DRINK

TASTED STRANGELY SWEET...

THAT'S ALL IT WAS?

A LIE...

A JOKE...

BUT STILL...

B...

THUP

AND
SO,

THE FILM
STUDIES
CLUB'S MOVIE,
"MYSTERIOUS
GIRLFRIEND Y,"

ENDED IN
A ROUSING
SUCCESS.

✂ END OF CHAPTER 70

SO YOU SEE,

WE ALL WORKED OUR VERY HARDEST ON THIS MOVIE.

PLEASE STAY AND WATCH IT TO THE END!

HUH?

SUWANO HAS...

WAS IT... A BOYFRIEND?!

THAT MEANS...

SHE DIDN'T COUNT THEM HERSELF, BUT SOMEONE COUNTED THEM FOR HER...

TO COUNT EVERY MOLE ON HER BODY, SHE'D HAVE TO TAKE OFF ALL HER CLOTHES...

IF SHE HAD SOMEONE SHE WAS THAT CLOSE TO...

BUT IF URABE AND I GET CLOSER, WILL I EVER GET TO DO THINGS LIKE THAT WITH HER...?

TH-THAT'S TOO EROTIC...!!

IF... IF SHE REALLY DID THAT...

"I WANT YOU TO COUNT MY MOLES..."

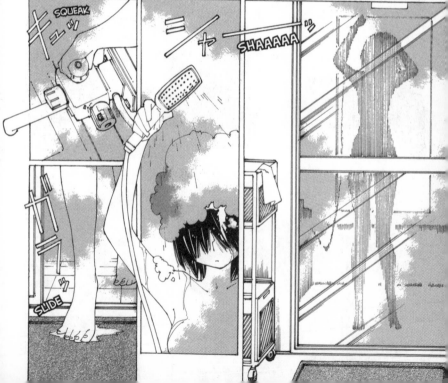

SHLP

SFF
ス...

I CAN'T SHOW YOU MY REAL MOLE...

WHAT? HUH?

A PEN ...?

HERE, TAKE THIS.

SO IF YOU REALLY WANT TO SEE A MOLE ON ME,

THEN INSTEAD...

IT'S A PEN.

WITH THIS PEN.

YOU CAN DRAW ONE

SOME-WHERE ON ME

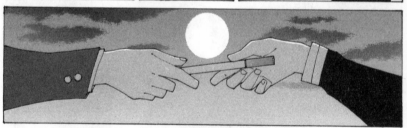

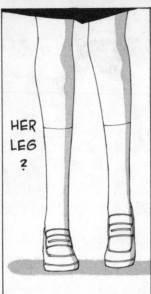

OR HER NECK?

HER LEG?

HER HAND?

AH...

IN THE LIGHT OF THE SUNSET,

IT MADE ME HOPE

WITH A SINGLE MOLE AT THE CORNER OF HER EYE,

THAT, SOMEDAY, I'D GET TO SEE THE REAL MOLE SHE HAS

URABE LOOKED SO ATTRACTIVE.

IN A PLACE THAT SHE CAN'T SHOW TO ANYONE ELSE.

LOOKING FOR MOLES IN THE BATH?!

WILL YOU STOP

SHE HAS A SISTER WHO'S MUCH YOUNGER THAN SHE IS.

LATER, SUWANO TOLD ME THAT

※ PS:

THAT'S 34!

I FOUND A MOLE ON THE BOTTOM OF YOUR FOOT!

AH!

END OF CHAPTER 71

OF THE "MYSTERIOUS GIRLFRIEND Y" FILM!

IT'S YOUR COPY

HERE, TSUBAKI!

URABE ON VIDEO WHENEVER I WANT! ♪

ALL RIGHT! NOW I CAN WATCH

THANKS!

OH!

THAT?

AH,

WHAT'S THAT?

HM?

THAT'S...

IT'S ALSO SOLD ON DVD AFTER THE FESTIVAL FOR 500 YEN PER COPY.

IS NOT ONLY SHOWN AT THE CULTURE FESTIVAL.

OUR CLUB'S SELF-PRODUCED FILM

EVERY YEAR,

WH...

WHAT DOES THAT MEAN?!

SALES COUNT...?

JACKPOT

OGI YAHAGI

BEST LIVE

THAT THERE'S A WEIRD MOVIE ABOUT TASTING DROOL.

WORD HAS BEEN SPREADING ONLINE

AND ON TOP OF THAT,

SOMEHOW, WE'VE SOLD 60 COPIES JUST WITHIN THE SCHOOL.

SO WE GOT 40 ORDERS THROUGH OUR WEBSITE FROM THE GENERAL PUBLIC!

AND MOST OF THOSE WERE BOUGHT BY OUR FAMILIES AND FRIENDS.

BEFORE THIS YEAR, WE NEVER SOLD MORE THAN 30 COPIES,

BUT THIS YEAR...

PEOPLE HAVE REALLY TAKEN TO IT.

BUT IT LOOKS LIKE

TASTING SOMEONE'S DROOL SEEMED KINDA ABNORMAL...

I THOUGHT THE THEME OF

THIS PICTURE WAS UPLOADED ONLINE...

IT LOOKS LIKE THE MOVIE'S BEEN INFLUENCING PEOPLE.

KLIK KLIK

WE'VE EVEN SEEN

STUFF LIKE THIS.

OF A GIRL PUTTING HER FINGER IN HER BOYFRIEND'S MOUTH,

JUST LIKE THE SCENE FROM THE MOVIE.

YOU SHOULD JOIN US, TSUBAKI.

SINCE THE DVD'S SELLING SO WELL, WE'RE THINKING OF THROWING A PARTY.

SO,

"MYSTERIOUS GIRLFRIEND Y"

HAS BEEN GETTING QUITE THE RESPONSE.

HMMM ?

HM?

THIS IS THE FIRST PEAR I'VE HAD

MUNCH MUNCH

THIS YEAR.

THERE WAS SOME FRUIT I USED TO EAT

THAT I REALLY LOVED...

EVERY YEAR, IN FALL,

OH, JUST ...

WHAT IS IT, URABE?

MUNCH

MUNCH

TA-DAA

THE FALL FRUIT CAMPAIGN IS UNDERWAY!!

WHIP

WHAT WAS IT?

...I CAN'T REMEMBER.

WE'LL FIGURE IT OUT THAT WAY!

LOOK FORWARD TO IT,

URABE!

IF YOU CAN'T REMEMBER WHAT FRUIT IT WAS YOU LOVED SO MUCH,

THEN, STARTING TOMORROW,

I'LL BRING A DIFFERENT FRUIT FOR DESSERT EVERY DAY.

HERE,

TSUBAKI.

TODAY'S DOSE.

SHLP

HM?!

SHLP

TASTES UNUSUALLY SWEET...

TODAY'S DROOL...

SOMEHOW...

REALLY?

HUH?

UH...

NOTHING, NEVER MIND...

THIS ROUTINE

WAS SUPPOSED TO BE OUR OWN THING...

SIGH...

MAYBE IT'S BECAUSE

OF THE PEAR OKA GAVE ME AT LUNCH.

IT WAS REALLY DELICIOUS...

URABE!

SEE YOU TOMORROW,

...

SORRY FOR THE WAIT.

SHLP

SHLP

GAH!!

AND OVER THERE.

SO...

NOW GIRLFRIENDS AND BOYFRIENDS TASTE EACH OTHER'S DROOL LIKE IT'S TOTALLY NORMAL...

THE INFLUENCE OF "MYSTERIOUS GIRLFRIEND Y" HAS SPREAD.

URABE
...!!

HEY...

AH...

SHLP...

SHLP

POP

YOU DO?

OH...

HUH...?

I'M NOT REALLY...

WHY DO I FEEL THIS WAY?

TSUBAKI,

TELL ME

THE REASON WHY.

I FEEL...

AND HEAVY...

SORT OF GLOOMY...

...FEELING GLOOMY

OR ANYTHING...

I...

I WONDER WHY?

A LOT OF DREAMS ABOUT THAT...

BUT I'VE BEEN HAVING

I DON'T THINK A ROUTINE LIKE OURS WILL ACTUALLY CATCH ON WITH OTHER PEOPLE.

NO MATTER HOW POPULAR THE MOVIE WAS...

WHEN THAT HAPPENS,

YOU'RE GIVING IT TOO MUCH THOUGHT...

SOMETHING FUN...

YOU SHOULD DISTRACT YOURSELF WITH SOMETHING ELSE.

FOR EXAMPLE,

EATING SOMETHING THAT'S TASTY...

AH!

...

BUY SOMETHING?

B...

HUH?

TSUBAKI!

I'M GOING

WAIT HERE FOR A MINUTE!

TO GO BUY SOMETHING!

DASH

URABE, WHERE DID YOU GO?

HAA

HAA

HAA

A PRODUCE STORE.

HERE.

TAKE YOUR MIND OFF THINGS!

HAVE SOME AUTUMN FRUIT.

I DON'T THINK YOU'LL HAVE ANY

OF THOSE WEIRD DREAMS ANYMORE.

OH...

OKAY...

THE DROOL-TASTING ROUTINE CATCHING ON.

I DIDN'T HAVE ANY MORE DREAMS ABOUT

FROM THAT NIGHT ON,

JUST AS URABE SAID,

HMM... NOPE.

CHEST-NUTS!

THE FALL FRUIT CAMPAIGN!

BUT CHESTNUTS ARE GOOD, TOO! ♥

ARE CHEST-NUTS EVEN FRUIT?

MNCH MNCH ♥

✂ **END OF CHAPTER 72**

WAS BOUGHT BY

OUR MOTHER.

BUT IT ONLY STAYS LIT FOR A MOMENT, THEN GOES OFF.

THERE'S THIS LIGHT-UP CHRISTMAS TREE WE'VE HAD IN OUR HOUSE FOREVER,

YEAH,

HUH?

A BROKEN CHRISTMAS TREE?

I THINK IT'S AT THE END OF ITS LIFE.

I WAS STILL REALLY YOUNG WHEN OUR MOM DIED,

SO EVEN AFTER SHE TOLD ME OUR MOM BOUGHT IT,

ALL I KNOW ABOUT THAT TREE IS THAT IT'S BEEN IN OUR PLACE AS LONG AS I CAN REMEMBER...

OF COURSE, IF WE COULD SPEND CHRISTMAS EVE ALONE TOGETHER...

IT'D BE EVEN BETTER IF I COULD SHOW IT TO HER THEN...

COME BY SOMETIME

SURE.

AND I'LL SHOW YOU.

TO SEE THAT CHRISTMAS TREE

I'D LIKE

SOMEDAY.

I WAS GOING TO INVITE HER TO THE MOVIES OR SOMETHING...

I SEE...

OH...

AT HOME, SINCE MY FAMILY WILL BE TOGETHER

FOR THE FIRST TIME IN A WHILE...

I'LL BE SPENDING CHRISTMAS EVE

BUT UNFORTUNATELY...

I'LL COME BACK

AS SOON AS I CAN!

U.T

YELLOW MAGIC

WHERE ARE YOU GOING

HEY...

HEY! AKIRA!

WITH OUR CHRISTMAS TREE?!

DASH

YANK

I'D LIKE TO SEE THAT CHRISTMAS TREE SOMEDAY.

Merry Christmas

GRAB

JUST

BORROWING IT FOR A WHILE!

Merry Christmas

AH...

IT'S ON!

Merry Christmas

WAIT... NORMALLY, IT ALMOST NEVER DOES! WOW... W...

MORE IMPORTANTLY, WHAT ARE YOU WEARING?!

IT TURNS ON JUST FINE! TSUBAKI,

AH...

BUT IT'S THANKS TO THIS LITTLE CHRISTMAS TREE...

THE CHRISTMAS TREE MOM LEFT US MAY BE FICKLE,

Merry Christmas

MERRY CHRISTMAS!

WELL

SEE YOU LATER,

TSUBAKI!

I FEEL LIKE IT WAS A CHRISTMAS PRESENT FROM MY MOTHER IN HEAVEN.

THAT I GOT TO SEE URABE SMILE TONIGHT.

IT COULDN'T BE

STILL, URABE WAS UNUSUALLY CHEERFUL TONIGHT ...

BECAUSE HER FAMILY GAVE HER CHAMPAGNE, RIGHT ?

IT'S ON!

Merry Christmas ♥

✂ END OF CHAPTER 73

NEW YEAR

THAT'S IT!

AND...

THERE!

POP

AKIRA!

DAD!

WAKE UP!

KLINK

AH...

YEAH!

SAME TO YOU!

I LOOK FORWARD TO ANOTHER YEAR TOGETHER,

TSUBAKI.

OUR FIRST DAY BACK TO SCHOOL IN THE NEW YEAR...

AND OUR FIRST ROUTINE OF THE YEAR.

SHLP

TSUBAKI.

HERE,

SHLP

COULD THE IMAGE I SAW IN MY MIND

AND THE SNAKE ON URABE'S CARD...

ACTUALLY BE CONNECTED SOMEHOW...?!

THE SNAKE ON URABE'S NEW YEAR'S CARD

HAD PINK STRIPES...!

AHH...

I SPENT WINTER BREAK

JUST EATING AND LAZING AROUND,

AND NOW I'M SO OUT OF SHAPE...

IT'S THE NEW YEAR.

MAYBE I SHOULD SHAKE THINGS UP

AND TRY OUT A NEW LOOK.

A NEW LOOK?

URGH...

ZWOOM

MEOW

URABE.

YOU'VE GOTTEN BETTER,

SLITHER SLITHER...

EVER SINCE I SAW THAT PINK STRIPED SNAKE AFTER TASTING URABE'S DROOL,

IT'S WEIRD...

I DREAM ABOUT THAT SNAKE EVERY NIGHT...

WHAT DOES IT MEAN...?!

I GUESS THIS IS THE YEAR OF THE SNAKE, SO MAYBE IT'S A GOOD OMEN ...?

HERE, TSUBAKI.

TODAY'S DOSE...

SHLP

YEAH... Y...

WHAT'S THAT...?!

UH...

TSUBAKI...

WELL,

SEE YOU,

AROUND URABE'S BODY...

SLITHER

AND IT MADE ME SEE THAT SNAKE!

YOU'VE BEEN WEARING PANTIES WITH A DIFFERENT PRINT,

YOU ALWAYS WORE WHITE PANTIES BEFORE, RIGHT?

SEE,

URABE,

WITH THE SLIGHTEST WISH FOR ME,

DID YOU

DRAW THAT PICTURE

OH, YEAH...

I DID DRAW THAT...

A PINK STRIPED SNAKE ...?

OH...

THE PINK STRIPED SNAKE ON YOUR NEW YEAR'S CARD...

YOUR BOYFRIEND, TO SEE THEM...?

EVEN IF

THAT WERE TRUE...

WERE YOU

SENDING ME AN INDIRECT MESSAGE THAT YOU HAD NEW PANTIES?

SHINK

SNIP SNIP SNIP SNIP

SNIP

THERE'S NO WAY

I THINK I'LL BE DREAMING OF THAT PINK STRIPED SNAKE FOR A WHILE LONGER.

I WOULD ADMIT IT TO YOU.

END OF CHAPTER 74

SO IT WAS JUST OUT OF OBLIGATION...

THAT SCARED ME...

OH... I SEE.

IN THE FILM STUDIES CLUB!

I'M GIVING THEM

TO ALL THE GUYS

MATSU-ZAWA...

AH... THANKS,

YOU WORKED REALLY HARD IN OUR MOVIE,

"MYSTERIOUS GIRLFRIEND Y," TOO!

HUH...?!

CHOCOLATE.

HERE, TSUBAKI.

COME TO THE CLUB ROOM EVERY NOW AND THEN!

TSUBAKI!

YEAH... SURE...

I'LL JUST DISPOSE OF THE EVIDENCE!

BEFORE I GO TO OUR USUAL SPOT,

OKAY!

STARE...

WOULD DEFINITELY GET MAD AT ME...

URABE...

AND IF THINGS END UP LIKE THAT...

KATHUNK!

POINTS!♪

WINTER SWEETS♪

SORRY...

BUT URABE IS SPECIAL...

MUNCH MUNCH

RIP

RIP

SLIDE

CHOMP

CHOMP

OUR USUAL ROUTINE...

OKAY, TSUBAKI,

S... SURE.

HERE, TSUBAKI.

SFF

OH!

RIGHT.

IS AN INCREDIBLY SAD THING FOR A BOY.

FROM HIS OWN GIRLFRIEND

NOT GETTING CHOCO-LATE

AH...

TAP
TAP

URABE...

IS IT

THAT GOOD...?

YEAH!

パキッ SNAP

REALLY GOOD!

THIS IS

MM!

REALLY GOOD!

ほぽんっ POP

ちゅっ SHLP

ちゅっ SHLP...

Y...

YOU'RE RIGHT...

IT'S JUST REGULAR CHOCOLATE...

BUT IT'S

REALLY SWEET...

GIVE ME

SOMETHING SWEET IN RETURN!

NEXT MONTH,

THEN, TSUBAKI...

OH...

SURE!

WELL,

OF COURSE IT IS!

IT'S CHOCOLATE FROM THE GIRL I LOVE.

IT'S TOTALLY

DIFFERENT FROM REGULAR CHOCO-LATES!

THUP

END OF CHAPTER 75

MY... YEAH, WELL...

MY FEELINGS WENT INTO IT, SO...

ARE THERE COOKIES INSIDE?

ONLY ONE OR TWO WOULD FIT IN A BOX THIS SMALL...

VERY SMALL.

IT LOOKS...

YOU DELIBERATELY GAVE ME A SMALL ONE

TO DIFFERENTIATE FROM THE ONE YOU GIVE YOUR GIRLFRIEND, RIGHT?

I BET...

YOU'RE GIVING URABE

IS MUCH BIGGER THAN THIS.

I BET THE ONE

IN CASE YOU'RE WONDERING WHY SUWANO AND I ARE ALONE IN THIS DARK, CRAMPED REFERENCE ROOM...

Y... YES?

TSUBAKI...

NOW,

SINCE WE HAVE THE SAME CLASS DUTIES,

OH,

AFTER YOU DISTRIBUTE THOSE HANDOUTS,

BRING ME THE 16TH CENTURY WORLD MAP FROM THE REFERENCE ROOM.

WE'LL BE USING IT IN CLASS.

OKAY.

IS WHAT OUR WORLD HISTORY TEACHER SAID...

I FIGURED IF I GAVE SUWANO HER PRESENT IN RETURN FOR VALENTINE'S DAY HERE, THERE'S NO WAY URABE WOULD SEE US...

Y...

YES ...?

TSUBAKI ...

BUT I NEVER EXPECTED THIS TO HAPPEN...!

YES, I DO!

Y...

I TOLD YOU THAT BEFORE!

DO YOU REALLY LOVE URABE?

I SAW THE PANTIES OF A GIRL WHO WASN'T URABE...

THAT'S THE FIRST TIME...

AND THEY WERE BLACK ♥...

I CAN'T GET RID OF THE IMAGE OF SUWANO'S BLACK UNDERWEAR...

WHEN I'M SUPPOSED TO GIVE URABE A GIFT IN RETURN FOR HER CHOCOLATE,

TODAY IS WHITE DAY,

TH... THIS IS BAD...

YET IN MY MIND...

AS IF...

IT'S

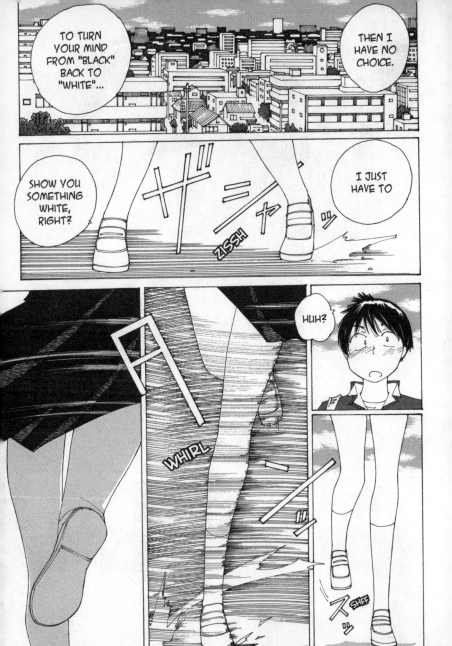

WHISH

WITH THE BOND OF DROOL THAT WE HAVE...

IT'S TRUE THAT LIES WON'T WORK

SURE!

S...

I WOULDN'T MIND BEING NUMBER 2...

IF I COULD GO OUT WITH YOU,

CHEAT ON URABE WITHOUT HER KNOWING ...

THERE'S NO WAY I COULD EVER

END OF CHAPTER 76

END-OF-VOLUME BONUS MANGA
RIICHI UESHIBA'S (FIRST) AUTOGRAPH SIGNING TOUR IN FUKUOKA 2012 11/3~4
SPICY POLLOCK ROE
OFFAL HOTPOT
HAKATA RAMEN
IN RESPONSE TO HEAVY DEMAND, RIICHI UESHIBA MAKES THE DECISION OF A LIFETIME!!
IN MY 20-SOME-ODD YEARS WRITING MANGA, I NEVER HAD AN AUTOGRAPH SESSION ...
I DON'T DO WELL IN FRONT OF LOTS OF PEOPLE...
WHEN I DO GO OUT, IT'S ONLY TO JUNKUDO BOOKS IN IKEBUKURO OR NAKANO BROADWAY!
MY CHIEF EDITOR, NASU* ...
WANT TO GO TO FUKUOKA, NOT TOKYO,
AND HAVE AN AUTOGRAPH SESSION FOR THE NEW EDITION OF "DISCOMMUNICATION"?
... SAID TO ME.
*EGGPLANT
OH,
WHILE WE'RE THERE, WE CAN VISIT OUR OLD SCHOOL, AND WE'LL GO DRINKING IN NAKASU AT NIGHT...
THAT SOUNDS LIKE FUN!
AND THAT THOUGHT STARTED IT ALL.
BEER
LEMON SOUR

AND THAT WAS MY ANSWER.

SURE, I'LL DO AN AUTOGRAPH SESSION IF IT'S IN FUKUOKA.

NASU AND I BOTH GREW UP IN FUKUOKA, AND WE EVEN WENT TO THE SAME HIGH SCHOOL, SO GOING SIGHTSEEING IN OUR OLD HOMETOWN IN FUKUOKA WHILE WE WERE THERE FOR AN AUTOGRAPH SESSION SOUNDED NICE.

DRUNK AND NOT USING MY BEST JUDGMENT

THERE WAS NOTHING I WANTED TO DO!

WAS IN NO CLUBS

WAS A YEAR AHEAD OF UESHIBA AND IN THE BRASS BAND IN HIGH SCHOOL

WHEN WE ARRIVED IN FUKUOKA, OUR FIRST STOP WAS OUR OLD HIGH SCHOOL.

MY FIRST TIME ON A PLANE IN OVER 10 YEARS

IT WAS SO CLEAR, WE COULD SEE BOTH THE SKY TREE AND MT. FUJI

THE DAY BEFORE THE EVENT, WE TOOK OFF FOR FUKUOKA FROM HANEDA.

SO,

IT'LL BE AT FUKUYA BOOKS ON NOVEMBER 4!

IT'S SETTLED!

WITHIN A FEW DAYS, THE SCHEDULE WAS SET UP...

FOR REAL?

THE VENDING MACHINE IN THE HALLWAY THAT HAD BEEN THE MODEL FOR TSUBAKI AND UENO'S FAVORITE HANGOUT IN "MYSTERIOUS GIRLFRIEND X" HAD BEEN REMOVED.

IT'S GONE!

I WANTED SOME PLUM JUICE...

WE TOLD THE RECEPTIONIST THAT WE WERE ALUMNI, RECEIVED VISITOR ARMBANDS, AND EXPLORED THE SCHOOL.

WE MET UP WITH NASU'S CLASSMATE, MR. F.

WAS THAT THERE BEFORE?

AND AFTER WE DRANK, WE CHECKED OUT THE NIGHT SCENERY FROM THE ROOF OF THE JR HAKATA CITY BUILDING.

BESIDES US, ALMOST EVERY-ONE THERE WAS COUPLES...

OHORI PARK IS THAT WAY!

AT NIGHT, WE DRANK IN NAKASU...

YEP! SURE IS!

FUKUOKA'S FISH IS STILL THE BEST!

BUT AS WE WALKED AROUND, WE SPOTTED MANY NOSTALGIC SIGHTS.

HELLO

CURRENT STUDENTS GREETED US VISITORS VERY POLITELY.

THEY'RE MUCH MORE CHEERFUL AND FRIENDLY THAN THE GIRLS WE KNEW IN OUR TIME!

I THINK THIS STOIC FASHION SENSE IS THE BEST.

PREP SCHOOL GIRLS LOOK REALLY CUTE.

I SAW A LOT OF SCHOOL GIRLS PASSING BY BEYOND THE GLASS DOOR. IT SORT OF REMINDED ME HOW IT FELT TO BE A TEENAGER.

DUFFLE COAT

OUR HOTEL WAS RIGHT NEXT TO THE K CRAM SCHOOL THAT I ATTENDED BETWEEN HIGH SCHOOL AND COLLEGE.

SO WHEN I SAT IN THE HOTEL LOBBY...

AND CHECKED OUT THE VIEW OF THE CITY. I LIVED IN FUKUOKA UNTIL I MOVED TO TOKYO AT AGE 19, BUT I HAD NEVER CLIMBED THE WALL TO THE FUKUOKA CASTLE KEEP BEFORE.

IF NOT FOR THIS TOUR I PROBABLY NEVER WOULD'VE CLIMBED UP HERE...

WE WENT UP A POINT THAT DIDN'T HAVE ACTUAL STAIRS, SO EACH STEP WAS HUGE

THE NEXT DAY, WE WENT TO FUKUOKA CASTLE AND CLIMBED UP THE STONE WALL WHERE THE CASTLE KEEP WAS SAID TO HAVE BEEN...

THEN WE ARRIVED AT THE VENUE, FUKUYA BOOKS.

The Latest from the Author

Riichi Ueshiba

I WATCHED THE COMPLETE DVD SET OF THE NHK TAIGA DRAMA "KUSA MOERU" (1979), AND WAS SURPRISED TO SEE WHAT A LOSER THE CHARACTER OF MINAMOTO NO YORITOMO PLAYED BY KOUJI ISHIZAKA WAS! BUT IT WAS VERY APPEALING AT THE SAME TIME. THE OPENING SEQUENCE WITH THE KAMAKURA WARRIORS RUNNING ALONG THE FOOT OF MT. FUJI WAS VERY COOL.

AFTERNOON
RIICHI UESHIBA AUTOGRAPH SESSION
2012.11.4 FUKUYA BOOKS

I KNOW BETTER THAN ANYONE THAT CALLING ME "SENSEI" IS RIDICULOUS.

I GREW INCREASINGLY NERVOUS AS WE HEADED FOR THE VENUE.

MY STOMACH HURTS...

WELL, READY TO HEAD OVER TO THE VENUE?

BY THE WAY, I WAS DRESSED IN AN UTTERLY BORING OUTFIT OF JEANS AND SNEAKERS...

I THOUGHT IT'D BE BEST TO SHOW WHAT I'M USUALLY LIKE...

LIKE THE CLOTHES YOU'D WEAR TO GO TO THE CORNER STORE...

← EXCUSE

WHEN THE EVENT BEGAN, I WAS TOO NERVOUS TO EVEN LOOK FANS IN THE EYE.

I TRIED TO AT LEAST GREET THE FANS

THANK YOU FOR COMING!

AS LOUDLY AS I COULD.

AFTERNOON
RIICHI UESHIBA AUTOGRAPH SESSION
2012.11.4 FUKUYA BOOKS

THE STAFF AT THE STORE HAD SET UP A SPACE LIKE A CUBICLE WHERE FANS COULD ENTER ONE AT A TIME FOR AUTOGRAPHS.

SO NERVOUS...

INSOMNI-ACTION NEW EDITION ①